Volume

A cautionary tale of rock and roll obsession

by Oliver Gray

A bit late — your neighbour had the last one !

Sarsen Press

Winchester, UK.

Design: David Eno and Judith Blake
Printed by: Sarsen Press, Winchester, Hants
Published by Sarsen Press

Contact Oliver Gray at P.O. Box 71, Winchester SO21 1ZE, UK
E-mail: oliver@revilolang.demon.co.uk

ISBN: 1-897609-81-7

One-Two

There I was, waiting for the kettle to boil and tapping my fingers to a nicely feedback-drenched track from the latest Afghan Whigs album, when a voice came from behind me. "Can't you turn that row down?"

I whirled round. "No, I bloody well can't!"

"I don't know how you can listen to it. There's no tune at all!"

This was terrifying. Surely, my father had risen from his grave, for these words, in fine detail, were exactly those I used to hear when attempting to tune in to The Hollies on *Saturday Club*.

On this basis, I swore that I would never impose my musical tastes on my children. I've endured Take That, All Saints and even quite enjoyed The Fugees and Robbie Williams, and I've never said a word against them. But it doesn't work the other way round. Every time we get in the car, my carefully-recorded Pavement and Sparklehorse tapes are instantly banished in favour of a bland pop station called Power FM. I'm not even allowed Radio 1 ("too much dance music").

So what is this "real music" to which my teenage daughter (for she it was who was ordering me to turn mine down) is so committed? Why, none other than the collected works of Celine Dion and, horror of horrors, Mariah Carey. We are woken daily by the lobotomised warblings of these easy-listening giants, not to mention "live" high-pitched accompaniments from the shower. And still I bite my lip.

We had feared drugs, early pregnancy and skinhead boyfriends. Instead, our daughter's way of rebelling is to save up her pocket money to purchase a Mariah Carey album. Well, I'm sure as hell not going to buy it for her.

Contents

Cautionary Note

Because I have lived about six parallel lives, some of the chapters just sort of merge into each other, rather than behave in a chronological fashion. You'll get used to it.

Dedication

To the women in my life, of course: Birgit, Annabel, Lucy, Marble, Toffee and whatever the chickens are called. I'm sorry I didn't have the imagination to write you a novel.

Thanks to: Tim Barron, Ian Binnington, Judith Blake, Alan Clayson, Paul Dominy, David Eno, Tony Hill, Mint, John Parish, Tony Rollinson, Deirdre Sharp, Dave Steele, Trevor Stevens, Chris Stonor, Richard Williams and loads of other people.

Soundcheck: Parish Hell

I'm sitting on a plastic chair in a brightly-lit "dressing room" which is actually the subterranean premises of a village hall playgroup. It is nearly Christmas and we are surrounded by glittering decorations. But the mood is sombre.

I'm having a conversation with Simon Edwards. Simon plays accordion, sings and is the heart and soul of a really good little roots-punk band from Bristol called K-Passa. They've just played a storming set, but Simon isn't happy.

On the way up from Bristol to Winchester, the band broke down on the M4 near Swindon. Worse, the cause of the breakdown was a tyre blowout, which hurled them across three lanes of the motorway, causing them severe terror. Having phoned to say they would be late, they procured another van and eventually made it to Twyford Parish Hall, the venue where we now find ourselves. Great.

Well, not really. The problem is that the replacement van was smaller, and they have had to leave two vital band members behind in Swindon: the new, allegedly both brilliant and glamorous fiddle player, plus Simon's girlfriend, who is the vocalist. Without them, the sound, not surprisingly, is dangerously one-dimensional. What is worse, the lateness of their arrival has meant that they have been unable to do a soundcheck. The amps have been left on settings which are not appropriate to the hall and the PA operator has had no option but to crank up the volume to a level way beyond that which the audience is prepared to tolerate.

There is lots of screeching unintentional feedback. The audience is not pleased. By the time K-Passa have finished their set, two thirds of the crowd has left. There is not the slightest chance that any of them will buy K-Passa CDs or recommend the band to their friends. It has, through no fault of their own, not been a career-enhancing evening for the band.

So here I sit with Simon. The other members of K-Passa are all in the hall packing up their gear, but Simon wants to talk. His eyes are glazed and distant, but his attention is focused: His band is in trouble, and he knows who to blame. It's the manager.

K-Passa's manager is a bloke called Jim, a self-consciously eccentric Bristolian who acts, faithfully but not very effectively, as their agent.

This summer, he has bumblingly booked the band into a whole series of eclipse celebration festivals which have gone bankrupt. In each case, K-Passa have turned up, played and not been paid. Simon Edwards, you see, prides himself on the fact that he has never missed a gig. If an audience expects him to play, he will. If he doesn't get paid, well, that's bad, but he'll still play.

That was why K-Passa hadn't done the obvious thing today and caught a train back home to Bristol when their van broke down. They have a professional pride which wouldn't allow them to do so. But manager Jim was in the van as well and the only proposition he came up with was to blow out the gig and call out the RAC to take them home. This suggested act of professional dereliction has finally convinced Simon that Jim can no longer be in charge of managing the band's career..

I add fuel to the fire. Not that I want to be critical in any way (Jim sounded like a nice enough fellow on the phone), but Simon was mentioning that:

a. they didn't know how to find their way to this very off-the-map venue, and

b. they hadn't realised that we would be providing food.

How could this be? I had battled with the computer to produce a detailed map of the area and I had also explained that food would be provided and even what it would be. And I'd spent nearly a day producing a vat of vegetable curry for the band to consume.

None of this information was passed on, with the result that K-Passa took a vital extra half hour searching for the venue as well as spending money unnecessarily on something to eat *en route*. I, in turn, was left with flowing rivers of uneaten vegetable curry, not to mention an impatient audience, incapable of comprehending why the performance wasn't all they had expected.

There was something else as well, seemingly insignificant but perhaps crucial. I'd seen K-Passa before and knew that an essential part of their normal performance was a call-and-response shout of "Bollocks" between each song. Now I couldn't give a bollock about swearing, in fact have personally bellowed back with enthusiasm on a number of occasions, but I had my doubts about the potential response of the audience in Twyford. It's a small village and a good half of the audience would be off to the local church the next morning. Maybe they would be delighted to shout "Bollocks", but maybe they wouldn't. On balance, I thought it better to err on the side of caution and ask Simon if he wouldn't mind drawing in his sails for one evening.

So before booking the band, I had a couple of surreal phone conversations with manager Jim:

"Jim, it's a bit embarrassing, but would it be okay for Simon not to say "Bollocks"?"

"Don't worry, moy dear, if oi tells 'im not to say 'Bollocks', 'e won't say 'Bollocks'."

"Can you make sure? I wouldn't want him to be uncomfortable in any way."

"Don't worry, moy dear. Oi'll have a word with him and get back to you."

A week later, having heard nothing, I rang him back:

"Hi Jim, any news on the Bollocks front?"

"Oh yes, moy dear, oi've had a word with Simon and he's fine. He's absolutely guaranteed he won't say 'Bollocks'."

Just to make sure, when I returned the contract, I added a rider:

"The artiste agrees not to say 'Bollocks' on stage."

(Well okay, it wasn't phrased precisely in those words.)

So that was that, except that, when I sent the undelivered directions ten days before the gig, I also included a note: "Don't forget, no Bollocks".

So it was time to introduce the band, and as Simon and I mounted the stairs towards the stage, I thought I'd better have a final check:

"Don't forget, Simon, no Bollocks."

"No Bollocks?" Simon was aghast. "What do you mean, no Bollocks? I can't not say Bollocks!"

"But I agreed it with your manager. It's in your contract."

"What contract? We haven't got a contract. We haven't agreed to anything."

Simon Edwards is a professional. Within a moment, he had regained his composure. He wasn't going to let me down. Unconvincingly, he replaced his Bollocks with stadium clichés like "Are you ready?" and "Do you feel all right?". But the point was that he hadn't been told about my request. It just re-emphasised what he was thinking: There was going to have to be a management shake-up.

K-Passa have been through many, many line-ups during the course of their (so far) twelve year existence, and Simon was in other bands (for example the Boothill Foot Tappers) prior to that. Simon claims that all the members are professional musicians, earning their living from gigging. Like heck they are: I am generously paying them £450, but the essence of what Simon tells me is that a good proportion of other gigs pay either virtually nothing or actually nothing.

So it's obvious to me: K-Passa, who in the right circumstances are capable of great musical heights, are in the same position as so many bands I have encountered before. Brilliance or otherwise, in the music business, have essentially nothing to do with it. They clearly have no realistic future. The days when they might have had a chance of breaking through into the mainstream, securing a conventional record deal and appearing on Top Of The Pops are long gone, but their profile on the "alternative" scene is on the wane as well. Simon Edwards really ought to be thinking in terms of seeking a career which, while not being such a helter-skelter of excitement, would at least provide him with some sort of income. I don't dare say it, of course, but somehow I sort of imply it.

Simon is angry. He is a single-mindedly determined person. He is convinced that he and his band still have a future and he will contemplate nothing else. For him, playing music is the only option. For a second, he almost looks as if he's going to suggest that I might think about going into management, but he reacts promptly to the look in my eyes. He is the sort of person we'll meet frequently in this book, a person of vision and dogged self-belief. Just the sort of person I'm not.

This evening has upset me a lot. I have made a misjudgement in one way, but in another way I haven't. The decision had been to book John Otway to headline the show and K-Passa to support. So far, so good. But, worried that the audience would want to dance, I have decided to ask Otway, whose show is more in the way of a comedy act, to play first. I thought that K-Passa could follow him, as a few bands probably could. Based on past evidence, I was sure this would be no problem, but I had reckoned without that burst tyre. In the circumstances as detailed, it didn't work. Otway had been incredibly funny and K-Passa had been incredibly tense. Given the burst tyre, I had thought that the audience would have had more understanding. But they didn't. Lots of them just buggered off, looking annoyed. One bloke even stood there shouting "Rubbish!" What did he want, blood?

There was nothing really for me to be so pissed off about. Lots of people had a great time. But in the precise terms I had set myself, the promotion had not been as successful as I had hoped.

Simon Edwards is, in one way, a lot like me. I can't imagine either of us ever reaching a day when, like any sensible person, we will say, okay, the time has come to bid farewell to silly rock and roll dreams and go off and do something which makes some kind of sense.

My immediate problem is this: I've written this book and now I need to find some kind of hook to hang it on. *Memoirs of a Rock & Roll Failure* is enticing, but then my eye is caught by John Otway's merchandising stall. Prominently displayed on it is his best-selling autobiography: *Cor Baby That's Really Me!* What is its subtitle? *Rock and Roll's Greatest Failure.*

Bugger! How could I have forgotten? It's been done before. And, later that evening, I find that not only has it been done once before, but TWICE.

It's 2.30 am. I have finally picked up the last fag end and cleaned up the last drop of vomit. The gig is over and I am in desperate need of a few minutes' peace and quiet. In the kitchen, I sit down with the brand-new copy of *MOJO* magazine. I turn to the Book Review section.

Well, that bloody does it. Heaping insult upon injury, there is a glowing review of a brand new book by someone called Ed Jones. This man is the ex-bassist of The Tansads, a raggle-taggle band remarkably similar in style to K-Passa. I had seen them at least twice at the Joiners Arms in Southampton. He's only gone and written his memoirs, hasn't he? And he's only gone and subtitled it *The Life And Times Of A Failed Rock Star.*

All this is more than a little depressing. But after a moment's thought, I suddenly realise that it isn't depressing at all. Otway, tish! Ed Jones, forget him! All they have done is not manage to succeed in the rock and roll business as performers. They have got absolutely nothing on me. After all, I have:

- not succeeded as a performer;

- not succeeded as a songwriter;

- not succeeded as a guitar player;

- not succeeded as a manager;

- not succeeded as a promoter;

- not succeeded as a publicist;

- not succeeded as a record company owner;

- not succeeded as a rock journalist;

- not succeeded as a broadcaster;

and, before too long, I will be able to claim that I have:

- not succeeded as an author.

All in all, that's got to be some kind of achievement.

I. Hurr

This is the original article which led to the writing of this book. When I had finished it, I realised that there was no magazine or newspaper into whose format it would fit. So here it is. If you don't like it, it will save you the trouble of bothering to read the rest of the book.

If I was a teenager today, I would try for a Liam Gallagher/Ian Brown hairstyle. My hair is a statement and always will be, even when I no longer have any. I'll probably have my head tattooed.

Upon my mother's mantelpiece there is a photo of me with a haircut which was imposed upon me by my parents. Their idea of the only acceptable haircut for a male was very short at the back, very short at the sides and parted on the left, with the front swept to the side, rather in the manner of people attempting to conceal a bald patch. To this day, my mother will point to the fading evidence and pronounce, "That's how I really liked you", and it genuinely is true to say that she has never really liked me since it went away.

In schools, even today, hair is of tremendous significance to those in power. Although there is no reason to believe that it is true, leaders in schools think that an unconventional hairstyle is a sign of evil. That this is false is plain to see. For example, I myself am a fine upstanding citizen with no criminal or anti-social tendencies, but I have tended towards confrontational hairstyles ever since I have had a choice. Currently, it's the only thing possible, a pony tail. This does mean often being derided for trying to be an ageing trendy, but it still demonstrates the required attitude of rebelling against convention. Daft really, in view of how deeply conventional I am.

Of youngsters I have known, those with the Mohicans and the green gel have turned into the most gentle and responsible family men while many of those with the most "appropriate" haircuts have turned into hardened criminals and wife-beaters. My own children are divided: Annabel would dearly love me to look "like everyone else's dad" and if I felt that I was causing her genuine embarrassment, I would cut it off. However, it seems that enough of her friends think I'm "cool" for her to be prepared to tolerate it. Lucy, on the other hand, specifically does NOT want me to look "like everyone else's dad". She looks tearful every time I suggest any kind of change. As for my wife Birgit, she doesn't show any sign of not wanting to be seen with me. We all enjoy knocking people's preconceptions and I know that many people have uttered the words, "He's actually quite nice really, despite the mess he looks". Mess! It's not easy to maintain an image, I can tell you.

I can trace the beginning of my personal hairstyle revolution to a front page story in the Gloucester *Citizen*. Terry Dene, a Fifties rocker so obscure he doesn't even appear in the index of *Beat Merchants*, became involved in a fracas in a Westgate Street coffee bar prior to his show at the Regal. The locals were so outraged that I started to be interested in the image of Dene and similar singers such as Billy Fury and Marty Wilde. I began to gather the existence of strange and wonderful things known as Square Cuts and Bostons, both of which were ways of arranging the back of your head (which you never actually saw outside of a very uncomfortable procedure involving holding up one mirror behind you whilst squinting into another held up in front of you).

My mother had heard of these dangerous options, so it was impossible to ask for them in her presence. Every few weeks, she would take me into Stroud to the barber's shop. I worked out a method which entailed going ahead to the barber's on my own while Mother chatted to a lady in the wool shop. In this way, I could be ensconced in the seat and have already requested the crucial variation ("Boston please, Bob") before she arrived. Obsessed as they were with the parting and its position, my parents would never be aware of my Boston. Invisible to them, to me it was everything.

To Jock Harley it was everything too, but in quite a different way. Mr Harley was my mathematics teacher. He was a small person who had come originally from Cornwall and thus had a strong accent which was ideal for imitating and grossly exaggerating by his pupils. Jock was obsessed with preventing anyone else from having hair with any kind of style, and would relentlessly pursue anyone whose neck or ears were sullied by anything more than millimetre-length bristles. His catch-phrase was: " Yoo, boooy! Git yore hurrrr kott!", which would ring out along the echoey, disinfectant-smelling corridors all break and every lunchtime.

The morning after my first successful duping of my innocent mother into not noticing that my haircut had deviated from the norm, I entered school with the completely justified fear that Jock Harley would not be similarly deceived. I was right: Mr Harley's life was dedicated to spotting such perversions.

"Grayyyy, booooy," I heard from a number of yards behind me. "Uzz thutt a Squayur Kott?!"

"What do you mean, Sir?", I offered, in an attempt to appear innocent.

"Down't playy gaymezz with mee, booooy. That izz oyther a Squayer Kott or a Bozzton."

It needs to be said at this point that Jock Harley very probably didn't really speak like a cross between Hermann Goering and a member of the Wurzels, but that's how he sounded when we imitated him, and that's how he will live forever. And so....

"And what'z moore: You appearrrre to be growin' yore soide whusskerz."

Beneath the terror, I felt a faint stirring of pride. In my just post-pubescent state, there was no conceivable chance of growing genuine Soide Whusskerz; however, many hours of combing small strands of hair (which actually wanted to grow behind my ears) in front of them had obviously had the desired effect, at least upon Jock Harley. He actually thought I was growing my Soide Whusskerz! My defeat (for him) was a triumph (for me)!

That night, the back-of-head mirror sprung into action and Plan B was adopted. It was important that Jock Harley should think I had been back to the hairdresser's as he had ordered me to do, so the Squayer Kott had somehow to remain in a form which was acceptable to my peers as being one, but would appear to Jack to have been removed. It was hard, but it was possible. Similarly, the Soide Whusskerz had to be slicked back in such a way that Jock would think they had been shaved off, but so that they would in fact still be available to be retrieved and reinstated on the way to the bus station and in time to impress the girls of St. Peter's on the bus. And I managed it!

Over the coming months (The Beatles had arrived) something akin to civil disobedience occurred at school. It became impossible for Jock Harley to size up everyone's Hurr. His head would have had to spin permanently through 360 degrees. He was forced to move on to ensuring that the Hurr didn't actually CUVVURR the EARZZ.

Which was, of course, the frontier that we would aim at pushing back next.

The next stage in my permanently ongoing hair fixation was determined by fan-worship of Tony Hicks, the lead guitarist of the Hollies. He always did have the world's best hairstyle and he still does. This is a very rare and precious gift.

When I first became interested in the Hollies, Tony had a hairstyle which, for the time, was perfect in its appropriateness for what he was doing (playing inspiredly casual lead guitar and singing harmony backup vocals in a combo which, at the time, prior to monstrosities such as "Jennifer Eccles", had considerable credibility). His hair (as displayed on the cover of *Stay With The Hollies*, their first album) was coiffed into an exquisitely Brylcreem-sculpted Eddie Cochran quiff which somehow didn't look like a teddy-boy. This contrasted with his colleague Graham Nash, who had a virtually identical style and an even more goofy grin, but merely looked a twat. For me it was crucial to be a Tony Hicks and not a Graham Nash. Whatever the elusive magic was, I had to have it.

Actually acquiring a "Tony Hicks" was quite out of the question, since, unlike a Square Cut or a Boston, it would have been impossible to disguise. But luckily, fate took a hand in the form of Beatlemania and the invention of the Beatle cut.

Tony Hicks: the Mildly Flattened Hamster Years
(Drawing by Lydia Metz)

You can trace on Beatles photos the arrival of the Mop Top style (in early photos they all sport teddy-boy quiffs), and all contemporary bands not destined for obscurity followed with alacrity. My style guru Tony Hicks adopted what to this day I consider to be the quintessential hairstyle by changing to a mop top which genuinely looked like a mop, i.e. it tumbled floppily (Flop Top?) from the apex of his crown to lie in a symmetrical sugar bowl style which needed no cosmetics or attention to keep it in perfect shape. I could almost surmise that he didn't even comb it, such was its casually impeccable state at the end of lengthy energetic live performances; on the other hand, I don't believe that Tony Hicks has sweat glands, actually.

But why am I using the past tense? Tony Hicks is still performing and he still has the same sublime head of hair (plus, no doubt, an ageing portrait in the attic). This desirable crowning glory can be viewed to best effect on the sleeve of the Hollies' 1966 album *For Certain Because*, but when the Hollies are next billed to play in your town, have a closer look at the fly posters. There, under the spotlight, stage right, clutching the cherry-red guitar, you'll see the mildly-flattened hamster that is the quintessential "Tony Hicks". And Graham Nash? Wouldn't you know it? He KEPT HIS QUIFF! At least for the time being. He became cool later, when he joined Crosby, Stills and Nash, but that's another story.

I worked hard on my Tony Hicks and naively believed that I approximately attained it; photos from this Sixth Form era reveal, however, that I was far, far away. The problem was the lack of texture and substance and a horrifying propensity for irritating little wispy, curly bits spoiling the overall picture. It wasn't until John Yorke came into my life that I learned a bit about how to tackle "butterflies".

****

Beginning university was quite a culture shock. For a start, I met John Vincent Yorke.

I'm not sure about the concept of retrospective respect, but John is due for some on account of something I didn't find out until recently. I knew that he had attended Eltham Green School and been expelled from it. I now know that these are two things he had in common with Boy George. John, anyway, was a wide boy who had sussed that he could get a year's free dossing at university before being asked to leave, and it seemed a pretty good option to him. So, nominally studying Sociology, he never actually attended any lectures or seminars or wrote any essays. John was free to party all night and spend all day sleeping and "smoothing".

Smoothing was a word invented by John and it meant a complicated but vital procedure necessary for attaining the perfect hairstyle. Its purpose was to eliminate "butterflies", which are those hated little wispy bits referred to earlier. The (correct) premise was that all butterflies must be killed at all costs and that if it took time, it took time. The derivation of the word was connected with the intended smoothness of the hair and the smoothness (= hipness) of its possessor.

So here's how to get rid of butterflies. First wash your hair carefully, rinsing several times. Dry very lightly, using a towel. During this process, take strands of hair between folds of the towel and pull down slowly but firmly from the top of the head to the end of the hair. Then switch on the hair dryer. Using a specially purchased round hairbrush, insert it kind of underneath the hair above the ears and very slowly draw the hair down to the ends with the brush, applying the dryer (set on medium heat) all the while. Just as you reach the bottom, gently twist the brush one more time towards the head, thus ensuring that the ends curl inwards, if at all. On no account may they curl outwards; the optimal result, of course, is complete straightness. Repeat the entire procedure all round for at least forty-five minutes or until hair is completely dry. Do not on any account go out in the rain or the wind, or all your work will be wasted.

Perfectly Smoothed. *For instructions, see this page.*

Tony Hicks, of course, steps straight out of the shower and achieves all this without any effort. Bastard.

John Yorke taught me how to do this and in our rooms we would spend Saturday afternoons preparing for the evening ahead. Favourites to emulate at the time were various Small Faces, the Action and, distressingly, in retrospect, Tich (out of Dave Dee, Dozy...), because they not only had no butterflies but also sported a little backcombed bit at the crown of the head, like a kind of fluffy skullcap. John was adept at creating one of these, but the shape of my head meant that it just refused to work on me. John was a Mod and I would initially have been interested in going in that direction, I suppose, but I was relieved that we were on the cusp of the transfer into general long-hairedness as a fashion. This meant that butterfly eradication was sufficient and that I didn't need to get into armache-inducing backcombing sessions.

So off we would go to the Saturday night gigs and do the little Mod dance which involved shuffling of feet, clicking of fingers but very little shaking of heads. The music came from The Mike Cotton Sound, Herbie Goins and the Night Timers or Geno Washington, and we thought the girls would be irresistibly attracted by our butterfly-free zones. Sometimes they were, but I didn't go as far as John, who refused to let girls run their hands through his hair for fear of disturbing it.

John had found his perfect hairstyle and stuck with it, but I was consumed with the desire for flowing locks and therefore continued to apply the anti-butterfly technology whilst growing the hair as fast as I could. I think I felt that the downward-stroking motions would make it grow faster, almost as if you could pull it out from an endless internal source (you can do this with a strimmer, did you know?). I now had new heroes to follow, in the form of Glenn, Trevor and Miles, three incredibly cool sociology students onto whom I latched. Both had perfectly straight, perfectly-smoothed shoulder-length hair and Miles had no surname. This later made me wonder whether he could have turned into Miles, the surnameless rock journalist, but I suppose we shall never know. One of my proudest possessions is a photo of me, Glenn, Trevor and Miles setting off to a Fairport Convention gig in Colchester. There is no wind and no rain and we all look spectacular. Just for that photo, it was worth all the effort. Unfortunately, the album also contains countless crap photos of interest only to lepidopterists.

So what became of John Yorke? He got a job packing records at Virgin Mail Order and was assimilated into the record industry, an ideal place for a lazy, vain, charming wastrel with flair. I only saw him a couple more times, but his anti-butterfly technique has been with me ever since.

******

No one will be surprised to hear that this interest made any further meaningful relationship with my parents a total impossibility. The shame of being associated with me was too much for them to bear, so they requested that I should come home as little as possible. It was fortunate that I was due for my year "abroad", a device which to the university authorities meant improving my standard of German but to me meant a glorious nine months of total turpitude.

I met Jochen Schmidt in the queue at the University of Kiel accommodation office, which meant that we ended up sharing a flat. Jochen, like all young Germans, had just completed his national service and thus was short-haired. Being similarly obsessed with musicians and their appearance, he aimed to change this as soon as possible, and thus was very keen to take lessons from me on the subject of smoothing. Outrageous as it may seem, in view of the fact that we were so poor that we could pay for no heating, transport and hardly any food, we spent our virtually non-existent cash on a HAIR-DRYER! And we never for a moment questioned the wisdom of such an action.

If I thought I was vain, Jochen Schmidt had me beaten hands down. In his ability to spend entire days in front of a mirror with hair dryer in one hand and brush in the other, he made John Yorke look like an amateur. He did, however, go to extremes. For instance, he refused point blank to set foot outside the flat if it was raining or snowing. This, in the bleak northern European climate of Schleswig-Holstein, was a real problem. There was also the little matter that the flat had no source of hot water, so every smoothing session had to be irrigated by an endless sequence of saucepans of boiling water (since the Germans have an aversion to kettles). The upshot of this was that the flat was permanently filled with condensation, resulting in freezing, damp beds and windows which were impossible to look out of.

The place to be and the place to be seen in Kiel was the Spektrum Club, now sadly a carpet shop. The DJ there was Paul Raven, later better known as Gary Glitter, although he can't have made much of an impression on me. All I can remember about Spektrum was many hours spent on the dance floor doing nothing but shake my hair. In contrast to the university hops, it was here important to be rooted to one spot on the floor and move nothing but the head, the feel of the flapping of the hair being a reassurance that it was indeed there and that one was indeed as hip as one thought one was. Jochen Schmidt and I would stand there and sway from midnight until three o'clock in the morning. The soundtrack was the then currently fashionable sort of track which lasted the whole side of an album, such as Iron Butterfly's In A Gadda Da Vida, various extended James Brown workouts and, curiously for a band noted for its brevity, an endless version of "Suzie Q (Parts 1 & 2)", by Creedence Clearwater Revival. Later, we would repair to Club 68, where we would sit cross-legged in corners and hope that girls would think we looked mysterious and intellectual. Jochen must have looked more mysterious and intellectual than me, because he would take far more girls back to the soggy sheets than I managed to. Maybe it was partly because I had an embarrassing tendency to fall asleep in the Club 68 and get thrown out.

The band that we worshipped was Free. Tonsorially speaking, it was hard to justify this, because the band was a hairstyle disaster area, with only one member out of four being really well-smoothed. Andy Fraser, the bassist, had an awful poodle-cut, singer Paul Rodgers' locks, though long and flowing, were coarse and unacceptably wavy, while Paul Kossoff....well, no wonder he got himself a drug habit. Drummer Simon Kirke, however, was the man. His hair was blonde, straight as a dye and fell forward to completely obscure his facial features as he walloped his drums in a wonderful minimalist fashion which has never really been given the acknowledgement it is due. That was what we were trying to look like as we swayed on the dance floor, and do you know, we probably didn't do badly.

One fantastic Tuesday evening, Free played live at the Spektrum club. It was the first time I heard "All Right Now". The entire band looked hopelessly out of it and played like angels. On the way home, I became involved in a bizarre episode which entailed getting arrested for fly-posting. It was a genuine mistake, since what I was actually doing was the opposite, i.e. REMOVING a poster of Free from a wall in order to put it up in my bedroom. When all this was explained, I was released amidst much hilarity.

The next weekend, we hitched to Copenhagen and ended up in the Tivoli Pleasure Gardens. Eager for further pleasure, we tried to impress some young girls by taking them repeatedly on the Big Dipper, but eventually impressed them much more by pretending to be members of Free on a night off from their European tour. Dark-haired Jochen Schmidt, slightly dishevelled from repeated goes on the "Ruschebeen", was Paul Rodgers and I, of course, was Simon Kirke. Just for one night, we got a mild feel for what it must have been like to be in a pop group, because yes, the girls believed it and yes, they were impressed. Once again, smoothing had proved its worth.

Twenty-five years on, Jochen Schmidt still lives in Kiel, still smoothing by day and grooving by night. He also still listens to the same records, which include *Those About To Die* by Colosseum, *A Doughnut In Granny's Greenhouse* by the Bonzo Dog Band, and *Bakerloo*, by (wait for it) Bakerloo. This little-known epic featured Clem Clempson, an excellently-smoothed guitarist, later to appear in Humble Pie and Colosseum. An original copy of this album is priceless; luckily, Jochen Schmidt won the National Lottery in 1990 and was able to obtain a mint version to replace the scratched one which I left behind in Kiel.

So, one way and another, nothing much has changed for Jochen Schmidt. The only difference is that his hugely impressive mane is totally white.

II. Tschairmany 1: Sharks

When I was fifteen, my father was keen to encourage me in what appeared to be a developing talent for languages. Via a convoluted web of acquaintances, he found me a German exchange partner by the name of Johann-Hinrich Möller. This person made it obvious that he didn't at all enjoy the kind of regimented existence that I had both at home and at school, and together we returned halfway across Europe to his home town of Schöningen, just by the East German border, in order to carry out the German leg of the exchange. There, I grew up a great deal in a very short time.

This applied particularly in the field of linguistic ability. As soon as we arrived, we sat down to a sumptuous meal of Johann's favourite dish, prepared specially to welcome him home: Eisbein. This innocuous-sounding item is, in fact, a pig's foot, and in case you have difficulty picturing a pig's foot, it consists of a lump of bone surrounded by a huge blob of fat, roasted in the oven. It came, as is the tradition, served with my two least-favourite accompaniments, namely Sauerkraut (pickled cabbage) and Kartoffelpuree (mashed potato).

After I had pushed this lot around the plate a few times, trying to compress it so that it looked as if some of it had been eaten, Johann's mother asked the inevitable question:

"Would you like some more, Oliver?" (Doubtless no Dickensian connotation intended.)

"Nein danke, Frau Möller. Ich bin voll."

It wasn't until days later that I was told that, far from meaning "I'm full", this actually meant "I'm drunk". They all kept impeccably straight faces and Frau Möller persevered:

"Is there a draught? Would you like me to close the window?"

"Nein danke, Frau Möller," I replied, confident in my memory of an obscure piece of vocabulary I had come across, meaning "hot and sticky".

"Ich bin schwul."

There was certainly a sharp intake of breath at this point, but again, it wasn't until much later that it emerged that I should really have said *Mir ist schwül*". My actual words had not meant "No thank you, I'm hot", but instead meant "No thank you, I am homosexual". I was negotiating a very sharp learning curve.

Johann-Hinrich had a guitar, a proper acoustic one with gut strings. He had had lessons and possessed a book of chords. Apart from German Chansonniers like Reinhard Mey, Johann was a big fan of Donovan, someone whom I had rather unfairly overlooked on account of his being a solo artist and non-electric. I started to approve of Donovan when Johann's song book revealed that you could make a reasonable stab at his entire works with a mere three chords. I learnt them and was immediately able to make a passable attempt at strumming "Catch The Wind" and "To Try For The Sun". My trump card was that I could impersonate Donovan's drawl without singing things like *Ketch ze vint*, and I soon realised that beautiful girls like Brigitte, Christa and Ute were impressed. I had liaisons with all three of them as well as with Jany, a French exchange student. All of them knew of this multiple faithlessness and none of them seemed to mind.

Music was becoming more and more interesting. When I got home, Jany sent me a copy of a record by the French singer Richard Anthony, with a message of love on the sleeve. The song was "J'irai pleurer sous la pluie", a French language version of "Crying In The Rain".

"In the chilly hours and minutes of uncertainty, I long to be, in the warm hold of your loving mind", I would bray, so everyone automatically assumed I understood and knew the words to all the English-language songs around at the time. This rapidly became a major burden, as a succession of people beat a path to Johann-Hinrich's door to implore me to decipher, interpret and, heaven forbid, translate their favourite songs into German. Foremost among these challenging lyrics was Barry McGuire's "Eve of Destruction". I got as far as "This old world it is explodin', sirens wailin', bullets loadin'" and I managed the chorus of "And you tell me over and over and over again my friend, how you don't believe we're on the eve of destruction".

This was pretty cool stuff, and impressed the youth of Schöningen enough to encourage them to approach me with other mysteries from the juke box of Amos's Italian Eiscafé, where we would congregate every afternoon after school to eat delicious ice cream and smoke as many cigarettes as humanly possible. I sucked up to one particular character called Ali who had a Beatle cut and I thought was especially hip. It turned out that he was a heavy-duty evangelical Christian and only had a fringe because that was just the way his hair happened to fall. I turned my attention to a girl who I think remains probably the most perfect human being I have ever seen, called Carla Jacobi. For her sake, I struggled for days with the Byrds' version of "Mr Tambourine Man". I remember walking the cobbled streets late at night, desperately trying to make some sense out of this mumbled gibberish:

"Take me for a trip upon your magic swirling ship,
And I like fish and chips
And my bathroom tap still drips,
And my feet too young to slip
Wait only for my boot heels to be wandering ..."

How the bloody hell was I supposed to understand or explain this stuff? Eventually I confessed to Carla that I was incapable of fulfilling the task she had set me and she completely lost interest.

Another prominent item was The Rolling Stones' "Satisfaction", which I first heard on Amos's juke box. A complete musical revelation, it nonetheless posed equally challenging lyrical problems and, just as with that damn Tambourine Man, I would run out of steam:

"When I'm driving in my car and a man comes on the radio, telling me more and more about some useless information supposed to fire my imagination ..." Yes, accepted the attentive crowd, but can you explain the political significance of these lyrics?

I was much more at home with the other German smash hit of the season, a version of "Brand New Cadillac" by an obscure band from Birmingham called The Renegades. They looked great in their American Civil War outfits. I've just been out to the shed to check that picture sleeve single - do you suppose it's valuable? The languid and, let's now face up to it, piss-poor performance had a charm all of its own, and I could relate to lyrics which were as empty-headed as rock and roll ought to be:

My baby drove off in a brand-new Cadillac,
She ain't never ever comin' back.

Baby baby baby please,
Can't you see I'm on my bended knees?
Your heart's so cold that it's gonna freeze.

Then, with a startled gulp from the singer, it lurches into a gloriously haphazard guitar solo that I can still remember every tiny nuance of today. I wonder what became of The Renegades? I hope they're all well.

Although my new friends weren't at all interested in such insignificant lyrics, the song was the highlight and climax of the live set of Schöningen's best (only) beat group, the Sharks. Another great band name, briefly purloined years later by a band formed by Chris Spedding and a post-Free Andy Fraser.

The Sharks had a great dayglo poster featuring their silhouettes throwing improbable guitar poses and it thrilled me utterly. Since you ask, yes, I do still have one in the shed. For what they were, they were absolutely excellent, a true Merseybeat style beat group of a kind you would never have expected to find in a small town in rural Germany. The girls worshipped them and so did the boys, and so, of course, did I. Johann was on nodding terms with them and I was desperate to belong to their scene, much like I have been with bands ever since.

Their trousers were wonderful, of a kind so preposterous that they never caught on in the UK. They were called *Hose mit Schlag*, which meant flared. But these were no ordinary flares. They were so wide that they completely covered the cuban-heeled winklepickers beneath them, but more than that, the flared bits had a pleat in them. And the pleat was held together by a little gold (plastic) chain. I promise it's true.

I coveted those trousers more than anything in the world, but they were to remain unobtainable, firstly for financial reasons but mainly because I would never have been allowed to wear them at home. Unlike the Boston Hurr Kott, they would have been impossible to disguise.

The thought of these trousers always brings to my mouth the delicious taste of something else which was new to me: the joy of German chips (*Pommes Frites*, pronounced Pom Fritz) with both ketchup and mayonnaise. Crunchy and cooked from frozen, these were a thousand times better than their soggy, vinegar-drenched

»the sharks«

The Sharks. Unfeasible trousers not illustrated.

English counterparts. Late one night, queuing in the Imbiss, I looked down and realised, from the magnificence of the Hose mit Schlag in front of me, that I was standing behind Wolfgang Baumann, lead guitarist of the Sharks. I had been introduced to him before, and hoped that my Englishness would make him want to know me. When he turned round, I smiled and nodded, but he just turned away. Probably my trousers were to blame.

Every Saturday, The Sharks played in a back-room, back-street club called "Beat Club", behind a pub called *Zum Goldenen Löwen* (Golden Lion). This environment suited me sufficiently for me to want to spend disproportionate amounts of the rest of my life in crowded, smoky, smelly, sweaty back rooms having my brains blown apart by loud music. I would drink too much beer, eat too many Pommes mit Mayo and spend much of the night throwing up into Johann's wash basin. To get it to go down the waste pipe, I had to plunge my hand into the vomit and swirl my finger round the plug hole. Then I would feebly try to remember the chords to "Catch The Wind" before passing out on the bed. I assumed nobody knew about this shame, but the room must have reeked of sick and besides, I was making frightening sea-lion noises. Of course they knew; they were just too polite to make a fuss.

One day, the entire teenage population of Schöningen climbed aboard several coaches and headed off to Wolfsburg, where, in a large warehouse-sized hall, a beat group competition was to take place. The Sharks had already won though several heats and this was the regional final. Each band had brought along its own gang of supporters so it came as little surprise that, as the flowing beer took hold, minor scuffles began to break out all around the room.

The Sharks played fabulously, looking and sounding every bit as though they were about to take on the world. It was obvious that they were bound to win, but they didn't. Instead, the judges plumped for a cheesy, lightweight combo fronted by a pretty girl, who had performed some dire versions of various current *Schlager* (pop songs). Instantly, the mood turned ugly, as the Sharks' supporters protested and the followers of all the other bands turned on us.

Like falling dominoes, a wave of fighting splashed right across the hall from wall to wall. Brigitte, the girl who had first befriended me, had in the meantime returned to her original boyfriend, a rather small and rotund person. Brigitte leapt onto a table, holding up her skirt as if being threatened by a mouse, and screamed for several minutes, while her boyfriend picked up a chair and stood in front of her, repelling boarders by brandishing a chair as if he were a lion tamer.

Not only was I a Sharks supporter but I also looked distinctive, in a striped Marks and Spencer jumper not available in Germany. Of course I had worn it to attract attention to myself, but now deeply regretted it. As I realised I was about to be beaten to a pulp, I did the only thing I could think of doing and bolted under Brigitte's table, folding myself up into the foetal position. From there, I could listen to the rumbling, crunching sound which characterises mass fighting. Winklepickers and cuban heels swished past various parts of my anatomy, but none connected, because I was so far under the table that my attackers tended to bash their knees before the kicks could land. Besides, in true Western film tradition they, too, were being tapped on the shoulder from behind and then being knocked out cold when they turned round.

I crouched under the table for what seemed like hours, only emerging when everything seemed to have gone quiet. Brigitte was still on the table, ashen-faced and quivering, while her boyfriend clutched a handkerchief to his bleeding temple. All around was total devastation. The entire place had been completely laid waste apart from, by some miracle, our table.

There was a wonderful result of all this. The riot commanded a front page news item in the next day's Bild-Zeitung. Entitled "Schlägerei beim Beat", it cited the Sharks as the chief culprits. This was a major triumph, since Bild-Zeitung is a mass-circulation tabloid. It was like being featured on the front page of the Sun, only better, and it meant that the Sharks enjoyed a brief period of national notoriety.

Twenty-five years later, I returned, out of curiosity, to Schöningen, accompanied by my wife Birgit. The visit was peculiar in the extreme, because virtually nothing had changed. The Golden Lion and the Beat Club were there, still featuring live bands and with unchanged decor.

Trembling with anticipation and fearing disappointment, we entered the hallowed portals of Amos's Eiscafé and approached the juke box. Oh Heaven! There, in amongst the current hits and Schlager, there they still were: "Satisfaction", "Eve of Destruction" and "Mr Tambourine Man". Of course, we put them on, guzzled ice cream and almost (but not quite) lit up a commemorative cigarette. Amos had retired but the café was being run by his son.

Without much hope, I enquired what had happened to the Sharks.

"Oh, Wolfgang Baumann still comes in here sometimes. He works in the woods as a forester. Would you like his phone number?"

I declined. If he had failed to acknowledge me in the queue for the chips, he was hardly likely to relish being phoned up twenty-five years later. Besides, I couldn't have borne to see him wearing ordinary trousers.

III. Beat Crazy

So here's the old cliché question: What was the first single you ever bought? Normally, the answer doesn't turn out to be anything particularly influential, and that's true of me. It was "Tie Me Kangaroo Down Sport" by Rolf Harris, which I guess I must have heard on Children's Favourites with Derek McCullough. Poor Uncle Mac was normally baffled by any new developments in music, but Rolf Harris was acceptable, along with "How Much Is That Doggie In The Window?" and my personal favourite, "Champion the Wonder Horse". In fact, listening to the entire programme every Saturday morning just on the off-chance that "Champion" might be played would also be the answer to that other vital query: "When did you first realise that rock and roll would rule your life?" Goose pimples, shivers down the spine, the lot. I didn't realise then, but I do now, that it all began with Frankie Laine.

"Tie Me Kangaroo Down" had everybody working unsuccessfully on wobble board construction, but the best thing about this single (I've just been out to the shed to check) was the B-side, brilliantly entitled "Nick Teen and Al K. Hall". In this, Rolf extols the virtues of his "two good amigos" (thankfully not "Two Little Boys") and warbles the immortal line "I'm still pure as the driven slush". This clever wordplay had an effect on my father who, for the first (and last) time ever would allow me to listen to a pop single in his presence. "That's actually rather clever," he would huff, reluctantly.

At the 1998 Glastonbury Festival, Rolf Harris played the acoustic stage in an epic performance which won over every cynic present. I optimistically called out for "Nick Teen and Al K. Hall", but he didn't respond. The poor chap was too overcome with emotion. He tearfully declared that day at Glastonbury to be the best of his life, and nobody felt like disagreeing.

It wasn't long before the DOCs made their world début. Good name for a band, eh? Why haven't there ever been any other bands called the DOCs? Short, snappy, vague narcotic hints, it's got the lot. Unlike us. We had nothing apart from cricket bats, cardboard boxes and knitting needles. But we did have a stage.

Duckworth, Oliver, Clewes. That's how the DOCs got their name. Roger Duckworth was my mate from school, Oliver was me and

Robert Clewes was my neighbour and friend. He was disapproved of by my parents because his dad had a midlands accent. I approved of him hugely because he allowed us all to watch *Ready Steady Go* every Friday evening on their black and white TV. My parents, by contrast, spent a lifetime disapproving of TV and not allowing one in the house.

Obviously, *Ready Steady Go* was a major influence on the DOCs. Being the drummer, my original role-models were the likes of Ringo, Charlie Watts and Dave Clark. On the sofa, one could arrange a biscuit tin lid as a hi-hat, another as a ride cymbal and a selection of cushions of different sizes and consistencies to correspond to the various drums. None of this presented any problems for the relatively simple patterns of any of these drummers. Ringo and Charlie we quite respected, but as for Dave Clark, oh dear, oh dear.

We were convinced that Dave Clark's records were played by a session drummer. This probably wasn't true, but it sure as hell looked like it to us. As he haplessly attempted to mime the *dadilly-dadilli-dadilli-dadilli-da* drum roll which characterises "Bits and Pieces", he would invariably reach the end of the supply of drums and wind up playing in thin air, while the sound continued to emerge. All this was achieved while sitting bolt upright in a white polo-neck sweater, his head wobbling like a chicken, his drumsticks hovering unconvincingly inches above the cymbals and his face split by an asinine grin.

There was amusement to be had, not so much in trying to copy Dave Clark's drumming (which was easy) but in attempting to reproduce his awful mannerisms and hideously un-rock and roll attitude. Of all the people we didn't want to be, The Dave Clark Five came right at the top of the list. It did appear that the organist, Mike Smith, who also sang, had a certain amount of talent and ability, but there was no magic such as The Kinks or The Hollies possessed.

Roger Duckworth's house had a barn attached to it, a barn with a hay loft. The DOCs would perform from this high, ready-made stage for hours on end, mostly Beatles songs from *Revolver* or *Rubber Soul*, but also quite a lot of instrumentals by Jet Harris and Tony Meehan. These could be sung without the difficulty of having to learn any lyrics, although it was important to imitate the exact guitar tone with your voice. We still had no instruments and cricket bats are hard to tune. The works of Jet and Tony invariably contained a drum solo, which I found very convenient. I learnt Tony Meehan's parts by heart and dedicated myself to finding cardboard boxes with different tunings, so I could ego-trip with my mother's knitting needles (she had several different sizes). Sandy Nelson's "Drums Are My Beat" was another great one for this approach.

Normally, the barn was completely empty apart from us. On rare occasions, the Moreland sisters from next door would come and listen in. We assumed that our efforts would make them lustful towards us, but normally they would retire in boredom after a few minutes.

My parents couldn't be allowed to know this was going on. That's why I had to be the drummer, since there was no chance that they would ever buy me a musical instrument. Popular music was a lower class occupation and worthy only of complete contempt. The worst term of abuse was "crooner", which they applied to people like Dean Martin and Bing Crosby, and pronounced like an expectoration of phlegm. The arrival of The Beatles was treated with total, utter incomprehension, certainly a potential end to civilisation. The only way they knew how to react to the musical revolution was to pretend it wasn't happening at all, and certainly had no conceivable application anywhere near our house or our family.

Roger and Rob had no such restrictions and both were bought extremely cheap and nasty acoustic guitars by their parents. These guitars had lethal steel strings. We didn't know how to tune them, we had no amplification, and we didn't know any chords anyway, so most of the time was spent miming (probably better than Dave Clark). Stardom didn't beckon for the DOCs, then, but we did work out one complete song because Roger had had the occasional piano lesson. The song was Billy J. Kramer's "Little Children", which, despite being a complete dirge, got to Number One. Actually, Billy did have one brilliant record, the Merseybeat-defining Beatles song "Do You Want To Know A Secret" (much too hard for us to contemplate) and the Dakotas were notable for having a guitarist with a glass eye. With the help of some sheet music, we managed "Little Children" all the way through, with piano, inaudible guitar, cushions and knitting needles. I hated it and in general, we realised that the traditional pastimes of bashing tennis balls against walls and charging dangerously round the lanes on push-bikes were better ways to occupy our time.

I do remember something just awful. We were playing cricket in Roger's garden and I was trying to bat when onto the radio came my first hearing of The Kinks' "You Really Got Me". It was just shattering and, like hundreds of thousands of others all over the world, I had my entire musical taste defined for life by that gloriously rebellious, simple yet genius-like guitar sound, riff and song. *Waagh Waagh Waagh Waagh Waagh ...* . The guitar solo (who cares who played it?) had the effect of making me no longer able to control the diarrhoea which had been brewing all day. And I was wearing cricket trousers. Never before or since have I felt so humiliated, but it is a measure of what good friends I had that I was never teased about it.

Every day, when I got home from school, I would sit in front of the fire with the tea and blackcurrant jam on toast that my mother would make me. On the radio (Light Programme) there were great early-evening music programmes, many of which were broadcast from Manchester. They would feature Bob Miller and the Millermen, Joe Loss and his Orchestra (with Elvis Costello's dad Ross McManus on vocals) and, most frequently, the BBC Northern Dance Orchestra. One programme was called "Here We Go With The NDO", and the format was the day's hits being covered, in front of a live audience, by the orchestra and various guest vocalists. This I could take or leave, but what was so exciting was the fact that the BBC was boldly introducing the new beat group phenomenon into this format. Most of the best bands seemed to come from the North, and groups like The Mindbenders, The Merseybeats and The Big Three shocked, amazed and impressed me with their ability to play, their accessibility and the excitement both of the R & B standards they covered and the original songs they presented.

One very noticeable thing was how quickly music was being transformed. A particularly striking band was The Swinging Blue Jeans. What on earth possessed them to call themselves such a daft name? When they first appeared on "Here We Go", they were called The Bluegenes and their most prominent instrument was a banjo. They did sort of swing and sounded like a cross between a skiffle group and a trad jazz band. But then The Beatles started appearing on the show and many bands came under their spell. The Swinging

Blue Jeans, who confusingly had one member called Ellis and another called Ennis, became a standard issue beat group and achieved fame with "Hippy Hippy Shake". Then, in a time-honoured tradition used slavishly by the record industry to this day, they followed it up with a ridiculous carbon copy. This version of "Good Golly Miss Molly" featured the same riff and structure, but despite actually being a better record, it was less of a success. By the time they hit their best form with a super cover of Betty Everett's "You're No Good", their star was on the wane, helped along by a dreadful album with an over-obvious sleeve picture of some blue jeans on a washing line. I've still got it somewhere and, what is more, the Swinging Blue Jeans are still swinging in 60s revival packages. I don't know whether that's inspiring or depressing.

At school, this type of music was not deemed to exist. Because I couldn't play any instruments, I hung around with people who could, and would be given jobs such as reading lessons between hymns at the carol service. Each year, there was a music competition between the various school "houses" and I became involved in a surprising turn-up when our house decided to do something neither classical nor choral: a live (from sheet music) performance of "Cast Your Fate To The Wind", an attractive piano instrumental which was a surprise hit for Sounds Orchestral. This was performed by my colleague Roger Green with the help of a person drumming who had never actually played drums and read his part from the sheet music.

I call Roger Green a colleague rather than a friend because he wasn't a friend. Everyone assumed he was because we had similar surnames and studied exactly the same subjects. But he was an ugly little shit and I thought I wasn't, so I found it very insulting that people would constantly confuse us or, worse, assume we were a single entity called "Grayngreen". I was allowed to compère the music competition, Roger Green made loads of mistakes, the competition was won by a surprise entry which trumped us by covering "Apache" by The Shadows, and several people congratulated me on my piano playing. Bastards!

Attempting now to put my old singles into some kind of chronological order of purchase, I find that I must, shortly after Rolf's magnum opus, have bought a Cliff Richard record. I undeniably have in the shed a copy of "Bachelor Boy". Turning it over makes me blush, because there we find the other half of this "Double A", called "It's All In The Game". This ballad contains references to kissing lips and caressing finger tips (odd occupation) which I found distasteful, being at the age when things like kissing and caressing were frightening and offputting. In fact, I must have actually been offended and corrupted by Cliff Richard, quite an achievement.

When my father's key could be heard turning in the lock, I would quickly switch off the radiogram and feign doing homework. Now and then, he would surprise me and lift the needle off the record, shouting "I won't have this rubbish played in my house". It was purely a class matter. Cliff and the Shadows were a terrible threat because they were uncultured and appeared to come from the lower classes yet still be successful. A couple of times, my father actually removed singles from the record player, snapped them and threw them in the bin. This is what happened to "The Rise and Fall of Flingel Bunt", a Shadows single which the DOCs were particularly adept at miming to.

It was and is hard to comprehend what gave my father the impression that we were above such things. Ours was not an upper class family by any means. My mother left school at fourteen and had only ever been an office worker and a housewife, while my father was, for much of his career, an insurance clerk. He was, however, extremely intelligent and obsessed with history, which was why he changed career late in life to train as an archivist. As a historian, he knew where our family "came from". We had been the "Grays of York" (it's still possible to visit Gray's Court, just by York Minster) but our side of the family had long since fallen on hard times. My parents were always hard up, and they only sent me to private school by denying themselves virtually everything, a peculiarly British piece of daftness which thousands of families still do today. But other strands of the family were, indeed, wealthy and considered themselves upper class, and my father was desperate for none of us to do anything which could be perceived as bringing shame on him.

I never forgave my father for his cruel treatment of my music. Our relationship was destroyed by his actions and words at that early teenage part of my life and only thawed slightly when he became old and infirm and I began to feel protective, even affectionate towards him. But it made me resolve never to behave in a similar way towards any music my own children may like, no matter how hard I find it to relate to. That is why, as I write, I can hear the wailings and shriekings of Mariah Carey wafting down the stairs and I won't, just won't complain. Oh God!

As far as pop music was concerned, King's School was an arid desert; such music didn't exist. When I now meet Richard Shephard, a contemporary at King's who is the headmaster of a Choir School, it would be reasonable to assume that we can't have a great deal in common. That is true, but we can still spend hours reflecting on what a terrible, terrible school it was and what a hopeless education it gave us. We reminisce endlessly about how abjectly poor most of the teachers were and how I was permanently getting into trouble because of my unhealthy obsession with all things which related to beat groups.

Plum was our German teacher. We thought he was mad, because he claimed that he spent the summer holidays writing French grammar books. Little did I realise that, as an adult, I would end up doing exactly the same. He naturally had little understanding for what I was doing when he entered the classroom prematurely one day to find me obliviously dancing on the teacher's desk doing my Freddie Garrity impersonation. "You were meant for me, everybody tells me so", I warbled, whilst dancing lightly from one foot to the other.

"Gray," intoned Plum, as he wearily filled out the detention slip, "you are absolutely pathetic."

Martin Gibson is by all accounts now a priest. At that time, however, he was a young teacher, physically in his early twenties but mentally still back in Infant School. Nowadays he would be hounded out of teaching for his lack of professionalism, but then it was fine for him to spend entire double lessons lying with his feet on the desk reading the *Beano* whilst expecting us to write endless notes on Beaumarchais' *Le Barbier de Séville*.

The Sixth Form Common Room was directly above Gibson's classroom and we discovered that there was a hole in the ceiling though which we could drop things. For safety's sake, we chose tiny pieces of paper which floated rather prettily. Gibson was so daft that he never managed to work out how it was that he was sometimes teaching in a light mist of confetti and that after each lesson his classroom floor looked as if it had been subject to a minor snowfall.

One day, Gibson was reading his comic as usual so, thinking that he couldn't see me, I decided to practice my Dave Clark mime. *Dadilly-dadilli-dadilli-dadilli-da*, I went (obviously silently and in mid-air, since I was miming), complete with purposely going off the edge of the desk to impersonate Dave Clark's incompetent miming. All went well until I inadvertently allowed one of my fingers to thwack the table, thus diverting Gibson from *Dennis The Menace* and alerting him to my non-Beaumarchais-related activity. He was furious.

"Gray!" he squeaked. "Stop being so childishly juvenile!"

Apart from being tautologous, this was hilariously ironic, coming from the most childishly juvenile person any of us had ever met. He berated me for several minutes in this vein; obviously he was under some stress.

Shortly after this attempted humiliation (actually, I gained much kudos from being accused of being even more childishly juvenile than Gibson), I had a piece of luck which greatly helped my academic career. Thundering across Rudge Common on my brand new Dawes (five speed derallieur gears, how cool can you get?) bike, I braked at the brink of one of the many craters created by the Cotswold stone quarriers who had worked there two decades earlier. I knew from experience that it was advisable not to plunge straight over without looking first to see whether any courting couples might be entangled in the relative privacy of the grassy crater. As I peered over the lip, whose startled eyes should greet me but those of Mr Gibson. Beneath his flushed visage was another flushed visage I recognised, that of Mrs Humphries, wife of the Head of Biology. I knew her well, because the previous Christmas I had played the angel in the Nativity play dressed in this lady's see-through nightdress. I must say that she had seemed particularly attentive towards me during the fitting sessions.

What could I do? He had obviously recognised me and I had equally obviously recognised both of them.

"Hello, Sir," I stuttered, before withdrawing from the scene of the crime, remounting my Dawes and retreating in some confusion.

In the subsequent lessons, he found it hard to look me in the eye, but when he did, I did my best to make my eyes convey the message "I know, Mr Gibson, I know. Just remember that." And sure enough, when my next scruffy and incoherent essay on Beaumarchais was returned, it had gained *"A+, très bien!"* This reward for discretion was extended to all further essays and thus it came as a surprise when, in the actual A-level exam, I barely scraped a B. But it wasn't a surprise to me, or to Mr Gibson.

Jock Harley was obviously as contemptuous of pop music as he was of unacceptable Hurr Kotts, but the headmaster, Mr Rufus, was an even bigger idiot. It's beyond belief that this person could ever conceivably have been appointed to a position in which he was supposed to be a role-model and figure of respect. His most obvious physical attribute was the most pronounced set of buck teeth in history. They were virtually horizontal, and because he smoked a pipe, were stained brown as well. Inevitably, he had pungent bad breath and a tendency to be unable to control his spittle, which, if one was unfortunate enough to be sitting in the front row, would encroach across the desk like the incoming tide.

For some reason, he taught us philosophy, of which he seemed to know little. This meant that, at least once a term, he would need to consult Grayngreen, the resident experts on German pronunciation:

"Um, Gwayngween, the famous German philosopher, now how do you pronounce his name again: Is it Immanuel Kant or Immanuel Kunt?"

With great enthusiasm, we would chorus back at some considerable volume:

"Kunt, Sir!"

Of course, in the grand tradition of crap teachers the world, over, Goofus Rufus remained completely unaware of anything untoward:

"Ah, Kunt. Thank you, Gwayngween."

"Yes, Sir. Kunt."

Goofus messed up any chances I might have had of fulfilling my father's ambition of getting me into Cambridge. Goofus misunderstood the entry regulations and made me waste an entire year of my life by staying on for an extra two terms in order to do completely unnecessary and subsequently completely useless S–

levels. Or maybe he wasn't so stupid and had his eye on the fees.

The deputy head was equally hateful. He went by the name of Turkey, this because he had allegedly previously lived in that country and liked to talk about it. He taught history, very badly, inevitably had a silly voice, and couldn't understand why, as the son of a historian, I didn't display any interest in his dire lessons. How, then, could he be expected to comprehend the deep cultural significance of Jet Harris and Tony Meehan?

One day, I was descending the stairs from the Sixth Form Common Room and, as I went, I tapped out the solo from "Diamonds" on the banister. Turkey was ascending the same staircase and our paths crossed.

"Hop hat, Hawaaay." ("Stop that, Gray.")

"Sorry, Sir," I replied, cheerfully. Well, of course I wasn't sorry, but I did genuinely mean to tell him that I wished I hadn't done it.

Turkey, however, didn't think I was sorry enough. He thought I was being cheeky.

"Hawaaay ... Hi hone hi ha hone a wah!"

("Gray, I don't like that tone of voice.")

Again, not wanting any trouble, I replied in what I thought was a non-confrontational way:

"What tone of voice, Sir?"

"Ha hone a wah, Hawaaay. Hee henn hunn!!"

("That tone of voice, Gray. Detention!")

But the detention was well worth it. Within minutes, the rumour spread that my innocent "What tone of voice, Sir?" had actually been "What bloody fucking tone of voice, you bastard?" For a few days, I was King of the Common Room.

Our Latin teacher was called Bog. Obviously, his actual name was Marsh and we were nothing if not predictable. Bog had a large, bushy, pubic-hair style beard and he also smoked an evil-smelling pipe. To complete the unappetising picture, he also had a pronounced nervous twitch, which would spring into action whenever he got angry, which was quite often.

Having tired of imitating Dave Clark (which was insufficiently challenging), I had been led into new drumming pastures by a new friend called Alan Jones. This was a cool person who lived down the road in Cheltenham and arrived at King's School fairly late on. This was a good sign, indicating that he had probably been expelled from elsewhere and was thus to be admired. TAJ, as he was nicknamed (Thomas Alan Jones) had an impressive Billy Fury-style quiff and one hugely respect-inducing attribute: His sister had actually gone out with and, so the rumour went, even been impregnated by Rolling Stone Brian Jones (along with half the female population of Cheltenham, but we didn't know that). Naturally, I was at the front of the queue to become pals with Alan Jones and actually we hit it off great. Alan drew my attention to The Hollies and in particular to their drummer Bobby Elliott, and we twice went to see The Hollies perform (sublimely) at Cheltenham Town Hall.

The transition from Dave Clark to Bobby Elliott was challenging indeed, because, while Clark was a tedious tub-thumper, Bobby was a "drummer's drummer", in that he was properly jazz-trained and generally several rungs above any other beat group drummer's skill level. We aspired towards Bobby's lightness of touch on the cymbals and ability to do real snare-drum rolls and precisely-timed excursions round the tom-toms. And so we had to practise.

We discovered that a particular desk in the Latin room was perfect for Bobby Elliott emulation. Different parts of the desk resounded in different ways and skilful use of all the fingers of both hands, plus the elbows (yes, the elbows) as bass drum and hi-hat pedals, could produce a passably accurate sound. This wasn't easy, in fact it was quite a work of art.

The song we liked to practise on was "Stay", the Hollies' third single. The drums on this speedy and perfectly-formed opus were tough to master, and I was triumphant when, after mid-morning break and while waiting for the arrival of Bog, I got all the way through the song without a single error. However, when I finished the last finger-thwack, the expected tumultuous applause failed to materialise. Instead there was a deadly silence as I looked up to discover Bog standing over me, hands on hips. In his Cambridge gown, he looked like some kind of demented vampire bat.

Fresh from his breaktime pipe, Bog's fury was such that he twitched almost as if he were having a fit. In my terror, I still remember that, as his face convulsed, a light mist of pipe-smoke issued from his beard and drifted across the room. He grabbed my arm and whisked me to the Head's office for six very painful strokes of the cane.

I would have done anything to gain revenge for this cruel treatment of a harmless bit of fun. But that would have entailed telling my parents exactly why I had been beaten, and I couldn't see their appreciation of Bobby Elliott's drum technique as being likely to be very profound. Yes, Bobby, it's all your fault.

So school in Gloucester was not much of a musical springboard, although it did have one claim to fame, in that Jimmy Young, the radio disc jockey, had once been a member of the school choir. He had spent his youth in the Forest of Dean and had a huge chart hit with his version of "Unchained Melody". However, since his credibility level was zero, his name wasn't one to drop.

I never met Jimmy Young, of course, but then neither did I meet either of the other two local music luminaries. My sister Faith revealed to me years later that she had been at Wynstones School with Mick Fleetwood, the bean-pole-like drummer of Fleetwood Mac. For a moment, this shock news almost made me feel a little warmer towards her, until:

"Such a shame. He was quite a pleasant lad and look what's become of him now."

I was aghast: This man was a national figure playing brilliant music in a world-famous band and Faith thought it was a "shame". It was incomprehensible.

The other surprising (if devious) connection came, amazingly, from my mother. When we had lived in Newent, Gloucestershire, Mother told me, our milkman had been Joe Meek. I had only been a baby at the time and thus not in a position to comprehend the significance of this, but it does open up the intriguing possibility that the milk in my baby bottle might well have been delivered by the world-famous and trailblazing producer of "Telstar" and countless other hits.

My mother, however, didn't see it that way:

"Such a shame. He could have had such a good, stable career. He could have taken over the family dairy. And now look at him."

Once again, I found this attitude beyond belief; in my eyes, Joe was a megastar. But when he eventually shot himself, a drug-addled, manic depressive with a criminal record for soliciting in public toilets ... well, maybe Mother had a point after all.

Shortly before I left school, two things happened which gave me a whiff of a connection to the music business. The first was the arrival at the school of Andrew Johns. He, too, was assumed to have been expelled from somewhere else and indeed he was a genuine rebel, surly, serious and cool. He possessed an electric guitar (a Gibson) and an amplifier (a Vox) and talked mysteriously and enticingly about his friends in London with whom he played in a band. Andy, it soon emerged, was the younger brother of Glyn Johns, who was the Rolling Stones' producer. I was within touching distance of the REAL world of rock and roll.

One rainy winter Saturday night, Andy's band came down from London and played at a school party in a youth club at Rodborough, a pretty village just outside Stroud. Parties at that time were strange events in that all that happened was that everyone paired up with a member of the opposite sex at the beginning of the evening and spent the next few hours lying in rows on the floor, with all the lights off, carrying out various levels of heavy petting. This was an unpromising environment for a band to perform in.

I was rivetted from the start, so much so that, in watching Andy's band setting up, I omitted to seek out a suitable partner. Thus it was that, when the band came to play (not very well, but excellently loudly), I stood watching them, wide-eyed and ringing-eared, rather than join in with the other activities. A deeply unattractive girl, the only one left, came over and tried to chat me up and I made her cry by telling her to buzz off and leave me in peace.

On the way home, I nearly died. Roger Duckworth had just passed his driving test and had persuaded his mother to lend him her Triumph car. Roger, having spent the evening groping Sally Moreland and consuming strong Whiteways cider, was keen to demonstrate a skill he had recently acquired, that of aquaplaning. The technique was to drive very fast along a rain-soaked road and then jam on the brakes, thus causing the tyres to lose contact with the road surface. You would then waft round in a circle, rather like a spinning top, creating the sensation of floating on air. On this occasion, Roger completely lost control of the car and we span round several times, eventually coming to rest upon the verge, just centimetres from a viciously jagged Cotswold dry stone wall. This was merely the first of several such escapades for Roger. Not many months afterwards, he wrote off five parked cars by bouncing off them as he failed to negotiate a bend. And still somehow avoided jail. Maybe it was because the village where it happened was called "Paradise".

Soon, Andy Johns left school and, far from seeking out further education like the rest of us, went straight into the studio netherworld inhabited by his brother. In a short space of time, he emulated Glyn's achievements by becoming one of the most in-demand record producers in the world. He engineered several albums each for The Stones and Led Zeppelin, as well as producing Van Halen and, most significantly, *Marquee Moon* for Television.

In my pointless third year in the Sixth Form (thank you, Goofus Rufus), they finally had to make me a prefect. My childish juvenility had meant that I had managed an entire two years without the formality of this promotion, which I gather was unprecedented. But now I was allowed to use the Prefects' Common Room and there, every Monday, we would dissect, virtually syllable by syllable, the previous day's edition of *I'm Sorry I'll Read That Again*. This brilliantly funny radio precursor to *The Goodies* and *Monty Python's Flying Circus* starred Tim Brooke-Taylor, John Cleese, Graeme Garden and Bill Oddie, the latter providing the songs.

One Sunday, the featured song was a minor masterpiece entitled "The Ferret Song". We decided to perform this opus at our end of term show, but it was impossible, even after the Monday repeat, to remember all the lyrics.

"Let's write to the BBC and ask for a copy."

The idea of actually striking up contact with the show's producers, that there were human beings behind the hilarity emerging over the ether, was both intimidating and exciting. I was delegated to write in to the Light Programme with our request. My letter was in-jokingly addressed to the show's mascot Angus Prune and contained references to another ISIRTA leit-motif, Rhubarb Tarts. Would it be possible to have a copy of the Ferret Song?

Virtually by return of post, we received an extremely friendly personal reply from the show's producer (and subsequently very big BBC cheese) Humphrey Barclay. He enclosed a copy of the much-coveted lyrics, together with a recommendation that they should be cooked slowly on medium heat for several hours.

Triumphantly, we rehearsed this literary epic:

I've got a ferret sticking up my nose,
It sticks its head out every time I blow,
How it got there I can't tell
But now it's there it hurts like hell
And what is more it drastically affects my sense of smell.

In their wisdom, the school staff deemed this song to be too childishly juvenile and of insufficient literary merit to be performed at the end of year show. Which just about tells you all you need to know about that place.

Those stupid extra two terms at school meant that I had a couple of months to spare before university. My father suggested I should get a job, which was how I ended up at the motor vehicle licensing centre in Gloucester. There, the mind-numbing banality of the filing work was enlivened by some of the obviously wanton female staff, in particular one called Kay, who also ran a band booking agency called the K and B Agency. One soul band she regularly booked was The Mike Cotton Sound with Lucas. Like Geno Washington, I think Lucas was an ex-GI who had decided to stay on. I certainly had never seen anything like it, when Kay took me along to a Mike Cotton show at Gloucester Guildhall. The evening frightened me, because a normally quite benign teddy boy who travelled with me every day on the 56 bus took part in a particularly vicious kicking of a young man outside the hall. Pointed steel toecaps rained down upon the head of this unfortunate youth, but I couldn't bear to look and I certainly wouldn't have dared to intervene.

All this time I was sporadically going out with a girl from the village called Rosamund, with whom I sort of sustained a relationship for the next five years. She was a Rolling Stones fan and shocked me by telling me she screamed all the way through their performance at the Gloucester Regal. I considered this behaviour most inappropriate and so took her to some concerts at the Guildhall which were much more sedate affairs. One I remember was by an acoustic rock band called Comus, whose lead singer brayed like Roger Chapman from Family. Another band we saw was John Peel's favourite of the time,

Principal Edwards' Magic Theatre. I thought they were overblown and over-rated, but we sat on the floor and said things like "far out, man". In the mad way that these things come around, almost thirty years later I actually met Lyn Edwards, the very Principal Edwards after whom the band was named. He was drumming in the orchestra pit for a pantomime at Salisbury Playhouse and revealed that he had taught guitar to Charlotte Hatherley of Ash. There you are!

Rosamund and I had a brief period of membership of the Gloucester Folk Club, which was held every Friday in the crypt of a church. Every cliché you could think of about folk clubs held true: They did wear Arran sweaters, they did put their fingers in their ears, they did sing the bastard "Wild Rover" every bloody week and they did expect you to sing along with their dreadful nasal dronings. And I was scared because the bloke who ran it had been Rosamund's previous boyfriend and was reportedly out to get me. Shudder! Roger Duckworth, meanwhile, had gone off to the College of Estate Management in London, keen to become a property mogul like his father. I visited Roger a couple of times. His girlfriend was called Sheila Gilhooly and Roger was absolutely affronted when she was comprehensively removed from his grasp by a disc jockey called John Peel, whom she had met at a recording of "Top Of The Pops". Sheila is now probably the most famous mum in the land, apart from the Queen.

On one occasion, Roger and I and some of his college friends went to a show at the Lyceum in the Strand, featuring The Who, The Crazy World of Arthur Brown and, I think, Jethro Tull. I remember this because it was the only time I ever literally "picked up" a girl, in that she (a complete stranger) was too short to see Arthur Brown's flaming headdress, so I put her on my shoulders. Although this was a suitably macho thing to do, after a few minutes it was utter agony. Then we somehow got split up from the rest and by the time we found the flat, bloody Duckworth had locked up and gone to sleep. Far from the hoped-for night of passion, we ended up sleeping on the stairs (not to be recommended at all). Two days later, I found a souvenir of the girl I had "picked up", in the form of a false eyelash, rather like a fisherman's fly, attached to my pullover.

This was a brilliant musical time to be growing up, and a wonderful time for university to be beckoning. But first, there was some farming to be done.

IV. Down on the farm

The bulk of my music in those school days came from the radio. In the time-honoured teenage tradition, I spent every evening under the bedclothes listening to Radio Luxembourg on a tiny transistor radio, which had been brought back from America for me by some friends of my parents called Mr and Mrs Ashwell.

Bernard Ashwell was the Cathedral Architect in Gloucester and glided past our house twice a day in his Bentley on his way to and from work. He was a kind, if varying tempered man, who gave me my earliest school holiday work, helping out (hindering, actually) in his office in Stroud.

The Ashwells' son, Michael, was a disappointment to his parents but impressed the likes of me. He ran a record shop called the Stroud Music Centre, where I was allowed to listen to the latest releases for hour after hour without buying anything. Michael eventually relocated to London, where he started up a very successful record distribution firm called Onestop. My parents spoke darkly and in whispers about the shame he had brought upon his family by not only getting involved in pop music but also by openly admitting to being homosexual. One Sunday lunchtime, he returned to Edge and infuriated my parents by telling me, over lunch, fascinating details about an American singer-songwriter called Phil Ochs. This really was the limit: pop music, homosexuality and now left-wing politics.

Not that my father was above exploiting me for his own political ends. In my early teens, I was sent off round the village on my bike to deliver leaflets on behalf of the Conservative Party. I quite simply didn't know what I was doing, but when I later plucked up courage to ask Rosamund out, I was challenged by her father Oliver, a Daily Mirror reader and firm socialist. He was a fine man who died suddenly at a young age from a brain tumour. I convinced him I had only been acting out of youthful ignorance.

I was attracted to Rosamund because she looked very much like Marianne Faithfull, with whom every young man was in love. On Rudge Common, there was a very tall tree which the DOCs used to climb. Right at the top of it, I carved the legend "I Love Marianne Faithfull" deep into the wood and, many years later, I climbed up there again and verified that, albeit faded, it was still there.

Unfortunately, I was hit by an attack of vertigo and it took over an hour to get back down. In order to check again, I would now have to chop the tree down, which would be an ecologically unsound thing to do.

When all that stuff about Mars Bars came up, I dismissed it on the grounds that My Marianne Would Never Do Anything Like That, and of course was proved right. At the 1999 Glastonbury Festival, I finally got to see Marianne Faithfull and she was everything one could have hoped and more.

Her records were, of course, played on Radio Luxembourg, a patchy station which nonetheless provided the only source of non-stop music in the evenings and at night. Different DJs represented different record companies, and I remember smoothiechops David Jacobs being affronted by the lyrical content of The Pink Floyd's "Arnold Layne" and vowing never to play it again. Jimmy Savile introduced a revolutionary sound when he gave the first play to "A Whiter Shade of Pale" by "Procool Haroom, guys and gals". My favourite was an enthusiastic man called Tony Hall, who played Decca records. His was the show on which you were most likely to hear the Stones.

The nephew of a lady in the village called Mrs Berry was a huge Buddy Holly fan who possessed every record Holly had ever made. He tried to convert me to Buddy Holly but I wasn't sure about the wavery voice and he seemed a little passé (no morbid pun intended). However, having listened to his records so many times, I knew all the words when I later discovered the happy fact that Buddy's songs, too, can be played with just three chords.

Just before I went to university in 1968, my sister Pippa married Colin Burnett, who was a farm manager. Knowing I was looking for something to do in the summer holidays, Colin offered me a job on the farm he was managing. The farm, mostly arable but with a herd of cows too, was called Carrimers and was just near Aston Tirrold, Berkshire.

The job was perfect, in that all I had to do was supervise the grain dryer, guiding in the trailers which brought the corn from the combine harvesters in the fields, checking its moisture and setting the furnace to dry the corn sufficiently for it to be stored safely. There was quite a lot of physical shovelling involved, but it was a nice independent job and it came complete with a free farm cottage.

All I had in it was a sleeping bag and a saucepan to heat up baked beans, plus of course the trusty transistor radio. In the evenings, I became completely hooked on pirate radio, in particular Radio Caroline, which had the best reception. As a result of obscure and devious deals with record companies, Caroline played a very peculiar selection of music. "Days of Pearly Spencer" by David McWilliams was to be heard about twenty times a day, as was my personal favourite, "Excerpt From A Teenage Opera", by Keith West.

Grocer Jack, Grocer Jack,
Is it true what Mummy says?
You won't come back, oh no no.

How mysterious this was. The world waited with bated breath for the rest of the Teenage Opera to appear, and the world is still waiting today.

Bizarre rituals took place on Caroline, such as the "Kiss In A Car Contest", whereby lovers were invited to draw up their vehicles on Frinton beach and flash their headlights to signal to the ship that they were getting it on in their cars, inevitably to the sound of Johnny Walker being romantic: "Take your loved one in your arms, lie back and think of Caroline. And here's Percy Sledge ..." No matter what dirt the tabloids dredge up on Johnny Walker, he will never lose his credibility with me.

Carrimers Farm was immediately adjacent to a large estate owned by Sir William Piggott-Brown, an aristocrat who was somehow connected through business to Chris Blackwell, the owner of Island Records. At the stage when I started work, Steve Winwood had not long left The Spencer Davis Group and joined up with Chris Wood, Dave Mason and Jim Capaldi to form Traffic. They lived and rehearsed in a (now famous) cottage adjacent to the track which marked the border between Carrimers and Piggott-Brown's land, thus giving birth to the immortal concept of "getting it together in the country". Most of the villagers, and indeed Colin and the farm workers, disapproved of these possibly drug-crazed townies doing things like leaving gates open and scaring the pheasants with their psychedelic music. I, of course, was entranced, and would take every available opportunity to volunteer to take the empty trailers back to the corn fields, which involved driving along that track.

One afternoon, I rounded the corner on my tractor. It had been raining for several days and the track was a quagmire. There, marooned in the middle of a puddle which was so big it could qualify as a small lake, was Steve Winwood, sitting in a tiny green Mini-Moke. I had seen the members of Traffic charging around in this vehicle before, but it was entirely unsuitable for muddy conditions. Maybe they thought it had jeep-like qualities, because it consisted of a jeep-looking top mounted on the chassis of an Austin Mini. Anyway, the water was up to the top of the wheels.

I regret now that I didn't show that I recognised him. Maybe I felt that it would compound his embarrassment. Now I like to imagine that it might have earned me an invitation to the cottage, but the truth was that I was in such a tizz at finding myself within feet of Steve Winwood that I just didn't know what to say.

"Do you need some help?" (Damn fool question.)

"I theem to have got thtuck."

Can he really have lisped? Surely not, but my memory is of being shocked by the wispy, whiny, puny speaking voice which emerged from those famous lips. It sounded so incongruous, having heard him bellowing "Somebody Help Me" and "Gimme Some Loving" on a hundred radio shows. He was very, very embarrassed, and looked so young, small and vulnerable.

I waded into the puddle, attached a chain to the bumper of the Mini-Moke and gingerly pulled it out, complete with its illustrious passenger. He thanked me diffidently and disappeared towards the cottage. The other workers, when I related the tale, were critical that he hadn't given me a tip, but for me, just to have done it was reward enough.

In Aston Tirrold itself there was quite a good village pub called the Chequers, and that was where Traffic and their friends would go in the evenings. One Saturday, Roger and Rob, my friends from the DOCs, came over to visit. This was an excruciating experience, because both of them had turned their enthusiasm towards the unsavoury occupation of rugby and had become members of Gloucester Rugby Club.

In the pub were a collection of cool-looking long-haired young men whom I didn't recognise. The landlord identified them as a band called Spooky Tooth, who were currently staying at the cottage. They kept themselves to themselves, chatting quietly in a corner, and the regulars seemed pleased to have them there. They were less keen on Roger and Rob, who, after a few pints, launched into a series of raucous rugby songs which became progressively more filthy until we were eventually requested to leave. Any credibility I had hoped to build up with Spooky Tooth or Traffic was lost there and then, and I scarcely showed my face in the pub again.

One thing I did do on a couple of occasions before leaving Carrimers was to venture down the track near the cottage late at night, when the bands would tend to play on a makeshift open-air stage. There I heard "Dear Mr Fantasy" and "Berkshire Poppies" and a number of extended jam sessions. God knows what they would have thought if they'd discovered me lurking in the bushes; Drug Squad, no doubt.

By the time the next summer came around, I had new friends and Colin had a new farm. This time, he was managing an even bigger spread called Stype, which belonged to the multi-millionaire Charles Clore. It consisted of several farms rolled together and was situated a couple of miles outside Hungerford, near Newbury. I rolled up to spend the summer stacking straw bales with three friends from university, Bob, Ian and Steve. The way we behaved was just incredible.

Again, we were given a cottage to live in, which rapidly became a slum. The nearest village was called Shalbourne, and social life centred around the village pub, called the Plough. We could have easily walked there, but Bob had an old Morris Minor, so of course we always drove. A little matter of the fact that I hadn't even had a single driving lesson (you can drive a tractor on L-plates), and that we regularly drove while blind drunk. Our idea of checking for traffic at a crossroads at night was simply to switch off the Morris's headlamps for a moment. If no lights were to be seen, we accelerated straight over the crossroads. We never considered the possibility of a cyclist or a pedestrian. I feel so ashamed.

Hungerford certainly wasn't a musical hotbed in any way, but in the Plough I met a young, curly-haired bassist called Chris. He was in a band called Ton Ton Macoute, from Newbury, who, amazingly later got a record deal and actually put out an album out Neon, one of the myriad "progressive" labels which the majors invented in the wake of the success of Harvest and Vertigo. From what I remember, the album featured flute as the main instrument and suffered badly from the fact that Ton Ton Macoute didn't have a guitarist.

Poor Chris, I nearly killed him. He and several of his mates used to charge around the area a lot in a red Mini. One evening, at dusk, I was hauling a huge trailer full of straw from one end of the farm to the other, which entailed pulling out onto the busy A338 Salisbury Road. As well as the very long trailer, the tractor also had a massive "foreloader" attached to the front of it. Called a "Farmhand", this was a viciously-hooked device for picking up and loading bales. It made coming out of side roads very awkward, because you had to be almost in the middle of the main road before you could see whether anything was coming.

It was completely my fault, because I put the tractor into the wrong gear. I chugged slowly out onto the main road, right into the path of Chris's Mini, which came screaming round the bend, far too fast, packed with him and four friends. He braked frantically and skidded, but all he could do was swerve onto the verge, where somehow he just managed to avoid hitting the tractor. They disappeared round the next corner, leaving behind the frightening smell of burnt rubber.

Shaking from head to foot, I at first thought that I had got away with it, but round the next bend, they were waiting for me. Gary, a huge, red-faced man mountain who had made threatening noises at us before on account of our being a load of smelly, layabout students who were trying to get off with the local girls, was standing in the road, holding up his hand for me to stop.

I locked the door of the cab because it was obvious that they were intent on dragging me out and beating me to a pulp. Gary, in particular, was beside himself.

"You fucking stupid fucking bastard, you fucking nearly fucking well killed us."

I decided it was politic not to mention that they had been speeding. All I could say was sorry, sorry, you're right, I was stupid, I'm so sorry.

Eventually, they drove on and I found my way back to the cottage. Obviously, Chris, Gary and co had been heading for the Plough, so I persuaded my fellow students that we should go to another pub in nearby Great Bedwyn. I was in urgent need of a stiff brandy. Of course, as soon as we entered, we realised that my enemies were there too. There was nothing for it. In one of the most courageous acts of my lily-livered existence, I went over to them.

"Gary, Chris, I've come to apologise. I know I nearly killed you and it was my fault. Can you forgive me?"

"Well ...," said Gary slowly, "we've been thinking about it and we reckon we've got to take some of the blame because we were going too fast."

I've never felt so relieved. We bought each other mutual rounds of drinks and from then on were accepted as part of the gang at the Plough.

With my first fortnight's pay, I bought myself a much-coveted pair of trousers. They were bright yellow hipsters, hugely-flared and made of a satin-like material. Yes, very funny, but absolutely perfect for the time. It now seems completely implausible that I could ever have had the figure to wear them, but I did. And I wore the yellow flares when we got invited to play one Sunday afternoon at the Hungerford Tennis Club.

Normally at harvest time it's a seven-day week on a farm, but it had rained a couple of days before and the baler couldn't work, so we were free.

One of the farm workers was a German ex-POW called Gerhard, who for some reason, had never gone home. Because no one could say "Gerhard" (not that it's that difficult), everyone called him Charlie. Even after all that time, he could hardly speak any English and he also had a pronounced limp. It thus seemed unlikely that, as was rumoured, he was having a protracted affair with a senior staff member at the local comprehensive school.

Obviously, Charlie wouldn't talk to us about such matters, but he did invite us to play tennis with his "friends", who were members of the local tennis club. I wasn't keen, since any kind of sport is alien to me, but I went along for the ride.

Charlie's lady friend's daughter was a most beautiful creature called Elizabeth, with long, flowing blonde hair and a mini-skirt which made her look like Anita Pallenberg or a Mary Quant model. All four of us lusted after her immediately, but as usual I gave myself no chance.

To see why, it's necessary to explain a bit about my colleagues. Bob was tall, olive-skinned, very handsome and soft-spoken, any girl's dream. The young women of Hungerford were easy prey for Bob, as he frequently demonstrated. Steve was skinny with a poor complexion and glasses, but with a quick wit and charm, an accomplished flirter. Ian was intelligent, blond and mysterious, one of those people who are ladykillers without really trying. And then there was me, shy, un-prepossessing, un-sporty. Who would the gorgeous Elizabeth choose?

On that Sunday, I didn't even speak to her, but a few days later, a mauve, scented letter from her arrived at the cottage, addressed to me. In her impeccably neat script, Elizabeth explained that she liked me and wondered whether I might feel the same way about her? It was obvious what had happened: She had got me confused with Bob or Ian, so I penned a polite reply, explaining her mistake and describing Bob and Ian so that she could decide which of them to contact.

Back came another letter. No, it was definitely me she meant. She was sure it was me, because I was the one with the yellow trousers. She was particularly taken with the yellow trousers, which was great, because that had been my purpose in buying them. As Elizabeth's second letter proceeded, however, she obviously felt a bit bad about implying that clothes were an important factor in judging a person. I am sure what she intended to write was something like, "Personalities are more important then outward appearances". What she in fact wrote was, "It's not the trousers that matter, but what's inside them."

Disappointingly, she never got to explore the contents of the trousers, because the relationship was unsuccessful. As she was teetotal and not remotely interested in music, it wasn't very sensible of me to invite her back to the cottage, get drunk and subject her to deafening hand-on-hip impersonations of Mick Jagger, while playing *Get Your Ya Ya's Out*, with particular emphasis on the introduction where Jagger teases, "I fink ah've lost a button on me traasers. Ya wouldn't want me traasers to fall dahn, would ya?" We went our separate ways and Elizabeth married an entirely different Mr Gray and lived, I assume, happily ever after. But I still have the letters in the shed.

Every night, on our drunken drives round the lanes, we would do stupid, life-threatening things. One night we drove onto a level crossing on the busy London to Bristol railway line and closed the gates behind us BEFORE opening the exit gates. And everywhere we went, we stole things. Not for any reason, just because stupid students steal things. They were signs, mainly, road signs, railway signs, even a sign advertising the famous Crofton Beam Pumps on the Kennet and Avon Canal. Invariably, we would wake up, wonder why on earth we had done such a stupid thing, and stack the signs (eventually upwards of twenty) against the sitting room wall. This was fine until the night someone suggested that Bob, Steve and I should pay a visit to Norlands College.

Norlands College is an establishment near Hungerford where nannies are trained. It's a very well-respected institution but to us it meant one thing only: Nannies are girls, so there were bound to be girls there. However, by the time we reached the top of the imposing drive, my alcohol-fuelled courage had worn off completely, so I stayed in the car while the others climbed in through a window. When they emerged, they had of course not found any girls, but they were triumphantly carrying some blankets.

"No more cold nights in that freezing cottage for us, lads!"

At the bottom of the drive, someone had the bright idea of going back for more. Why not? So back we went, only this time the inevitable caretaker was waiting for us. Boy, was he angry. However, in my state of relative sobriety, I had an idea. Before anything else could be said, I piped up:

"We realised how stupid we'd been as soon as we got to the bottom of the drive. We decided to bring the blankets back. We're really sorry for what we've done."

This calmed the caretaker down a bit, so that on the way home we were exploding with self-congratulation. He hadn't carried out the Citizen's Arrest on which he had plainly been intent, and we had managed to get away with it. Or so we thought.

A couple of days later, Steve borrowed Bob's car to drive to London, but was stopped by the police in Hungerford. The caretaker had, of course, noted down the car's number. Steve was forced to tell the police where we were living. Okay, son, we've got you, now where are your accomplices?

By a miracle, we were at home when they knocked on the door. Bob kept them talking for a minute or two on the doorstep, while I frantically hurled all the stolen signs into the bathroom. If they'd found them we'd have been looking at a serious punishment, and my subsequent career in the teaching profession would never have been allowed to have taken place.

Bob and I were interviewed in separate rooms, and luckily we both said the same thing, viz. my cock and bull story that we had been on our way to return the goods. We were both formally cautioned (those words about anything you say being taken down and used as evidence are pretty chilling), but we never heard another word. That wouldn't have been the case had either of the policemen, as we kept expecting, asked to use the bathroom. Then, the words "shit" and "fan" might have come into play.

For my last couple of weeks at Stype, I was delegated to the chicken house. This place was as vile as any battery chicken unit may be imagined. The de-beaked birds were crammed five or six to a cage, where they shat through wire mesh onto a shelf below. To combat the non-stop cacophony of clucking, the radio was played full blast all day through a series of speakers, allegedly to soothe the chickens. Not when I was on. I kept it tuned to the newly-inaugurated Radio One, where the birds were suitably traumatised by Tony Blackburn and Jimmy Young. I can't hear "Hey Jude" without thinking of the chicken house and of Raymondo enquiring, "What's the recipe today, Jim?" Sure hope it's not chicken.

Right at the end of my stay, the chickens were all sold. In a change of policy, the shed was to be given some new role. A huge lorry rolled up and a couple of surly, tattooed blokes grabbed handfuls of chickens by the neck and threw them with great cruelty into wooden crates. If one looked a bit scrawny, they would casually wring its neck and toss it into the bushes. I hopelessly tried to appeal to their better nature and get them to treat the helpless creatures more kindly, but they had no better nature and simply thought I was mad.

Steve then got called in. His job was to creosote the outside of the shed, using a high-intensity paint spraying device which worked off the power take-off of a tractor. I, meanwhile, was inside the shed trying to clear the shit off the shelves, ready for the cages to be dismantled. I thought I would approach the job by shovelling it all onto the floor first, before transferring it to a wheelbarrow. The trouble was that there were mountains of the stuff, and I hadn't realised that, when it is disturbed, chicken shit lets off a smell ten times worse that if it is left to stand. As I contemplated the scene of ammonia-stenching devastation, Steve called out:

"Can I start?"

"Yes, sure, put it in gear."

Now what I meant was that he should put the power take-off in gear, but Steve thought I meant the tractor itself. Zombie-like, he put the tractor into gear and watched as, unmanned, it drove straight through the walls of the shed and out the other side.

Colin's face as he arrived to find the steaming piles of shit, misdirected creosote and a Desperate Dan-style tractor-shaped silhouette in his shed was truly a sight to behold.

Although not at all a vengeful kind of person, Colin got his revenge when I visited the farm again the following Christmas. Being broke as usual, I begged him to let me do some casual work over the Christmas period, perhaps allowing one or other of the farm workers the odd day off. This provided me with a couple of good (only in retrospect) shit stories.

The cows were kept indoors in the winter, which presented a sanitation problem. Since they spent the whole day shitting, where was it all to go? The designer of this particular cattle unit had devised a simple but effective system. The floor consisted of metal slats. The shit fell though these onto a concrete floor about a metre below them. The clever bit that was that this floor was on a slight slant, so that the slurry (liquid shit, since you ask) swished down into a lagoon at the bottom of the shed, ready to be pumped away across the fields. Fine, except that the concrete had not been laid at a steep enough angle. This meant that, every now and then, someone had to descend beneath the slatted floor and, with the help of an implement like a sort of rubber broom, encourage the shit to move.

That winter, it had got so deep that someone had to spend a day down there. That someone was me. I was dressed in a luminous yellow diver's outfit and lowered into a bath of liquid shit up to my thighs. But I was too tall to fit below the slats standing up, so had to hunch my head to a position where it was inches above the brown soup, whilst I struggled desperately to push the glutinous mass towards the exit. I sometimes wonder if my tendency to claustrophobia may have started there. All the while, naturally, the cows were up above, intermittently crapping on my head. Just think, there are people who do jobs like this for a living.

Once outside, the slurry got pumped over the fields to a pit where it was stored ready to be used as Spring fertilisation. This operation was conducted through a narrow pipe and propelled by a powerful electric motor. On Christmas Day, there was bad news. It had snowed in the night, and the sub-zero temperatures had frozen the slurry inside the pipe. The trouble was, no one knew exactly where the blockage was, so I was sent off to find out. This entailed using a pitchfork to disconnect the various points where the lengths of pipe were attached to each other, to see if there was a free flow of slurry or not.

Unfortunately, when I eventually located the place where the blockage had occurred, Colin, back at the cowshed several hundred metres way, had switched on the motor, so that a high-powered jet of liquid slurry blasted out of the pipe and hit me with a force strong enough to knock me flat onto the ground. I don't recommend the experience, and neither do I recommend the subsequent one, which was being forced, by my sister, to strip completely naked in the snow before being admitted to her house.

Told you I had some good shit stories.

V. Jaded Hack (1)

When the *Stroud News and Journal* ran a front page story about my newspaper the *Edge Gazette*, they jokingly referred to it as a rival publication and noted that I had no ambition to be a journalist, preferring the idea of becoming an archaeologist. But the signs that I was going to be entrapped by the printed word were there, even though the *Edge Gazette* was entirely handwritten.

The concept was straightforward. The paper consisted of just one copy, which was passed from household to household for a "penny a read" in aid of the Church Roof Restoration Fund. Most of the population of the village of Edge was reasonably well-off, so many of them paid a shilling or so, and most issues of the *Edge Gazette* made a couple of pounds, which were gratefully received by the vicar, Dicky Bird. What he didn't know was that, when I delivered the cash, I always took the opportunity to check out the outhouse in which parishioners dumped their left-over newspapers for recycling, also in aid of the Restoration Fund. Some anonymous member of the congregation regularly dropped off back copies of "Parade", a girlie mag to which I otherwise would have had no access. So I was not only corrupted by Cliff Richard but also by his beloved church.

Private Enterprise At Edge

Joint editors of the " Edge Gazette " preparing their copy for the latest edition are 11-years-old Oliver Gray (left) and Tim Douglas.

"That's how we used to like you, dear."

The *Edge Gazette* didn't have a music column (well obviously, my parents read it) but even at the age of eleven, I regret to say that there were business politics involved. Initially, the paper had two sections, one general one written by me, and something called the *Children's Gazette*, which was written by a neighbour called Tim. This was a young man whom I was encouraged by my parents to associate with because his father was a Naval Commander, but as an editorial team, it didn't work. The poor chap had some kind of learning difficulty which meant that he spoke in a slow, lugubrious voice, and also that he had very poor handwriting. Considering that the entire *Edge Gazette* was handwritten, this was a problem, and one or two local children complained that they couldn't read their "section".

So I instituted a take-over bid for the *Children's Gazette* and literally bribed Tim with sweets and the offer of a post as Business Manager (a definite promotion, he was assured) until he let me write the whole paper. In the end, he got bored and resigned, which suited me fine. My megalomania was allowed to run rampant, and the final edition of the *Edge Gazette* weighed almost as much as the Sunday Times, with a Sport Section, an Entertainments Section and a Colour Supplement. But by then the church roof had been restored and thus the raison d'être of the *Edge Gazette* was no more.

The reporter from the *Stroud News and Journal* was right. I did want, as much as anyone that age can have career plans, to be an archaeologist. But, now he came to mention it, maybe journalism wasn't such a bad idea after all, although I didn't think about it until the time for post-O-level decisions approached. I had often had items published in the King's School magazine and, in my last week in Schöningen, I had penned, in not very accurate German, an article for the school magazine there. Schöningen was brilliant, said the article, but I didn't like the grumpy old widows who sat in their windows and scowled at any young people who passed by. This went down well (except, presumably, with the grumpy widows, but they wouldn't have read it anyway).

A classmate called Mike Sayer left school to work on the Gloucester *Citizen*, a paper famous for once having reported that raiders had threatened a bank manager with an iron bra. I was interested in doing something similar (training to be a journalist, not brandishing an iron bra) but my father wouldn't hear of it. Journalism was a disreputable career and besides, I was destined for university. The only trouble was that it wasn't at all the university he had in mind.

My father, who had been at Cambridge himself, wanted to exploit his contacts there. He really thought that his friends would be influential enough to get me into Cambridge, even though I wasn't intelligent enough. It might have worked if I had had some sporting talent, but I didn't, so instead I ended up travelling by coach to Cambridge for a hopeless interview followed by an even more hopeless entrance examination which I virtually had to leave blank on account of not understanding any of the questions. When I showed my father the paper, he looked at it as uncomprehendingly as I now look at much of my children's GCSE work. The world moves on.

On the way back from the interview, I lost my suitcase, containing all my A-level notes. I had to suffer the indignity of copying them all up from Roger Green (of Grayngreen). Eventually, after several weeks, the suitcase was returned. Apparently, an old lady on the coach had been met by a care worker at Banbury. He had mistakenly taken my case as well as hers and had left it in her hallway. For three weeks, she had been too frightened to open it, thinking it might contain a bomb. I returned to my own notes with alacrity, because obviously they were much better than bloody Green's. Unfortunately, with all the reams of paperwork, there was also a banana which I hadn't got round to eating. Now, on the very rare occasions I think of Goethe or Schiller, the inimitable aroma of stale banana always comes to my nostrils.

And so, having also been rejected by Oxford, Bristol and Durham, I ended up at the University of East Anglia, or UEA, as it is known to everyone. This turned out to be a spectacularly good choice of university for a number of reasons. Like Sussex in Brighton and Essex in Colchester, this was one of the "new" universities, which meant that they were hotbeds of student militancy, primarily because they were so "new" that there wasn't much in the way of established procedures. Academically, you could get away with doing practically nothing, which was most pleasant.

I was billeted at an old RAF station at Fifers Lane, Horsham St Faiths, which was where I met most of the people I would stay friendly with. A disadvantage of these "Halls of Residence" was that you had to travel to the university and back by coach. However, this was made up for by the fact that you were given a gigantic full English breakfast before you left. Apart from that, you had to cater for yourself.

I got off to a terrible start in that I was put in a double room with a guy called Sebastian who was a classical musician and had rather eccentric habits and mannerisms. On top of that, as I undressed each night, I could see his beady eyes observing me over the bedhead. After a few days, he declared that he was homosexual and asked me whether I was as well? I replied in the negative and realised that, for both our sakes, a transfer of room might be appropriate. That was how I got to live next door to John Vincent Yorke, the butterfly exterminator.

Horsham was administered in a fairly benevolent way by a gentleman called Oliver Wilson. He was so kind and helpful when I approached him about the problem with the accommodation, and how did I repay him? By being a complete dickhead.

The records show that, during that first year, I had to receive several warnings about constantly being noisy enough to disturb other students until two or three in the morning. This I would tend to do by playing music very loudly on my newly-purchased Crown record player, an extraordinary white plastic device from Japan which was considerably smaller than the LPs it was playing, which stuck out way over the side. The music was mostly the sampler albums that you could get very cheaply, promoting albums by artists on progressive labels. *The Rock Machine Turns You On* was a favourite, with lots of American artists like Blood, Sweat and Tears and Moby Grape. Another goodie was the first Island Sampler, *You Can All Join In*, which had the added advantage of a cover featuring a picture of all the artists photographed together. This gave me a good opportunity to casually mention Traffic, Spooky Tooth and the cottage, as if they were my best friends.

Almost everybody had these samplers because they were so cheap, but the trick was to buy one or two of the albums being promoted on them. Most people would buy Jethro Tull or Free, but to be cool, you had to have one of the more obscure ones. I bungled here by opting for Wynder K. Frog rather than Nick Drake. If you had a Nick Drake album, the girls thought you were sensitive and understanding. I made up for this by buying *Super Session* by Mike Bloomfield and Al Kooper, which was regarded as a good muso record, but my trump card was *Love Chronicles*, an album by Al Stewart which caused a sensation by being the first record ever to use the word "fucking". This I would play at loud volume to show how progressive I was, and thus would cause neighbouring students to complain to Oliver Wilson.

There is another letter from him in which he noted that "at midnight, you and Mr Besley saw fit to push the cricket sightscreen half a mile from its designated position. If you do not want me to take further action, please make sure it is replaced by midday." And, shame of shames, one night, we ordered a huge Chinese meal and had it delivered to Mr Wilson's door. Oh, how we sniggered as we hid in the bushes and watched the hapless restauranteur being sent on his way by a baffled Mr Wilson. And oh, what twats we were.

We clubbed together to buy food for evening meals. One bloke from Devon called Rick had an enormous greatcoat with deep pockets and used to steal masses of food from the NAAFI supermarket which was anachronistically still on site. But then he refused to share it with us, citing the fact that he was taking great risks by stealing the food. It had a sort of twisted logic, but we resented it and started being horrible to him. When he re-entered my life out of the blue in the late nineties, I found him to be a delightful person and felt quite ashamed that I had been beastly about him behind his back.

The big controversy at the time ('twas the Swinging Sixties, remember) was whether male and female students should be allowed to co-habit. There was serious student unrest when Oliver Wilson wrote to a female student, suggesting she was illegally living with her boyfriend on campus. The letter was leaked and articles appeared in the press about what a den of iniquity the university was, which was undoubtedly true.

Two girls we knew, called Liz and Mandy, were outrageously promiscuous. They shared a room just next to the Horsham breakfast room and often, if there wasn't an early lecture (or even if there was), we would visit them for coffee. There was always music on, and in particular I remember they had both the early Traffic albums. I adored songs like "Feelin' Alright" and "Who Knows What Tomorrow May Bring?", which latter had a clever stoned Steve Winwood Hammond organ solo.

Poor old Liz. I quite liked her but she was a hopeless case. Nicknamed "The Wet Fish" by male students, because she allegedly just lay back and let it happen to her, she would sleep with absolutely anybody. One night, after a party, I found myself alone with her outside my room. She was hanging around in the corridor, obviously expecting to be invited in. But I remembered the wet fish and all the people I personally knew who had slept with her, plus all the ones I didn't know. I couldn't face it, said goodnight and shut the door. From my friends, I actually gained respect as the one bloke who HADN'T slept with the Wet Fish, but as for Liz, she was as simple a prey for drugs as she was for sex, and sadly died at a young age.

As it happened, Rick the Nick was a very good Hammond player, and Hammond organs featured high on the early UEA agenda. I loved Steve Winwood's playing, especially on the jazzy instrumentals which formed the B-sides of early Fontana Spencer Davis singles. Rick was a fan of Jimmy Smith and some of the earliest gigs I attended at UEA were by Mike Carr and Tony Crombie ("Hammond Under Pressure" was their slogan) and also the aforementioned Wynder K. Frog. I had already purchased his album "Out of the Frying Pan" on the strength of a track on "You Can All Join In". When Wynder K. Frog appeared at UEA, it was the first time I guess I had been to a "real" gig as we know them: The band had a brass section, a nicely seedy rock and roll image and were, to my ears, staggeringly loud. Mick Weaver (WKF's real name) still is the greatest and nowadays can be found caressing the keys with Taj Mahal and The Phantom Blues Band.

In the following weeks came gigs by Elmer Gantry's Velvet Opera (for some reason, the students were negative about him because he had a bit of a camp image, very tolerant I'm sure) and also The Alan Bown!, shortened for reasons best known to himself from the Alan Bown Set. It was the day after that that I took my first step to becoming, oh God, a rock writer.

There was a weekly magazine at UEA, read by virtually everybody, called *Chips*. It had a music column called *Popinion*, written by a student called Chris Foren under the pseudonym of "L'étranger". Foren's claim to fame was that he knew a pirate radio DJ called Keith Skues. *Popinion* was a singles review column in an era when no self-respecting student bought singles. Plus, Foren insisted on unnecessarily mentioning Keith Skues several times each week.

Now anyone who has read this far will have discerned that unnecessary name-dropping is not entirely an alien concept to me. But Foren only had one name to drop, and it got on people's nerves. Having hugely enjoyed those first few live gigs, I couldn't understand why Foren never even mentioned any of the live music at UEA. So I approached him.

"Good idea."

"What?"

"Good idea. Why don't you do a live music column to run alongside my singles column?"

It was as simple as that. Foren was influential on *Chips*, so I immediately had not only an outlet, but a regular and widely-read one.

My bluff had been called, and the opening salvo was far from auspicious. The first *OLLIPOP* (sad but unavoidable title) must have been in early 1968 and was a retrospective on some recent concerts. Praised as the most memorable gig was the appearance of Savoy Brown, which had indeed been impressive. These heavy, long-haired bluesers, starring the well-smoothed Kim Simmonds and the gormless "Lonesome" Dave Peverett had initially baffled but then won over the audience, more used to soul bands. Most of them good-naturedly sat down on the floor and shook their heads to the beat, but some complained that they couldn't dance, and that was the theme of the inaugural *Ollipop*: Be tolerant, man.

Other highlights covered included The Pyramids, the first reggae band I'd experienced, and The Move, for whom the approving adjectives "mean" and "cool" were reserved, in particular for Ace Kefford and the dark-glassed, spiky-haired Trevor Burton. I thought it was fantastic that a band having pleasant Top Ten hits and appearances on mainstream TV shows could put on such a loud, heavy, aggressively "couldn't give a fuck" live performance. "Brontosaurus" wrote the template for heavy metal. And as for Roy Wood, if he isn't in the Rock and Roll Hall of Fame, induct him immediately.

The final gig of the 1968 Spring term was The Jeff Beck Group. What joy! Here was another chart hero refusing to behave as he should. With Ron Wood and Micky Waller, he performed a set of vicious blues and R & B, studiously ignoring all calls for "Hi Ho Silver

Lining". On lead vocals was a pencil-thin, strutting Mod with shades and a unique hedgehog haircut. His name was Rod Stewart, and he's never been as good since.

The soul groovers who wanted to dance had had their day, because the social secretary, a burly, determined Welshman called John Morgan, had an agenda of "progressive rock". He pulled off quite a coup by arranging for Pink Floyd to visit UEA, in a surprising but clever double bill with Fairport Convention (because both were represented by the Bryan Morrison Agency). Being now UEA's official Rock Bod, I was keen, if not confident, to try and do some interviews. But, apart from the friendly-looking Sandy Denny, the Fairports looked scary. Tyger Hutchings, in particular, seemed aloof and unsmiling, so I decided to go for the brilliant guitar player with the Bolan-style corkscrew hair.

"Excuse me, have you got a few minutes to spare?"

"Only if you ask extremely intelligent questions."

As Elizabeth from Hungerford would have said, it's not the trousers that matter. Despite the total change of appearance since those days, Richard Thompson was as affable then as he is now.

This version of Fairport (there was never a better one) still contained Iain Matthews as well as Sandy Denny, who was cheerful and relaxed. On drums was Martin Lamble and later that night I met a girl who knew him from home in Golders Green. She went on to become his girlfriend and they were still going out together a few months later when Martin was tragically killed in a crash in the band's van.

The interview revealed exciting things such as the fact that they would describe their music as "electric folk" (goodness), that they never had trouble winning over audiences and that, if they had to compare themselves to any other bands, they would say Big Brother and the Holding Company. At the time, I was astonished: There didn't seem to be any similarity between Sandy Denny and Janis Joplin. History was to prove, however, that there were, indeed, a number of similarities, not least in their volatility and their embracing of the darker side of the rock lifestyle.

The Fairports gave a revelatory performance. Sandy broke the audience's hearts with her versions of "Who Knows Where The Time Goes" and Leonard Cohen's "Suzanne" and we sat cross-legged on the floor, enraptured. The atmosphere intensified with the arrival of the Floyd, who were headlining. The light show, so innovative for its time, wafted and flickered over the band as they played endless, mesmerising versions of "Astronomy Domine" and "Careful With That Axe Eugene". They looked so frightening on stage but they, too, were happy to be interviewed. Roger Waters was particularly magnanimous towards Fairport, calling them "the best electric folk this side of anywhere".

Asked to classify their music, they declined, just calling it "our thing", but they did explain that the music was improvisational to a large extent, with no two performances ever being the same, and that, since the departure of Syd Barrett, the bulk of the writing was done by Roger Waters and Rick Wright. Their forthcoming album, they revealed, was to be called "Saucerful of Secrets".

That day marked my growth into someone who was always going to like good music regardless of category. This was because, despite the brilliance of the evening, there were still a few soul groovers in the audience who complained that they couldn't dance. To them, I signed off the column with a pompous but sincerely-meant put-down: "To those who went away mumbling discontentedly, I would say don't criticise what you don't understand, because any sort of sincere invention is valid."

Blimey! Bob Dylan put it more succinctly.

Next up was Tyrannosaurus Rex. They were booked for a reduced fee, stepping in at the last minute to replace The Spencer Davis Group, who had an illness problem. Pushed by John Peel, this embryonic acoustic version of T-Rex consisted of Marc Bolan and a percussionist called Steve Peregrine Took, whom John Yorke knew, from his days at Eltham Green School, as Steve Porter. This gave me a good "in" with the band, although John did mess things up a bit by greeting the ultra-cool hippie with, "All right, Stevie mate? How ya doing?" as Tyrannosaurus Rex emerged from their van.

Tyrannosaurus Rex were promoting their album "My People Were Fair And Had Sky In Their Hair" and Marc Bolan turned out to be my easiest interviewee ever, even though the reporting of it was of the customary uninspired standard:

"Bolan and Took believe implicitly in John Peel's sincerity. They don't care if people ignore their records: 'We'll do our thing as long as we're happy doing it, that's the way it is, man.' But they are worried about what they see as the deterioration of the Pink Floyd since the departure of Syd Barrett."

This simple paraphrasing was a poor journalistic technique which continued throughout the reign of *Ollipop*.

There was plenty of action in Norwich town as well as at the university. The Progressive Club, later called the Cat Trap Club and finally called Bang! was a tiny room run by Gerry Welsh, one of those eternally optimistic promoters who doubtless lost his shirt for the love of music. Bands I saw there included Free, The Deviants (who we didn't think were musical enough), The Pretty Things, Caravan and Locomotive, a Midlands band who had a great single called "Mr Armageddon". Plus the ubiquitous Keef Hartley.

We used to laugh a great deal at Keef Hartley, because he had absurd delusions of grandeur, considering that all he did was drum, and not particularly interestingly at that. Keef Hartley albums, on the other hand, always featured large photos of the man in an Indian headdress, plus a lengthy list of credits: The Keef Hartley Band, Photos by Keef Hartley, Design by Keef Hartley, Co-ordinated by Keef Hartley, Executive Producer Keef Hartley, etc., etc. Then, if you searched the small print, you could find: Vocals by Miller Anderson, Guitar by Miller Anderson, Songs written by Miller Anderson. So in fact, they were to all intents and purposes Miller Anderson albums. The slightly-built Scot was a superb guitarist and a good singer too, rather in the style of Frankie Miller.

In 1999, I spotted an advert saying, implausibly, that Miller Anderson would be playing in a grotty bikers' pub near Portsmouth. Out of curiosity, I went along, but I wish I hadn't. Miller had put on masses of weight, sprouted a bushy beard and was playing blues standards over a karaoke-style backing track. Stuck in the corner of this godforsaken pub, he was totally ignored by the fifteen or so customers, who talked loudly throughout. Birgit and I insisted on clapping after each song, which seemed to startle him a bit. I felt like crying.

One of the best nights at UEA came courtesy of my old acquaintances Spooky Tooth. The impression this band made is hard to describe, so revolutionary were they in an era spanning well-behaved beat groups and progressive rockers. They had the equivalent of two

Steve Winwoods in the form of keyboardists Gary Wright and Mike Harrison, who both sang. With the veins standing out on their necks, they howled wildly emotional vocal lines across the stage at each other. This was particularly mind-boggling in a twenty-minute epic called "Evil Woman", which contained a very long but not cliché-filled guitar solo by Luther Grosvenor. Could that have been his real name? Who was to know, but in his shoulder-to-toe leather overcoat, not moving his body an inch as his fingers tortuously attacked the fretboard, he was rock and roll cool personified. There was also an unusually upfront bassist, Greg Ridley, and a drummer who defined the power gained from restraint. When Mike Kellie re-emerged in one of the greatest bands of the Seventies, The Only Ones, it came as no surprise.

The interview with Spooky Tooth went well, even though, unsurprisingly, they didn't remember me from Aston Tirrold. I gleaned lots of interesting information but, having never learnt shorthand, conveyed it in the same odd odd way as usual, merely laid out as a series of facts, rather than as quotes:

"They were brought down when 'Sunshine Help Me' was a flop, and also admit that they made a mistake in releasing 'The Weight' as a single. They play a lot of university dates and enjoy them. A new LP is coming soon, on which they will try to get nearer their stage sound than before."

Around this time, there was an outing to London for Cream's farewell concert. This was a good experience, but not particularly because of Cream, who had certainly reached their limit and droned on and on with the kind of endless guitar soloing that was giving progressive rock a bad name. But also on the bill were Yes, who still had Peter Banks on guitar and were quite snappy, yet to descend into their famed musical self-indulgence. Opening the show was a trio called Taste, featuring a young Rory Gallagher. One aspect of this concert was the fact that, the Albert Hall being what it is, we actually had to sit BEHIND the bands, which gave a bit of an unusual perspective. We had an unrivalled view of the rears of the Marshall stacks.

When Free eventually played at the university, I knew I had finally found my kind of music. Paul Rodgers was so macho, doing impossible splits in his skin-tight trousers, manipulating the microphone stand like no one before, and barking out the songs in a voice and style which would be copied for decades. The sparseness of their music appealed: the bass used almost as a lead instrument, the hard but unfussy drums (a stark contrast to currently-fashionable show-offs like Jon Hiseman), and the trebly vibrato style of the unhealthy-looking, disgracefully unkempt guitarist. He stayed at the back of the stage, leaning back against the amp and pulling grotesque faces, but otherwise avoiding guitar hero poses.

This was Paul Kossoff, and it was Paul I homed in on for the interview, because I was intrigued that this wild man could be the son of the gentle and benign David Kossoff, who I had often heard reading Bible stories on the radio. The report in *Ollipop* gives a good idea of the naive style of the column:

"Andy Fraser, Free's bassist, is a mere 16 years old, and very accomplished too. The lead guitarist (the bristly one on the right) is Paul Kossoff. He studied classical guitar for five years and has been playing blues for two. Paul and Andy do most of the writing. On March 10th, their first LP emerges, entitled 'Tons of Sobs' (yes, they hate it too!). They were terrifically together on stage, but will they come across well on record? We shall see. Career-wise, nothing particularly exciting is coming up, which is sad. Ambitions? A hit, they say, is not the greatest objective, merely recognition and the chance to make a living out of what they enjoy doing."

I saw Free a number of times over their career and watching the decline of Paul Kossoff was heartbreaking. On the final occasion, at the Colston Hall in Bristol in 1972, he collapsed twice onstage and the show had to be curtailed. That is one of the many reasons why I am unashamed in not being interested in drugs. People like Hendrix, Kossoff and Cobain, who destroy themselves before they get to scratch the surface of their potential, are the high-profile cases, but what about all the other thousands of ruined lives?

Towards the end of my second year at UEA there was another excellent double bill, headlined by the Nice, whose single "America" had charted, despite its great length. Now down to a trio, they were popular with students because of what appeared to be an anti-establishment stance and because Keith Emerson stuck knives into his Hammond organ. I interviewed the bassist Lee Jackson, who was gratifyingly anti-pop:

"We refuse to put classifications onto music. We prefer just to call ourselves a 'musical group'. We don't like the fashion of calling any musician who isn't a cretin a genius. We look forward to playing at places like the ICA where we don't have to think about pleasing the masses."

This was the kind of thing I liked to hear, but I had less success with the support group, The Idle Race. I wanted to quiz Jeff Lynne about his association with Roy Wood of the Move (with whom, although I didn't know it, he would soon form The Electric Light Orchestra), but Lynne was furious. He only wanted to talk about the new Idle Race single "End of the Road", and refused to continue the interview. Something similar happened soon afterwards when I tried to interview Joe Cocker. He was so drunk that all I got was a series of unbelievably filthy jokes and some unprintably scurrilous gossip.

Ollipop led to a number of such humiliations, but few were worse than that handed out by Jon Hiseman. Colosseum had come to play at UEA and I had been promoted by the new Social Secretary, Neil Merchant, to being resident DJ for the gigs. I got to stand behind the curtains and play music in between the bands. On this occasion, I had acquired a highly-prized American import copy of Ten Years After's live extravaganza "Undead" and, having ostentatiously carried it round under my arm all day, was eager to show it off. I placed the needle onto my favourite track, an immensely long (and, in retrospect, rather preposterous) version of "Woodchopper's Ball". After a couple of minutes, Jon Hiseman's moustachioed face appeared round the curtain:

"Excuse me, young man. Could you turn off that infernal row? We're trying to do a soundcheck."

Also playing that term was Bakerloo, who featured Dave Clempson, who later ended up with Colosseum before joining Humble Pie. For me, Colosseum was another Keef Hartley special. Although they called themselves Jon Hiseman's Colosseum, the best songs were written by their guitarist James Litherland. "Elegy", from the first Colosseum album, is a superbly poignant song.

The humiliation at the hands of Jon Hiseman was as nothing compared to my second encounter with Sandy Denny. Fairport's return visit to UEA was not a success, because Sandy had a bad throat and was also in a black mood. At first she refused to go on, but the Social Secretary waved the contract in her face and insisted.

She coughed her way through the first song, but during the second, her voice gave out completely. The band left the stage and I had to rush back to my post to put on a record. Sitting backstage on a flight of steps was Sandy Denny, just in the process of lighting up a King Size Benson and Hedges.

"Do you think that's a good idea?" I enquired, remembering what a warm, friendly person she had been on the band's last visit.

"What do you mean?"

"Maybe smoking a cigarette isn't a very good idea if you've got a bad throat."

"Well," replied Sandy, "you are just a pathetic little creep and you can fuck right off."

The last ever *Ollipop* adventure was the best, in that it involved my original favourite band from way back, the Hollies. You know how you feel when a band lets you down, betrays the musical faith you placed in them? How must fans of The Frantic Elevators feel about Mick bloody Hucknall whining "My Way" in a dicky bow? Or what The Thompson Twins became? Or The Leyton Buzzards turning into Modern Romance? Well, that was how I felt about The Hollies at that point.

I'd stuck with them through thick and thin, bought every single (yeah, yeah, the shed) and also every album, out of the purest admiration for Tony Hicks, who I secretly hoped would go solo or start up another band. As people sneered at all my Hollies albums with their cod-psychedelic sleeves, as they dressed up inelegantly in beads and kaftans and performed songs like "Fifi The Flea", I still kept the faith. It was confusing, though, because the bassists kept changing, Allan Clarke kept leaving and returning, and, to be truthful, I hated his voice anyway. And when I met them, things were at their worst.

Amazingly, the goofy Graham Nash had turned out to be the most credible in the band, going off to America to work with David Crosby and Steve Stills. The only reason that I admired Tony Hicks (apart from his hairstyle, obviously) was his snappy little guitar solos, and he'd completely stopped doing them. On "Stop Stop Stop", he played the banjo, and on "On A Carousel" there was an appalling steel drum interlude which was inserted, pre-recorded, into live performances. For Christ's Sake! The only saving grace was that Nash had been replaced by a fairly cool character from The Escorts called Terry Sylvester.

Hell hath no fury ... Just think of those Frantic Elevators fans. When the early Hollies had covered classics by Chuck Berry, the Everley Brothers and Roy Orbison, they had done so with flair, and even added character to them. But now, they had done something unforgivable. They had not only recorded but actually released an abomination of an album called *Hollies Sing Dylan*. In this, they took all the master's most commercially accessible songs and ritually disembowelled them. Their big band swing version of "Blowin' In The Wind" must surely be a candidate for worst cover version of all time. And now, Neil Merchant had booked them for the UEA Rag Barbecue.

This bold event, which took place in Earlham Park, Norwich in summer 1969, was doomed, as are all events which have no clear rationale. Set up as a proper festival (we had to build fences of almost Glastonbury proportions to keep out fictitious gatecrashers), it starred (wait for it) The Hollies, Marmalade, Dave Dee Dozy Beaky Mick and Tich, Spooky Tooth and The Soft Machine. The idea was to draw in punters from outside (although the Beat Group era was all but over) as well as muso students (who, of course, wouldn't be seen dead anywhere near Dave Dee and the like). Spooky Tooth wisely didn't show up, Soft Machine played a cursory set and disappeared, and the event was a financial catastrophe.

Determined to get the interview with The Hollies, I chased them round all afternoon and evening. Before the gig? Too busy. After the gig? Too tired. What about at breakfast the next morning? Okay, when are you leaving? Eight o'clock? Bloody hell! There was another problem, in that I had a visitor for the weekend, in the form of Elena, a Yugoslavian girl I had met at Easter in London. John Yorke had secured me a job serving at the Railbar in Euston Station, a distinction which, I recently discovered, is probably the only thing I have in common with Damon Albarn, apart from drinking too much.

Elena didn't speak a single word of English. so we communicated by looking at each other approvingly. Except that, on the day of the Rag Barbecue, we didn't even do that, because I spent the whole time swanning around being important backstage, while she had no backstage pass. By the time I'd finally fixed up the interview, Ian

Wingfield had stepped into the breach and, judging from the leers he was giving out over the next few days, what passed between them was more than admiring glances. But I had no time for all that, I had to be at the Castle Hotel at 7 am.

Thank goodness, The Hollies had changed out of their white stage suits and looked more or less as they ought to. They immediately started asking the questions I'd hoped they wouldn't: Had the students liked their act? Had the barbecue been a financial success? It was obvious that they, too, were unsure of their career path and were still trying to recover from Graham Nash's departure. And they were on the defensive about the Dylan album:

"Does the issue of the LP indicate a drying up of impetus after the departure of Nash? Yes, although there are several new songs ready now and they are adjusting to the new situation. Why had they recorded already familiar numbers? Simple (from Tony): It's sad but true that people just don't buy Hollies LPs, so they were going for the people who only buy records with familiar songs on them. I doubted whether this market actually existed, but this weeks' album chart proves their point."

Some clever dick entitled the article "Ollie's Hollies".

Before leaving, I did extract one scoop from Tony Hicks: "We've found a song for a single. If it comes off, it'll be another "Whiter Shade of Pale". Sure enough, "He Ain't Heavy, He's My Brother" appeared a few weeks later and made almost anyone temporarily forgive the band their sins. Unfortunately, it wasn't long before the sins became unforgivable. They recorded an album called *Hollies Sing Hollies*, in response to those who said they couldn't write songs. And, later on, another one in a similar mould, called *Confessions Of The Mind*. On this opus, there's a track by Tony Hicks, called "Too Young To Be Married":

Tew yerng tew be married,
Tew yerng tew be free - ee,
Tew yerng tew be marr - eed,
But what could they dew?
They were gonna have a bay - bee.

I'm a faithful sort of chap, and I still go to see The Hollies today, when they come round. But my love affair with the band ended with *Hollies Sing Dylan*, and so did *Ollipop*. Germany beckoned.

VI. Tschairmany (2): Kiel-Hauled

I picked Kiel for my "year abroad" because it was easy to pronounce.
No, that's not true. I picked Kiel because Germany has hardly any
coastline and Kiel looked as if it might be a seaside resort, with
some blue beside it on the map. It was also enticingly close to
Denmark and all points north.

The journey was horrible, the customary stormy crossing to
Bremerhaven in the company of hundreds of drunken, aggressive
squaddies, followed by a train to Kiel, a station which, as a terminus,
had a frightening finality about it. The end of the line. Now life gets
serious. Which it did.

Having nowhere to live, I checked into the youth hostel, and even
that was an effort, because it was over on the other side of the fjord,
miles from the centre, in a very dodgy area of town. It was as vile as
all youth hostels are, a barracks filled with farting, belching, snoring
blokes with stinking feet. No wonder women divorce men; I would
have nothing to do with them if I could help it, at least nothing
involving shared domestic arrangements.

In the youth hostel I met several people. One was a pleasant
oceanology student called Uli, with whom I agreed to start looking
for accommodation, since single rooms or flats were simply
unavailable. The other two people were a couple of English guys
called Dave and Frank, who were working as washer-uppers in the
hostel.

Dave was good company, a gentle Yorkshireman who was trying
to busk his way round Europe. A very good folk-style acoustic
guitarist, he nonetheless wasn't earning enough to exist on and
therefore had to stop every now and then to save up some money
by doing a temporary job. The other Englishman was Frank, and
Frank was trouble.

He was a deserter from the British Army of the Rhine, which was at
least something in his favour. But he was also a drug dealer and a
wholly untrustworthy person, the kind who would smile as he
twisted the knife in you. But for all that, he was sort of superficially
likeable in a situation where you're homesick and grateful to have
another English person to talk to.

Also in the youth hostel for a short while was a colleague from UEA called Ian. Ian had a fabulous idea which worked fabulously well. His girlfriend lived in Copenhagen, and that was where Ian was going to spend his "year abroad". But he was supposed to be studying German, not Danish, so he had chosen Kiel because of its proximity to Scandinavia. After a few days in Kiel, Ian moved to Copenhagen, where he remained for the entire year.

How could he get away with this? Easy. Every couple of months, he would pen a letter to his tutor in Norwich, put it in an envelope and send it to me in Kiel. I would put a stamp on it and post it on to Norwich. Hey presto, Ian was in Kiel. But, to be frank, he needn't have even done that. Owing to the aforementioned "newness" of UEA, there were no systems in place at all to check up on us. I could have spent the entire year in Timbuktu and no one would have known. You didn't even have to write a single essay.

The only way they might have become suspicious would have been if I had come back no better at German than when I went out. In fact, I came back with my German massively improved, which, to be fair, was the purpose of the operation. I ended up getting quite a good degree, which Ian didn't. Not surprisingly, his German hadn't improved at all, although he was a dab hand at Danish.

Every day, Uli and I would catch the tram to the accommodation office at the university, always in vain. There was a vast queue of others in the same position, because Kiel was a small town with a big university. There simply wasn't anywhere to live.

On the fourth day, we noticed an old tramp-like man going into the office. At the front of the queue was Jochen Schmidt (whom we didn't know), who overheard that the old man was offering a flat for three students. "I'll take it", said Jochen, and then picked us to be his flatmates. He says today that he picked me out because I had long hair and, being just out of military service, he didn't, but wanted to. At any rate, we had our flat.

It is very difficult to describe the awfulness of Harriesstrasse 14. It was on the second floor, but the toilet was *auf halber Treppe*, which meant it was outside the flat, halfway down the stairs, so that it could be shared by two floors. Initially, I shared the bigger room with Uli, while Jochen had the smaller room to himself. In no time at all, however, we were infiltrated by Frank, Dave and an assortment of down and outs, most notably a long, greasy-haired native of Kiel, called Charlie, and a friend of Jochen's, called Peter, who had a job gutting cod at the fish market and smelt accordingly.

Any combination of these could soon be found lying or stumbling around the room at any time of the day or night, without any suggestion of contributing to the rent. Dave was okay. One day, he and I found an old piano which someone had put out on the street for *Sperrmüll*, which is a system whereby you put out old furniture and it gets collected by the council. Or impoverished students like us steal it, which is permitted too. Six of us lugged the unbelievably heavy instrument up the stairs and Dave and I had the odd jam session, which was hard because I had zero musical ability.

Charlie fell instantly under the spell of Frank and so, unfortunately, did Jochen. Frank had ready takers in these two for hash, but also for a variety of other pills which he carried. Very quickly, Uli moved out, sensible chap, and I was left marooned as the only non-drug taker. As is the way in such an environment, I became the fall guy, constantly being sniggered at. They wouldn't let me sleep, I had not the slightest hint of privacy, and they more than obviously wanted me out. But if I have no other positive character traits, I can certainly stick to decisions, even if they make no sense.

I should have gone somewhere else, anywhere, even back to the youth hostel. But I wasn't going to be pushed out. It was stupid, because the flat was just horrible. In the winter of 1969, temperatures in Kiel plunged to minus 20 and stayed there for weeks. The sea, and I promise this is true, froze over so that you could walk out on it. Harriesstrasse, being a very steep hill, became like the North Face of the Eiger, especially if, like me, you wore fashionable but hopelessly impractical stack-heeled boots. The only way up it was on all fours.

The first band to come to Kiel was yet again, Spooky Tooth. They were really, really good, angry and aggressive, and of course my new-found friends were very impressed. Charlie was convinced that he could see needle marks where he thought Mike Harrison had been injecting himself. I couldn't discern any such thing, and assumed that Charlie was imagining it. He probably was, but the point is that Charlie, far from being shocked or disgusted, was impressed. This was what he aspired to.

A couple of years later, I became curious as to what had become of Charlie and asked Jochen.

"Very sad. He died of a heroin overdose."

I temporarily escaped from this hell into another one. I appealed to Jochen's better nature by saying I could no longer share my room with these maniacs and asking if I could move in with him. The flat had no heating of any kind apart from a coal stove, but we had no money to buy any coal. Occasionally, someone would steal a pile of newspapers from a newsagent's front step, but the effect was brief and negligible.

We had absolutely no money. The Mensa canteen at the university did *Eintopf* (a bowl of stew) for 70 pfennigs and that was what we lived on, although now I come to think of it, we had money for beer. Cigarettes were less of a problem, because English one-shilling pieces fitted the cigarette machines. I brought a big bag with me, so we were never short of Peter Stuyvesants. In the evenings, I soon got into the habit of drinking a bottle of cheap red wine (69 pfennigs from Aldi, absolutely evil), which was the only way I could get to sleep. Inevitably, I would wake up after a couple of hours and shiver for the rest of the night.

I have always had a love-hate relationship with Jochen Schmidt. Enthusiastically affable, he can be the kindest, most considerate person in the world. And he can be a complete bastard.

After agreeing to let me share his room, he abused my friendship on a number of occasions. Frank, thank goodness, had been picked up by the Military Police, and Dave had moved on, leaving just Charlie, who did nothing, and Peter, who stank of cod, in the other room. It would have been all right, but often Jochen would have visitors and they would lie around smoking dope as I tried to get to sleep. They all talked complete shite for hours on end. As an advert for smoking joints, it was terrible. Obviously, in the type of environments I frequent, I have been offered joints on hundreds of occasions. It was the time in the Harriesstrasse which made me decide always to refuse, on the grounds that I don't want to waste my time talking, and presumably thinking, bollocks. (Yes, yes, I know what you're thinking.)

The other unforgivable thing that Jochen did was have loud, violent, shrieking sex with a variety of women while I was in the room.

There really can't be many worse things than trying to get to sleep to an accompaniment of a creaking mattress, grunts, gasps and groans. Occasionally, he returned late at night from the harbour with hideous, aged whores he had picked up there. I was quite relieved when he got a steady girlfriend, called Juliane. At least she probably didn't have anything catching.

Temporary rescue came in the form of a very straight student called Hardy, whom I met in the Mensa. Seeing my plight, he kindly invited me to spend Christmas with his family in Wilhelmshaven, on the North Sea Coast. They were all extremely kind to me, except that they made me wear a headband at mealtimes "for reasons of hygiene". But their house was warm and it was a welcome, if brief respite.

Hardy, who had a car, had to return to Kiel straight after Christmas, but I stayed on for a couple of extra days, with the plan of hitch-hiking back. This went badly wrong, because I became stranded, on my own, late at night at a motorway service station called Stillhorn, just outside Hamburg. The café closed at 11 o'clock, so, beginning to feel ill, I tried to sleep in the relative warmth of the toilet block. After only a few minutes, the door flew open and three large men with an Alsatian burst in.

They were wearing plain clothes but they identified themselves with Drug Squad badges. I was in a state of panic, because I was wearing a greatcoat which Frank had left behind. God knows what might have been in the pockets. I must have looked a cert for a successful bust, long-haired, unshaven and pale. They went away disappointed, but just to make the point, they forbade me to sleep in the toilet and arranged for the caretaker to lock it.

It was apparent that I was being gripped by 'flu. I had a raging temperature and uncontrollable shivers. There was no alternative (there being no traffic whatsoever) but to lie down and sleep in the snow.

A couple of hours was all that I managed. Feeling fit to die, I walked aimlessly round among the parked lorries until first light, when I trudged across some snowy fields to a bus route and travelled free (which is something you can do in Germany as long as no inspector comes along) into the centre of Hamburg. There I did the only thing I could think of doing: I rang up Johann-Hinrich's dad (the one from Schöningen), who was a manager of a branch of the Volksbank. When I explained my plight, he arranged to transfer me enough cash to catch a train back to Kiel. Kind man.

What awaited me in Kiel was less pleasant. I arrived back to find a man, some kind of drunken sailor, asleep in my bed. Jochen had met him in a pub and "thought I wouldn't mind". With the kind of rage which can only come from feeling very ill, I threw this interloper into the street and, just for good measure, stormed next door and ordered Charlie to leave as well. Peter I couldn't dislodge, much as I'd have liked to, because, with his fishy income, he contributed to the rent. Peter, unbelievably, later implied that my throwing Charlie out was the factor that drove him to drugs. Like hell. The person who did that was behind bars in Mönchengladbach.

We made various attempts to get some kind of work in order to help us survive. One job entailed delivering leaflets advertising a dry cleaners in the town of Rendsburg. We were supposed to climb right up to the top floor of each block of flats and deliver the leaflets though each door. After a while, the temptation simply to stuff handfuls of the leaflets through the ground floor letter box became too strong to resist. Unfortunately, the boss had cleverly posted some lookouts on the top floor of various blocks and, after three days, he announced that he was sacking us for not doing the work properly. We were actually quite pleased, because the job was deadly dull, so we asked for our wages for the thousands of flyers we actually had delivered. He refused to pay us on the grounds that we hadn't delivered all the leaflets. His attitude when we protested was, "Yeah? What are you going to do about it then?"

Then we got the chance to do door-to-door delivery of eggs, the bright idea of a local farmer, who offered us a percentage of the price of all the eggs we sold. This seemed a great idea in principle, but in the eight hours we spent climbing up and down the tower blocks, knocking on each door and greeting the householders with a cheery, "Good afternoon! Farm-fresh eggs!", we failed to sell a single egg. Having a door slammed in your face every two minutes was pretty demoralising, and ten percent of nothing, as they say, is still nothing. It may sound soppy, but that is why I always buy a copy of the Big Issue, even if I have no intention of reading it.

An enthusiastic young man called Günther offered to pay me for writing a revived *Ollipop* for a student magazine called *Ouzo*.

Professional journalism! This was tempting, but the German students' appetite for rock and roll gossip was not big. In fact, they were completely baffled as to why anyone could be remotely interested in such matters. The column was discontinued after two weeks and of course I didn't get paid. Stupid thought in the first place.

Things didn't improve much from there, although there was a respite in the form of a relationship with a girl called Sabine, who was the friend of Jochen's girlfriend Juliane. I didn't fall for her exactly, but I did badly need a warm person to lean on. Like a fool, I managed to get myself into a reprise of the Stillhorn incident when Jochen, Peter and I hitched to Lübeck, where Sabine's parents lived. While the other two watched a soccer match, I endured a very stiff *Kaffee und Kuchen* with the family, who were obviously horrified at the state of this apparition their daughter had invited into their house. On the way back, we once again got stranded in the middle of the night in a godforsaken village called Bad Schwartau, where we had to sleep in the open air on a garage forecourt. At least this time we were able to offer each other a little body heat.

Sabine suddenly suggested a trip to Berlin. As there was absolutely no reason to stay in Kiel, I agreed to go with her, and contacted Knut, an old friend from Schöningen days, who had a flat there. Fortuitously, he was planning to go away for a month and wanted someone to look after his flat for the whole of February. Things definitely seemed to be looking up as we travelled by train to Berlin, giving me my first opportunity to experience the activities of the DDR border guards, who ran mirrors underneath the train to check that no refugees were hanging on to it, and insisted that I should hold back my hair so that they could compare my ears with those on the elderly passport photo. It came as a relief when they finally put the green stamp in my passport, but Berlin brought little improvement in the quality of life.

Sabine was keen to check out the folk clubs like Danny's Pan and the Steve Club, which seemed odd because she hadn't previously shown any sign of being interested in music. Suddenly, she announced that her real reason for coming to Berlin had been to find her ex-boyfriend, a folk musician with a drug problem she felt she should help him with. She had now found him and therefore no longer wanted to be with me. I couldn't really do anything about it, so Sabine disappeared, never to be seen again.

Knut's flat was at least warm (he had left behind a supply of coal) and I dreaded what might await me back in Kiel, so I stayed put for a couple more weeks, feeling mightily sorry for myself, and making a bit of cash by joining a group of students doing illegal nocturnal fly-posting for a travel company. This was an incredibly cold job which entailed getting covered from head to foot in flour and water glue and constantly looking over your shoulder for fear of being apprehended.

Eventually, I hitched a lift back to Kiel on a lorry and had a repeat procedure of the "show us your ear" ritual, this time outside in the snow. I had to stand to attention for five minutes while the guard scrutinised my ear from the warmth of his sentry box. But Spring was finally arriving.

Musically, and in other ways too, things began to look up. Back in January, The Soft Machine had visited Kiel and I had been shocked when, walking past the station the next morning, I spotted them leaving town. The ancient Transit was actually being driven by Mike Ratledge, the square-shaded organist who only the night before had seemed to me to be a star. Next to him, in conditions of obvious great discomfort, sat Hugh Hopper and Robert Wyatt. The rock and roll illusion was beginning to reveal itself.

When Steve Winwood left The Spencer Davis Group, he was replaced by Eddie Hardin. Eddie was an even better Hammond player, a tiny, bouffant-haired man who used the Hammond's bass pedals to great effect and was prone to throw the heavy instrument around rather like Keith Emerson did in the Nice. This new Spencer Davis version didn't last long and Eddie and drummer Pete York went out as Hardin and York, dubbed as "The World's Smallest Big Band". They were signed to the Bell record label (if you keep reading, you'll come across that name again), but the reason they broke through so big in Germany was a bootleg album recorded live at the *Fabrik* club in Hamburg.

In 1970, they were absolutely huge in Germany, so much so that vendors sold the "Hardin and York Live" bootleg album from stands in the street. I took to them enthusiastically, inspired by the Hammond sound I loved so much and the gigantic Leslie speakers which blasted out the sound into the audience. I also liked their strange choice of material (an incongruous medley of "Norwegian Wood" and "Like A Rolling Stone", for example) and the brilliant drumming of Pete York, the only drummer I had (have) ever encountered who could do a ten-minute solo without even threatening to be boring. This he achieved by not merely being highly skilled, but by humorously taking the piss out of the entire concept of drum soloing. Anyway, Hardin and York played twice in the Mensa in Kiel, and there were also concerts from Steamhammer and Renaissance, whose singer was Jane Relf, sister of the Yardbirds' Keith, who was also in the band.

As the weather improved, so did the mood. In June, Jochen and I joined a gang of people travelling down to Hamburg for a two-day festival held on a racecourse. This event featured most of the best-known UK bands of the time, including Black Sabbath, Humble Pie and Uriah Heep. We slept outside and woke up covered in dew, but it was worth it. Finally, on July 15th, Free came to Kiel, playing in the tiny Spektrum Club. "All Right Now" had just been released and no longer did they have the attitude of "just doing what we enjoy doing"; Free were up for it in a big way. My freeze-frame of that night is of a lascivious Paul Rodgers pinching the bottom of a girl who walked across the corner of the stage. She turned round and delivered a mighty slap to his extravagant stubble. Paul Kossoff played a blinder but looked ill, ill, ill.

Day to day existence consisted of sitting round at the university (academic work was unthinkable; Jochen Schmidt took nine years to complete his degree) and spending the evenings either at Spektrum or a student disco called Tamen-T. There, you could only pull if you were willing to dance to "Sugar Sugar" by the Archies or "Venus" by Shocking Blue. I wasn't, but was known on several occasions to fall asleep standing up at the bar. I never actually collapsed, just had to be nudged back into consciousness.

Normally, Jochen and I would stagger back to the Harriesstrasse at about two in the morning, when Tamen-T closed. On the way home was a snack bar which we called *Bitte schön* because of the exaggerated politeness of the lady who ran it:

"Guten Abend. Bitte schön?"
(Order your food.)

"Bitte schön."
(Ask for something else.)

"Bitte schön."
(Say *"danke schön"*.)

"Bitte schön."
(Pay.)

"Danke schön."
(*"Bitte schön,* oh bugger, now you've got **me** going.")

By now, having advertised in the local paper, I had several students I was tutoring in English, so could afford the speciality of the house, meatballs with red cabbage and fried potatoes. Well, you had to be there.

One night, at *Bitte Schön,* a dream came true. I put a Mark into the fruit machine, an annoyingly parsimonious device known as the Golden Seven. Oh joy! It got stuck in the winning position, spilling out over two hundred Marks. I held my hands outstretched in the cup where the winnings came out, so that the clattering wouldn't attract attention. The winnings continued until the machine was empty and all my pockets so full that I could hardly walk. I tried to look unobtrusive as I walked out, but sauntering was difficult in the circumstances. In celebration, we went straight next door into a pub and drank a good proportion of the money immediately. Afterwards, we surmised that, far from switching off the machine, the landlady would probably have merely said, *"Bitte schön!"*

In the summer, I got the nearest I would ever get to being a drug fiend. "Kater" Weimershaus, a demented medical student, invited us out to his house in Strande, a beach resort up the coast. Kater had a reputation for driving through the streets of Kiel in his Citroen 2CV brandishing an imitation pistol. On the way to Strande, he also demonstrated his patent method of filling up with petrol for free, by jumping up and down on the rubber pipe which brought the petrol from the pump. The syphoning effect this created allowed several litres to enter the tank before a suspicious attendant approached, at which point Kater drove off. He assured us that, on principle, he never paid for petrol. The principle was that he didn't want to pay.

In Kater's flat he, Jochen and I sat around with three girls while Kater distributed "Cappys". These were tablets called Captigun, which Kater nicked from the clinic where he worked. The idea was that they were supposed to keep you awake all night, rather like babies do. In a moment of conformity, I took one, along with everyone else, and then spent the entire night pointlessly awake, listening to Procol Harum's *A Salty Dog* album over and over again. Why? I'd much rather have been asleep. And I felt shit the next day.

Before I left Kiel, we dragged the piano down to the beach and set fire to it. Then I returned for yet another, slightly less wild, summer stacking bales at Stype before returning to UEA. This final year was quite different from the preceding ones, in that, in theory, one really was supposed to work. In practice, I fell in with a "bad lot" in the form of a gang of people who had all spent similarly dissolute "years abroad" in Europe. We occupied a new, purpose-built student accommodation block called Waveney Terrace and called ourselves, sadly accurately, the "Waveney Wankers", as we spent most evenings having water fights in the corridors. This started early on with one student simply lobbing a sponge at a neighbour in jest, and ended up with people filling entire waste bins and emptying them over whomever they wanted to annoy. Interestingly, no one declined to join in and there was much fun to be had eavesdropping on the consultants who were brought in to analyse why there were obviously major teething troubles with the building's plumbing.

Luckily, work would have been difficult anyway, because we were permanently on strike. The music scene at the university had collapsed completely, probably as a result of the disastrous Rag Barbecue of two years before, and the only gigs were a couple of outside promotions at Norwich Lads' Club. One featured Yes at their most self-indulgent (bloody Steve Howe and bloody Chris Squire in ridiculous Eskimo boots) and the other was a hopelessly out-of-it Traffic, who had expanded but not improved. "The Low Spark Of High Heeled Boys" lasted twenty-five minutes and poor Chris Wood looked (was) on his last legs. My only personal musical outlet that year came when I became resident DJ on a radio station set up to entertain a sit-in. I regret to say that I can't remember what we were sitting in about, but we received some praise from one local resident who complimented us on our choice of "wake up" tune at 7 am, when the speakers would be pointed out of the windows of the block where we were sitting in and turned on full blast:

"That's a damn good tune, that is. Sets me up for the day. What's it called?

It was The Internationale.

Having brought back a bag of two pfennig pieces from Germany, I was able to stay in close telephonic contact with Rosamund, who was studying to be a primary teacher at Rolle College in Exmouth. Two pfennig pieces, in a happy synergy with one shilling pieces for German cigarettes, exactly fitted the sixpence slot of British telephone boxes. Rosamund invited me down to Exmouth for a weekend music festival.

This was a great time. On the first night they had Arrival, who had just had a chart hit with "Friends". This was a good song which was nonetheless annoying, because one of the lines went, "We all have friends who have friends by the river", which was patently untrue. Still, they were good, as were Mogul Thrash the next night. They were the reason for my hitching such a ridiculous distance, because they had been formed by James Litherland, who had wisely moved on from Colosseum. The final attraction was Osibisa, an African dance band. In the canteen before the show, one of them made a suggestive remark about Rosamund, but I decided not to challenge him, as there were eight members in the band. Rosamund and I had a nerve-wracking time deceiving the night porters, since Rolle College had yet to lift its rules about "co-habiting".

Suddenly, in mid-1971, I had a degree and nothing to do with it. I had made half-hearted approaches to a few newspaper training schemes, but, just as I had known back at school, they were seeking school leavers, not graduates. Yet another summer at Stype, this time completely on my own, put off the evil day, but, just to make sure, I applied for the last refuge of those who can do nothing: a teacher training course at Bristol University.

I was rescued by Ian, the student who had spent his German year in Denmark. He was thinking of going back, did I fancy coming along? It seemed a good idea, so in October 1971, there I was back in Kiel. A few enquiries soon led me to Jochen Schmidt. With a new blonde girlfriend called Ingrid, he was living in something akin to an opium den, on the top floor of a derelict hotel, the ground floor of which had been turned into a disco called the Pupille. He seemed pleased to see me; however, the first few minutes of conversation revealed that not only did both he and Ingrid have crabs, but that the entire building was infested with white mice, the legacy of a previous tenant who had bred them and then allowed them to escape.

I would never have moved in, were it not for the fact that I unexpectedly got offered a job. A menial, badly-paid one, to be sure, but still a job, making photocopies and being a general dogsbody at the University English department. Merely being there was fantastic, because you could say, "Yeah, actually I work at the University" and people were instantly impressed, thinking that you might possibly be a lecturer or a professor or something. No, honestly.

The unfamiliar pleasure of having an income, however insignificant, gave me the courage to ring Bristol University and request them to defer my application for teacher training, which they agreed to do.

So I moved into something akin to a cell above the Pupille. That this was a mistake soon became clear. The disco stayed open until 3 am, but all you could discern were the bass notes. This wouldn't have been such a problem to anyone not interested in music, but to me it was hell, because I couldn't stop myself from trying to identify the songs from their bass lines. I took to staying downstairs in the Pupille until closing time, often falling asleep on one of their sofas and having to be woken up.

I thought that a trendy Englishman such as myself would be an ideal DJ for the Pupille, but Dieter, the current DJ, saw me as a rival. On the only occasion he allowed me a slot, I got so drunk to calm my nerves that I sent the needle skidding across the record I was trying to play, thus annoying the dancers. That was the only chance I got. The only live music the Pupille ever presented was a concert by Alexis Korner, which ended in controversy because Dieter claimed he didn't have any money to pay him.

Life upstairs was barely tolerable. The heating broke down daily and the bathroom carpet was provided by an ever-deepening pile of *Melody Makers*, which I bought weekly at the railway station, ensuring that we all had black soles on our feet. The white mice were everywhere, so it was unthinkable to bring any girls back. One night, Jochen and I explored the cellar kitchen area. It was exactly as it had been abandoned, years before. The grease-filled pans were still on the hobs, but the whole room was infested with a seething mass of thousands of mice. We quickly slammed the door shut and ran for it.

Existence in this hideous environment being so unpleasant, I returned home to spend Christmas with my family. I really should have known better, because Christmas seems to be completely jinxed for me. My parents were staying with my sister Pippa and her husband Colin, who by now were on yet another farm, this time near Basingstoke. My father found my hippie image completely unbearable, worrying even here, many miles from any friends or relations, that people might think the worse of him if they saw me in that state. On Boxing Day, I came down to breakfast having forgotten to shave. Father refused me permission to sit down at the table, saying he wasn't prepared to eat breakfast with someone who was unshaven. Maybe I should have cracked some joke about Elizabeth's adage that it's not trousers that are important but what's inside them, but instead I just cracked, full stop.

"Father, I'm twenty-three, I'm working at a university," (had to get that one in), "you just can't talk to me like that any more."

"I don't care how old you are, there are certain standards that must be adhered to."

"So that means that you love me if I shave, but you don't love me if I don't."

"Yes."

"In that case, I can't stay here any more."

I rushed upstairs, threw my bits into my bag and ran out of the house, aware of my mother's sobs but unwilling even to say goodbye to any of them. If I found the mice and lice of the Pupille preferable to this, things must have been bad.

It was only when I reached the main road that I realised that I had, in the short term, nowhere to go. I walked the five miles to Basingstoke, caught a train to Stroud, then trudged four miles in the dark from Stroud up the hill to Edge and down the lane to Rosamund's house, by which time it was past midnight. I threw some pebbles at her window in an attempt to wake her up. Unfortunately, the only person to hear was her father Oliver, who, having doubtless been terrified by the ghostly sounds I had been making, went completely apeshit.

"What the hell do you think you're doing, prowling round here in the middle of the night? I've a good mind to call the police."

Having been refused admission, I had reached the end of my ideas as to what to do. I walked down the sunken lane, crawled under a hedge, covered myself with leaves and branches and fell asleep. In the middle of the night, I was awoken by heavy rain. Within minutes, my womb-like creation had turned into the shower scene out of "Psycho" - only a lot colder. Sleeping in the open air in the middle of winter was becoming a habit; this was the third time in two years.

Back in Kiel, our favourite pub was a student haunt cum pizzeria called *Heinrich VIII*. When the Welsh band Man played in Kiel, they noodled on seemingly for ever and then went for a meal afterwards in *Heinrich VIII*, as did the considerably briefer and more inspiring MC5. Even though it was in a gig series dubiously entitled *This Is Pop Time*, we all approved of the MC5's riotous show at the Eichhof because they had such an anti-establishment image. When they then repaired to *Heinrich VIII*, I was inevitably designated as chief interpreter, haplessly attempting to translate answers to questions such as, *"Warum sollen wir die Marmalade hinausstossen?"*, "Can you explain the rationale of the White Panthers?" ,*"Was bedeutet 'Motherfucker'?"* and *"Ich will meine Mutter nicht ficken"*.

Luckily, Wayne Kramer was building a gigantic pyramid of upturned beer glasses which eventually, shortly before it reached the ceiling, collapsed, sending shards of broken glass all over the pub. The MC5 were asked to leave.

Jochen, myself and Albrecht Schwab, an ex-merchant seaman now studying law, ended up in relative civilisation, following a litigation-strewn eviction from the Pupille, in a nice city-centre flat, underneath a Transcendental Meditation Centre. Rosamund came to visit me there, and we really seemed to be getting on okay, as I returned to Bristol to face the inevitable teacher training. If you don't know what to do, you might as well give teaching a go.

The year in Bristol was one of the least musically eventful of my adult life. I found a minuscule flat behind the hospital, cold but at least with a gas meter. I played the most recent album by Free, *Heartbreaker*, which demonstrated only too graphically how the collapse of Paul Kossoff had immobilised the band. The bay window overlooking the city provided a good stage for half-hearted Paul Rodgers impersonations. But mainly, I was involved in writing lesson plans. Teaching was something which demanded serious concentration, otherwise you were doomed.

The only musical interest that year came in the form of a concert at the Victoria Rooms by local heroes Stackridge, who combined comedy with prog-rock in songs like the epic "Purple Spaceships Over Yatton". Other than that, Rosamund and I lived a life of unprecedented and uninteresting domesticity (apart from my occasional unauthorised late-night outings to the Dugout Club). Rosamund taught at a Primary School in the village of Chew Magna and had to be sensible about preparing lessons, so we lived separately, but spent most of our free time together. We almost drifted into marriage. Thank goodness we didn't, because we would undoubtedly have become a statistic.

At the end of my teacher training, I was once again in a position of not knowing what to do. I half-heartedly answered an advertisement in the Times Educational Supplement from an agency looking for English teachers to work in secondary schools in Germany. I was taken on and spent the years from 1973 to 1976 in the northern city of Bremen.

During my time there, I had a few musical adventures, mainly based on the fact that the German pupils loved all the songs I could play with the thee chords I had learnt in Schöningen all those years before. I bought a songbook which contained hundreds of British and American folk songs and details of how to play them. With the help of another English teacher called Peter Jackson, I learned three more chords, namely the three *barre* chords used by Status Quo (filched originally from Chuck Berry). This made it possible for the two of us to play a few lamentable gigs as a duo and one not quite so lamentable one with a drummer, a bassist and my Woolworths guitar and plastic wah wah pedal.

Compared to Bristol, Bremen wasn't too bad for gigs, as the list in the back of this book demonstrates. But the time in Bremen was crucial in my life for quite a different reason. Since this is a story not strictly connected with a book about music, I shall tell it in the form in which it appeared in the *Independent On Sunday* during 1999.

Intermission

Where Love Leads ...

I took up my first teaching post in 1973. I was 24. It happened to be in North Germany, where a shortage of English teachers meant that work was readily available. They particularly needed people to take classes in the Oberstufe, which was pretty responsible work. As well as teaching the students for their Abitur (A-Levels), I was responsible for detailed marking of coursework for five different classes.

Anyone who knows about love at first sight will understand the next bit. I walked into the first lesson on the first morning and was lost forever. The quiet, rather shy seventeen-year-old girl in the second row made my heart leap, my stomach churn and all the other traditional but true symptoms. We've never known why, but then you can't explain things like this. Birgit wasn't particularly good at English, certainly never drew attention to herself and, above all, was completely uninterested in me. The advance grapevine had marked me down as spoken for, and besides, you don't look at teachers like that. And, despite the wild feelings in me, I realised that I could never look at a pupil like that either. It was out of the question.

Except that anyone who has felt like that knows that rationality flies out of the window. I did one hilariously naff thing by lending her an LP by a band called Camel with a song called "Lady Fantasy" marked with an asterisk; she never even noticed. After a year, fate intervened in the form of a friend of Birgit's organising a party and inviting me. On the way home, I asked if Birgit would like to share my umbrella and, in the teeming rain, we briefly kissed outside her front door. I remember dancing home, Gene Kelly-like, and being horrified yet amazingly elated in the morning. Birgit's diary merely reads: "Elke's party, Mr Gray." But there is no sign of doubt.

Mysteriously, we both started organising parties like there was no tomorrow, always inviting loads of other people to disguise their true purpose. We both intuitively understood what was happening, and that it was completely right, yet in the eyes of most people, entirely wrong. Birgit's diary regularly starts to read: "Got home at 2 am / 3 am / 5 am". The mixed feelings of passion, love, terror and inability to fight it return to both of us today as we look back over that amazing time. It was nearly two years before we could "go public", two years filled with adventures, scrapes, near misses and numerous doomed attempts at ending it. Practically every sentence I write seems like a line from a crass pop song, but, as Birgit's mother never failed to say: "Some things are meant to be."

One of the most helpful aspects of the relationship was that Birgit's parents rapidly found out what was happening and supported it. They also could feel the "rightness" of what was developing, they liked me and they were interested in their daughter's happiness. But the way it came out was memorable. Birgit's unwitting father agreed to find me a second-hand car and we all drove out to a small village garage to inspect it. "It'll be ideal for you to take your fiancée out in," said the dealer.

"Fiancée? Don't be daft. This is her English teacher," protested Birgit's dad.

"No way," replied the dealer. "Have you seen the way they're looking at each other?"

That evening, it all tumbled out. And was given the seal of approval.

This made everything a lot easier. Added to that, we were sensible. We continued to go out with groups of other students, none of whom suspected what was happening after they said goodnight. We would drive long distances to cinemas, theatres and pizzerias in other cities, with poor Birgit crouched on the floor in the back of my VW Beetle. We even took a four-day break in Copenhagen, where I had a friend who was in on the secret. The diary reveals a level of activity which scarcely seems credible, eighteen years of marriage and two teenage children later. Boy, was it love.

On frequent occasions we would decide that it had to stop, that the stress had become unbearable. These interludes would normally last a day or two before bowing to the inevitable. Things which would start these doubts could be pretty unpleasant. One evening, we were indiscreet on a tram, only to become aware that we were being observed by another pupil from Birgit's class. "That's it," I thought, "I'm sacked". But amazingly, he never said a word. I reckon he must have woken up and assumed he'd imagined it.

At school, we were so discreet that it was probably almost noticeable how distant we were. I remember when Birgit had just emerged from a dreadful oral exam and was sitting in the corridor in floods of tears. Even the most cold-hearted teacher would have comforted her. I had to walk past without casting her a glance.

The only matter of disagreement, which niggles to this day, was the fact that my determination not to show Birgit any favouritism meant that I erred on the side of caution in marking her work and awarding her all-

important marks (which would have a crucial influence on A-level grades, university admission, etc.) It worked in that no one suspected any preferential treatment, but maybe I could have been a little more generous.

On several occasions, we had to attend social events like parties and gigs and pretend not to have any relationship other than the teacher-pupil one. To this day, my flesh creeps at the Richard Thompson song "The Way That It Shows": "Your gaze of compassion, just a little too right ... A slip of the tongue, a squeeze of the hand, that's the way that it shows."

For make no mistake, this was a serious business. The fact that we felt we had to go through with it is significant. Even though Birgit was obviously over the age of consent, her parents approved and I wasn't hugely older than her, from an educational point of view, it would undoubtedly have been a sacking offence.

And then, in early 1976, it all became dark, nasty and very frightening. The local authority where I was working realised that they no longer needed foreign teachers, and the teaching unions demanded that the "guest teachers" should not have their contracts renewed. This meant, effectively, that I was to be sacked.

In a situation which was crammed with ironies that nobody could have suspected, a huge protest erupted. Students, parents and staff all agreed that it was essential that I should stay. The entire school went on strike, there were protest marches in the city centre, a TV documentary was made and the story was front page news in German newspapers, both regional and national. At one stage, my landlady reported that two strange men had been snooping around my flat, in the wake of a Communist paper implying that I was being removed for alleged left-wing sympathies. I was and am convinced that the men were either from the tabloid press or the local authority, seeking evidence on which to sack me.

If only they had known what to look for, they would have found it in abundance. As it was, they left empty-handed. The protests failed, my contract was duly terminated and Birgit and I relocated to England, where we have lived happily ever after.

None of the above will be comprehensible to anyone who has never been hopelessly in love. To those people, I can never explain. But I believe most people will understand.

VII. School Daze

Going to see The Rolling Stones at Knebworth in the summer of 1976 was a big mistake. I went on my own, Birgit having not yet arrived in England, in my little blue Beetle. Driving had, until then, always been fun, something I looked forward to and volunteered for. Any distance, any time. For some inexplicable reason, I took my Super 8 silent movie camera with me to Knebworth. What a strangely futile thing to do. Lynyrd Skynyrd wibbled on for hours and hours (maybe an advantage of silent film after all) and I can remember absolutely nothing of the Stones' performance, so it can't have made much of an impression.

I have made four attempts in my life to see the Rolling Stones. The first was in Hyde Park in 1969, on the occasion of the embarrassing poem and the dead butterflies. It wasn't altogether a success. Someone from UEA had the bright idea of trying to sell Rag Mags to the captive audience, so a group of us drove up from Norwich in a van full of very poor quality rag magazines. Trying to sell these smutty and unfunny items to the assembled "love and peace" throng went down very badly indeed, and the Stones' Hells Angel retinue before long told us to sling our collective hook or risk being propelled into the Serpentine. We gave up.

The day should theoretically have been rescued by a meeting with Rosamund, who travelled up from Exmouth to see her favourite band, the Stones. Unfortunately, neither of us being familiar with either the geography of London or the magnitude of the event, we made insufficiently detailed arrangements, viz: "Meet you in Hyde Park". Needless to say, this didn't occur (there were a quarter of a million people there) and I, of course, got the blame.

The Rolling Stones also came to Bremen in 1976 on their "Black and Blue" tour. They played at the *Stadthalle* and obviously it was a big deal. Unfortunately, it was right in the heart of the time of panic about my affair with Birgit and the political shenanigans surrounding my sacking. It was crucial that we should not be seen together, so, not for the first time, I tried to be sensible and insist that we should try not to see each other. Birgit was upset about this (as was I) and the evening was tense because we were both there, saw each other, but didn't communicate. But anyway, I never really enjoyed any shows in the *Stadthalle* much, because it was a huge, characterless concrete cavern of a place.

I would love to say I saw the Stones in 1963 at the Station Hotel, Richmond on Thames, but I didn't. If you want to see them nowadays, you have to go to some horrible stadium such as Wembley. We did make it there in 1982, but all I can remember is being uncomfortable, claustrophobic and unable to either see or hear. Oh, and having to park miles away and walk for ages through a sea of litter.

The most ridiculous Stones débacle was when we attempted to see them in Wembley in 1992 (gluttons for punishment, perhaps, but people kept saying, "Aren't you going to see the Stones?"). I sent off for tickets at enormous expense, put them away in a safe place and completely lost them. Even when we later moved house and totally removed every single item except for the light bulbs (well, including the light bulbs actually, but that's another story), they still didn't turn up. In the vague hope of maybe being able to get substitute tickets, we travelled up to Wembley anyway, but of course, nothing was doing. We gave in when we heard the distant strains of "Jumpin' Jack Flash" wafting on the wind from behind the walls, and instead went to see Wilco Johnson at the Half Moon, Putney. It was not an adequate substitute.

There is a reason for mentioning all this. After the Knebworth show, it took several hours to get out of the chaotic car park. In the dark, I found the profusion of bright headlights confusing and frightening. Then, when I got on the motorway, I had my first-ever panic attack. Lights seemed to be coming from all directions and I found myself unable to be sure of where I was supposed to be going and what I was supposed to be doing. I felt I wasn't in control of the car and that I was about to pass out or even die. I struggled to the next exit, baffled and scared, and parked up, dazed and shaking.

Later on in the night, the traffic diminished and I was able to drive back relatively normally to Basingstoke, where I was doing some work on Colin's new farm. In the morning it seemed as if it had been a bad dream, but unfortunately it was one which would recur. Colin sent me up to Aldershot in a Land Rover to collect some tractor parts and it happened again, this time in daylight, and I had to return using small side roads. Another bad night-time attack came shortly after that, when I had been to see The Heavy Metal Kids and an embryonic XTC at the Brunel Rooms in Swindon. Again, I was terrified by all the vehicle lights on the M4, and felt that I had lost control over both myself and the car.

The position was that, having lost my job in Bremen for reasons which were beyond my control and for which I was in no way responsible, I felt deeply resentful that I was being forced to start a new job in a new school. Henry Beaufort School, a good comprehensive in Winchester, was a perfectly reasonable place to be, but I didn't want to be there. I felt that I had done well in Bremen and had been brought up to believe that if you do something well, you get rewarded. But in fact, I had been punished. I wasn't in charge of my own life.

Thank goodness, Birgit had decided to risk coming over to England as well, and had found herself a live-in job as an au-pair with a lovely family in Winchester. For my part, having lived in nice, self-contained flats in Bremen, I only managed to find a tiny, damp, unheated room in a shared house, which I had got through advertising in the local paper. This, believe it or not, was actually the best of the available options.

God knows how I would have survived the transition if it hadn't been for the unswerving support of Birgit. The working conditions couldn't have been more different from those in Germany. Long teaching days, less autonomy and far less respect from the community at large, as well as a salary roughly half of what I had been earning in Bremen ... Was it any wonder that I felt resentful?

I survived the first week or so all right. I remember the first staff meeting, during which the deputy headmistress berated the staff for allegedly being lax on the matter of uniform. Enormous detail was gone into about what constituted "acceptable" or "non acceptable" items of clothing, the difference between various types of dot and stripe, and the precise number of inches above the knee the girls' skirts were permitted to be. This was obviously a matter of life and death for the deputy head. As far as I was concerned, coming from a school environment in which only teaching and learning were considered to be important, I felt as if I had landed on another planet.

At the end of the week, I found myself a GP and made an appointment. Had he ever heard of this strange driving affliction? No, but he was sure it was merely stress and anxiety. He prescribed two sorts of pill, one of which I stopped almost immediately after Birgit looked it up and discovered it was an enormously strong and highly addictive anti-depressant. The others were standard tranquillisers, to be taken before attempting to drive. Bafflingly, the label said that one should avoid driving after taking the pills. It also said, "Caution with alcohol", which was so vague that I just carried on drinking as usual.

In the second week, the panic symptoms ("I'm losing control, I'm about to fall over") started to appear in lessons. I consulted the only person I could think of, who was the male deputy head, Roy Bone. He was kindness personified, and said I should have some time off and get medical help. It helped enormously that Roy was not negative or judgmental in the way he responded to my difficulty.

I then spent a couple of weeks in my box of a room just sobbing and feeling that the end of the world had come. Most evenings, Birgit would come round and comfort me, and I'm sure I took her far too much for granted in my perception that I had been badly mistreated.

Nowadays, it's well known that Benzodiapezam initially creates the same symptoms as it is designed to combat, and I am now sure that this was what was happening in the classroom. The symptoms I felt weren't real panic attacks but the effects of the drug. My constant thought was that I could possibly get by without driving but I couldn't possibly survive without teaching. What was I to do?

It didn't help that the conditions in the rented house were so unbearable. The main tenants were a girl who worked in an office in Winchester, and her boyfriend, who worked for the County Council. Their lifestyle was unbelievably tedious. Every evening, they would sit side by side on the sofa watching TV until it finished, not saying a word to each other. They said that I was welcome to join them! Sometimes I did, because upstairs it was even worse. On the other side of the paper-thin wall lived a young music teacher who was some kind of nymphomaniac. Her endless high-volume nocturnal activities with her macho pilot boyfriend brought back hideous memories of Jochen Schmidt in Kiel. Twenty years later, I was approached by a teenage pupil:

"My mum says do you remember her? She used to share a house with you on Bereweeke Avenue."

"Of course I remember her," I replied. But I didn't explain why.

Things settled down a bit and I was able to go back to work. But the price was that I was permanently on Valium. I didn't think it was an addiction, but I had been told to take them whenever I planned to drive, and I planned to drive every day. As we now know, lots of people in those days were regularly prescribed repeat prescriptions of Valium, but I felt terribly ashamed, particularly in view of my steadfast opposition to drugs. Of course it wasn't a recreational drug, but I still felt weak and stupid and I didn't tell anyone about it apart from Birgit.

In the evenings, we would meet in town at a pub called the Bakers Arms, which had a good juke box. Even this was a worry, because one of the regulars was a handsome Rhodesian called Peter. I found him loathsome because he would forever promote the virtues of the Apartheid system in a loud voice, and I had several heated exchanges with him. What was worse, if I arrived late, he would chat Birgit up, telling her I was a wimp and a waste of time and that she should have a real man like him. He even knocked on her door and asked her out. Thank goodness she resisted, because, like me, she saw something very sinister in him. A couple of years later, he received a prison sentence for killing his girlfriend.

There wasn't much to do in Winchester, but before long I had got my slot reviewing gigs for the Hampshire Chronicle, so we spent a lot of time at places like Southampton University and the Gaumont. Musically, school life was a little better than it had been in Bremen. There were a couple of school bands and I soon met a pupil called Greg Watkins who shared my penchant for Camel. With Greg and a couple of other students and staff members, we formed a band called the Weeke Jokes (a reference to the suburb where the school was situated) for a one-off performance at a staff party. This wasn't much of a success, but a couple of people danced to humour us. It was a relief to everyone, on and off stage, when the disco returned.

Greg was the first of many students whom I corrupted into listening to music their parents didn't approve of. Unfortunately, he isn't a very good case study. His father wanted him to stick with the Hampshire County Youth Orchestra, where he was deemed to have a bright future. At one stage, the orchestra's director was even asked to approach me and tell me to desist from distracting Greg from his true calling. Greg (this defies belief but it is true) claims that my rendition of the intro to Chuck Berry's "Roll Over Beethoven" was what inspired him to take up the guitar, to which he has been a slave ever since. Over the years, it has been painfully obvious to me that Greg, in his determination to sustain a career as a professional musician, has frequently been subsisting on the breadline or below. And, oh God, it's all my fault.

Greg and I fell out quite seriously when I espoused punk and enthusiastically turned my face against all things prog-rock. He saw me as betraying the faith, I saw him as being insufficiently open-minded. Greg currently fronts a Dire Straits tribute band, so he is one pupil with whom I can truly be said to have failed (but only on a musical level).

Another aspect of school life which I inaugurated was the Friday lunchtime Rock Club. This was an oasis of mild misbehaviour which entailed students bringing their records to the school Music Room to play. It was fun, and I had a (sometimes difficult to maintain) policy of not expressing opinions about people's tastes. The first year was laid back, with Yes and Genesis, the second year was a brutal battle between the old guard and punk, which punk won, and by the third year it was wall-to-wall Crass and Poison Girls anarcho-punk. I loved all of it, especially the latter days when people would vie with each other to locate the most obscure indie singles and would challenge me as to how much vinyl swearing I would tolerate (any amount, as it happened).

All the while, and over a number of years, I was trying absolutely everything I could think of to conquer the driving phobia. Every person I consulted agreed on the cause: If you have a big upheaval in your life over which you have no control, it often expresses itself in an unexpected and seemingly unconnected way. Examples of the type of thing that can spark it off are divorce, sudden bereavement or, as in my case, loss of a job. The result can be panic attacks, such as fear of heights or agoraphobia. Mine just happened to choose to express itself through driving.

I consulted a series of psychiatrists and psycho-therapists. One person I went to just made things worse. Despite his opulent house, his leather chaise-longue and the long series of letters after his name, he showed no sign of being able to relate to the condition. He also lived in a place only accessible via a busy road, so that didn't help. Another one tried really hard to help me by coming out in the car with me, the idea being to overcome the phobia by confronting it.

In theory, it was a sound approach, but after a couple of sessions, he was so shit-scared that he told me he didn't dare continue. I didn't blame him.

Yet another psychotherapist thought that group therapy might help. Unfortunately, the other participants had quite different phobias, of bats, mice and snakes. They didn't empathise with my problem and I didn't empathise with theirs. There is one particular lady in Winchester that I still dart into doorways to avoid, lest she should engage me in conversation about worms. Homeopathy wasn't any better. The white-coated expert was obviously a charlatan and sold me some pills which I knew were made of sugar.

The most helpful person was a local acupuncturist, although it was a bit awkward. Her daughter was one of my pupils and kept walking in to find me spreadeagled on the couch, looking like a pin cushion. The acupuncturist also treated several members of Winchester's "arty" fraternity and would regale me with information about their personal problems. I could only assume that she was also telling them all about mine. What she did do, however, was teach me good relaxation techniques, which I have found useful in a variety of situations ever since.

Finally, I found a sort of way to solve the problem. Annoyed at my GP's insistence that there was nothing for it but to "keep taking the tablets", I changed to another doctor. He immediately said I should stop taking the tablets and also stop driving.

"Stop driving?"

"Why not? Millions of people don't drive. What's the big deal?"

He was right. I can drive short distances on small roads and luckily, Birgit is an excellent driver who enjoys nothing better than blasting along motorways. The tranquillisers went down the toilet and in my retirement, I plan to research and write a volume entitled *How To Drive From Land's End To John o'Groats Without Encountering A Dual Carriageway*. It's bound to be a best-seller.

At the end of the 1976-1977 school year, I failed to break the habit of working in the summer holidays. This time, instead of opting for the farm, I decided to teach English in Bournemouth. I don't know what made me choose Bournemouth but I guess that, as usual, it was an advert in the Times Educational Supplement. It's strange to think that I wanted to teach during the holidays, but the year had been so awful and the hankering for EFL teaching was so strong that there I suddenly was, in South Coast Fun heaven.

England was deemed to be hip, England was cheap, English language skills were vital, and well-meaning parents all over the globe thought it a good idea for their non-linguistically-inclined children to be sent to Bournemouth for the summer in order to be taught English. Their offspring were delighted to be given the opportunity for a month's pure hedonism and to be assumed to be doing something for their education at the same time.

Bournemouth provides all the necessary facilities, except, perhaps, for sunshine. Pubs and clubs abound. In fact, the Old Christchurch Road consists of practically nothing but. On every corner are Language Schools, many of them scruffy rip-off joints but a few of them international leaders in their field. The Eurocentre, where I ended up, was renowned for having been behind "English In Situations", a huge-selling book by Robert O'Neill, which provided foolproof ready-made lessons. This book had provided me with all my preparation when, during my final months in Bremen, my mind was on other matters. Lesson plans, which in more conscientious times had run to half a page or more, then consisted of "O'Neill, Page 24", or even simply "O'N. P. 24". The interesting thing was that these lessons were no better or worse than those which I had spent hours preparing, and no pupil would ever have noticed the difference.

So I arrived at the Eurocentre expecting an academic institution of great vibrancy, but O'Neill had, of course, long since moved on to fame and fortune. It was just a language school, a good one, sure, but nothing particularly special. The students were, in the main, there for a good time rather than to learn.

The welcome party, held at a disco called the Maison Rouge, featured a band called Luther, who were usefully loud. This meant that it was sufficient just to shake your head and tap your feet and that it was possible to avoid conversation. Just as well, since God knows what I would have said to anybody.

The work was really hard, because one couldn't just regurgitate O'Neill's lessons in this environment. There was a strictly controlled syllabus, as this was supposed to be an intensive course which brought results, and was being paid for. It was difficult, often, to work out exactly what and how one was supposed to teach, and almost every day I had a splitting headache. What I should have been doing was having a rest.

On the first Friday, there was a "getting to know you" staff outing to the New Forest. We drove in a mini-bus to a tiny pub called the Queen's Head in a village called Burley. It was here that I got my first inkling of what the real world of rock and roll might be like. In the Queen's Head there was a band.

It certainly wasn't promising. A small blackboard in the car park declared, "Tonight Live: The Freshly Layed Band". Horror was my initial reaction: such abuse of the English language. Surely it should be "laid"? But maybe not, since the atrociously-designed poster depicted an obviously stoned and very confused dancing chicken. Anyway, it was a shit name for a band.

You don't often find good bands in pubs, especially not in country pubs which clearly haven't been designed for noisy music. There wasn't a stage and there wasn't room for many people other than band members in the tiny public bar where The Freshly Layed Band had set up. But this was a real gig. You could tell that because there was masses of equipment, a full-scale light show and, yes, a man fiddling with an "out-front" mixing desk. Not very far "out-front", because there were barely two metres between the band and the bar, but "out-front" nevertheless. I had never actually seen the like before. While the rest of the Eurocentre staff sniffed and entered the other bar to spend the evening talking shop, I found myself being lured into the Freshly Layed trap. It was a decision which was to have a crucial effect on the future course of my life. I instantly felt the need to join in in some way. No longer could music remain at arm's length, I needed to be closely and intimately involved at a hands-on level.

Undoubtedly this wouldn't have happened if The Freshly Layed Band had been a standard pub band. After a moment, I'd have shrugged and returned to my new colleagues in the other bar. But they weren't. They were intriguingly different, like no band I had ever heard before.

They were kind of heavy metal in the sense that there were a good number of very fast wah-wah guitar solos. But they certainly weren't a conventional heavy metal band. They didn't preen or pose about and they didn't have a screeching vocalist shouting "Do ya feel all right?" They seemed to be playing their own songs and, above all, they were funky. Perhaps they reminded me of late-night marking sessions in Bremen, listening to the British Forces Broadcasting Service's "alternative" disc jockey Alan Bangs playing tracks by Little Feat.

I stood and watched them, trying to dissect their appeal. The funkiness was clearly emanating from the rhythm guitarist, a short, rather stout bloke with a beard. On the face of it, he wasn't the most instantly appealing member of the band, in that he didn't move at all and he didn't even look particularly friendly.

The bassist was tall, lean and obviously stoned. He kept his head down and held his bass guitar in a curious manner, at right angles to his body. He seemed to be working telepathically, both with the rhythm guitarist and with the tiny drummer, who was sitting on a stool so low that he had to reach upwards in order to hit the drums. The sound they were making just didn't seem conventional in any way that I could identify, yet I felt myself drawn to it.

On that night, there were two people who stood out particularly. The singer, far from the conventional hard-rock frontman, was a quite seriously overweight man dressed in red dungarees. He sang in a fairly conventional way, without any overstatement. The lead guitarist, on the other hand, was the only member of the band who really looked the part: concave stomach, long flowing curls, white flares and fingers so fast that they were a blur.

My immediate thought was, "You don't see bands like that in Winchester. Why not? And how can I get them there?" After the set, I approached the band and, rushing off to rejoin my colleagues in the mini-bus, just had time to pocket one of their gig lists.

It turned out that The Freshly Layed Band were, in the immortal phrase, "Big In Bournemouth", so big, in fact, that they regularly sold out the 800-capacity Town Hall. It was here that I met Jim, an immensely likeable maniac speed freak who was the band's manager. He somehow held down a full-time job in the local planning department, which we later felt might explain a series of incomprehensible and scarcely negotiable mini-roundabouts in the centre of Poole. Jim was keen to find new gigs for the band and welcomed my offer of finding somewhere for them to play in Winchester.

But was there anywhere? I was determined not to be outdone by some poxy pub in the New Forest. If there wasn't a venue in Winchester, I'd make one. For the rest of the summer, meanwhile, I moved from my awful Bournemouth digs into a much nicer room in the house of Tim Holt, who was the funky little FLB rhythm guitarist. His girlfriend Sally, who was the sister of Nick, the drummer, made me huge breakfasts and sumptuous suppers, and I must have weighed a stone more when I returned to Winchester to recommence school.

In Winchester High Street, some unfamiliar fly-posting had been taking place. Large posters had appeared, simply proclaiming "BA". BA? What could it mean? Then someone added "Riverside" in felt-tip underneath the name. And finally, a couple of days later, the jigsaw was complete: "25 September". Obviously it was a band and obviously I had to go and see them.

The Ba turned out to be the quintessential punk band and the Riverside the ideal punk venue. The room was tiny, above a run-down pub at the bottom of town, and was full of spiky-haired urchins of the type always to be found hanging round the city centre. They grabbed each other by the lapels and pogoed like crazy as the

"Bus Garage Café, well it's okay." The BA at Winchester Art School. (Nick Jacobs on left, Mark Hudson on right).

Ba, four confrontational students from the Art School, blasted out a bare half-hour's set of two-minuters by the likes of the Velvet Underground, plus their very own tear-jerking tribute to Winchester Bus Station:

Bus Garage Café, well it's okay,
Bus Garage Café, well it's okay,
People hanging round the tables,
Drinking their tea,
Should be bloody grateful.

The Ba were very rough and very ready but had lots in their favour, such as a sneering "who are you looking at?" frontman by the name of Mark Hudson, and a choppy guitarist called Nick Jacobs (later a Blue Aeroplane), who played his Telecaster left handed and upside down. Most usefully for them, they had a competent manager by the name of Tim Rostron, who ensured extensive coverage in the local press. Unbelievably, Tim Rostron was later to become a rock critic for the Daily Telegraph!

The floor of the Riverside bounced and creaked dangerously, but I guessed that if it could cope with that amount of concerted pogoing, it could handle more or less anything. I made contact with the landlord, who was one of those dour types who was reluctantly willing to do anything if it might help him to sell more beer. Negotiations then began with Jim about finding a mutually convenient date and The Freshly Layed Band was duly booked to play at the Riverside in December.

Like many promoters before and since, I had given no thought as to how to attract any customers. In the end, we put a poster in the sole city record shop, I told all my pupils (scarcely any of whom were interested) and every evening I went round putting up posters in the local colleges. These would always be pulled down by the authorities, so the next day I would doggedly return and replace them. We then got into trouble for handing out flyers, which I had run off on the school banda machine, in city centre pubs. Most of the landlords, quite reasonably, objected to us trying to coax their customers into a rival establishment and promptly showed us the door. In the end, we took to simply standing in the High Street, handing out flyers to anyone who looked like a potential customer.

The gig was a sweaty, sold-out success. The tiny old lady behind the bar, so small she could barely see over the top of it, ran out of beer and had to send down for more. Birgit turned out to be the perfect door person and bouncer, one steely glare from her being enough to intimidate any potential trouble makers, of whom there were a few. The only worries came in carrying a mountain of heavy equipment up and down the slippery fire escape, and in trying to divert the hapless hotel guests, who doubtless had been anticipating a quiet evening in an idyllic cathedral city, away from the bathroom which was rightly theirs. This had been commandeered by the band as a dressing room, for which read skinning-up room.

In the meantime, I had found another band I was determined to put on in Winchester. My unreliable Beetle needed repairing and I was recommended to seek out a young man called Paul, who lived in the city and was a VW expert. While he worked, he listened to a demo tape by a band whose singer he knew: The Soft Boys. The wonderfully crazy music which wafted from the Beetle's tape player entranced me, as did the words. The chorus of one of the songs went,

Where are the prawns?
Down by the sea,

while another one started,

Feel like asking a tree for an autograph,
Feel like making love to a photograph,
Photographs don't smell,
Waaaaaaaaauuurrrgh.

The backings tended to sound like a mutant version of The Byrds. And this came from Winchester?

Well, not exactly. The band, Paul told me, was based in Cambridge but their leader, Robyn Hitchcock, had been at Winchester College. His father, Raymond, had written the cult novel "Percy", for which Ray Davies of the Kinks wrote the music when it was turned into a film. Could Paul put me in touch? Certainly. Would they be up for a gig? Probably. This was good news, because in the music papers, a "press buzz" was rapidly building up around The Soft Boys.

The venue was the problem, because the fee the band required meant that the Riverside was out of the question. However, there was a reasonably-sized hall attached to the Art School in the city centre, and I came to an agreement with the Social Secretary there: We would pay them to hire the hall and they could also have all the bar profits. As this was a win-win situation for them, I thought it was more than fair, but I did, through inexperience, do some silly things. Security was insufficient. Having never been there before, I didn't realise that the Art School was a place where people always expected to walk in for free, and got nasty if they couldn't. The admission price, incidentally, was 60p in advance and 70p on the door. Another error was to book a Camel covers band, led by my prog-rock loving pupil Greg Watkins, to be the support band. This was not what Soft Boys fans wanted to hear and people talked loudly all the way through their set, creating a bit of a bad atmosphere.

There were also sound problems, and after the show, the Social Secretary accused me of profiteering. In actual fact, we had made a loss, but profit wasn't and never has been my motivation in putting on gigs, which in the circumstances is just as well. I was offended and we had a row. This caused immense complications because we had already advertised a return visit by the FLB, to take place at the Art School. This now had to be relocated back to the Riverside and all the publicity re-done.

Worst of all, I then made a terrible pig's ear of attempting to interview Robyn Hitchcock for the *Chronicle*. We met in the Eclipse pub, by the cathedral, where he consumed five pints of Guinness in an hour and talked complete gibberish. The trouble was that it wasn't stupid gibberish but highly intellectual gibberish, several miles over my head. I felt severely intimidated and was unable to gather a single usable quote. It's a measure of my love for his music that I have seventeen Hitchcock albums, despite the fact that every attempt I have made to have dealings with him has been disastrous.

For getting on for a year, Birgit and I began to follow The Freshly Layed Band around. This is hard to explain, because they didn't at all fit in to my rapidly developing penchant for punk and new wave, but we loved them. The regular concerts at Bournemouth Town Hall were wild affairs and a live album recorded there sold thousands of copies. Sally Buckle would cause great entertainment as she sold her home-made food like a fishwife:

"Cahm on, get yer Ploughman's 'ere!", she would shriek. Luckily, the punters didn't realise that dear Sally manufactured the chicken liver paté in bulk in her bath.

There was plenty of excitement as the FLB progressed through the 1978 *Melody Maker* Band Contest. At Southampton University, in an early heat, I saw what seemed to be an early example of the "cynical rock journalist" syndrome, when Allan Jones, editor of *Melody Maker*, remained poker-faced throughout the evening, showing no sign of enjoyment. It was only in later years, when I would have to judge a number of such contests myself, that I realised how essential it was not to let a soul see what you were really thinking of the horrors being played out before you. At any event, the FLB did well, winning the semi-final at the Marquee and only narrowly losing the final at the Roundhouse. On both occasions, we joined a gang of drunken and stoned followers who travelled up to London by coach to demonstrate their support.

Over the following years, Birgit and I promoted a variety of bands (mostly those perceived as "up and coming") at various venues in the city. Most gigs were reasonably uneventful, the main feature being that we almost always lost money. There was one event, however, that was both horrible and had serious repercussions. Luckily, it was not one of our shows.

The Art School Union had become even more notorious for its poor security and dangerous atmosphere. Nevertheless, I would occasionally go there because it was often the only place in town with live music. On that particular occasion, a punk band from Southampton called Stratejacket was playing and the atmosphere was chilling. The floor was swilling with beer and, because the only drink on sale was Newcastle Brown, there were plenty of heavy bottles flying around the place.

Somewhere in the pogoing masses, some incident took place to which someone took objection. Words, maybe even blows were exchanged. It was probably a bit of a "Winchester - Southampton" thing. At any rate, at some stage a member of the crowd left the hall and went up to a pub near the railway station, to get reinforcements. On the way back to the Art School, one of the gang picked up a heavy crowbar from a building site.

The first anyone knew of what was going to happen was when the door swung open and the men entered.

"That's him," shouted someone, at which the man with the crowbar walked up to a frightened-looking member of the crowd and smashed him on the head with it. The crowd parted as the young man fell to the floor and the attackers ran out of the room. I had seen it all. The head injury was appalling. Together with Kevin Rayner, a member of The Ba who was working behind the bar, I tried to stem the flow of blood with a bar cloth. It was obvious that the victim was lucky to be alive.

When the case came to court, I was called as a witness. The case swung on identification of the attacker (I had to say I couldn't be 100 percent sure, since the situation had been dark and confusing) and how the blow had been dealt.

I remembered that the bar had been raised above the attacker's head before being brought down on the victim.

"Is this the weapon?"

"I believe so. It looks like it."

"Please take it in your hands and show the court how the blow was dealt."

I knew the bar was going to be heavy and that the defence lawyer was hoping that I wouldn't be able to lift it. But I knew what I'd seen and so summoned up all my strength and raised the bar above my head, much to the lawyer's visible annoyance.

The accused was convicted and it turned out that he had had a record for violence. Now, by all accounts, he is a reformed character. In a weird footnote, Stratejacket's guitarist, Nick Petford, who had changed into a quiet singer/songwriter with an album out on Stick It In Your Ear records, later came to live next door to us. He is now Dr. Nick Petford, an expert on marine biology, who is occasionally interviewed on Radio 4.

Of daily life at school there isn't much to say. I coped well enough to stay out of any form of trouble there for over twenty years, for the first few of which I was also writing for music papers, going out to gigs non-stop, doing radio shows, promoting gigs, managing a band and, just by the by, organising school trips. How did I manage? No idea, but it wouldn't have been possible without the help of my wife. Oh, and the tranquillisers.

The school trip thing isn't strictly relevant to this book, but very occasionally, foreign exchanges offered the odd musical experience. Most of the adventures were of an altogether more stressful kind, as I tried to illustrate in an article published in *Teacher's Weekly* in October 1990. Here's an extract:

Every so often, something happens to remind you just how enormous are the responsibilities you bear on your "holiday". One that sticks in my mind took place on a boat train heading for our destination, the sleepy North German town of Cloppenburg. Thirty of us were ensconced in our six-person compartments, mostly dozing in an attempt to recover from a night crossing during which all sleep had been denied by the persistent attempts of some very drunk squaddies to ravish our third-year girls. As fate would have it, however, three of these girls had met some attractive young lads on the train.

Unbeknown to me, they had been invited into the next-door carriage for a chat (and possibly a cigarette). And even if I had known, it would hardly have been possible to confine everyone to their compartment for an eight-hour journey.

It was without a care in my heart that I decided to carry out a quick inspection. Where were the girls? In the next carriage? Oh, fine, I'll just go and make sure they're okay.

There was, however, a problem. Continental trains have a disconcerting habit of splitting up into different sections, which head off in different directions. Instead of another carriage, all I found was a securely-locked door and a window looking out onto the receding railway track. The girls and their new-found friends were at that very moment speeding off towards Copenhagen. You may imagine the feeling in my stomach.

As it turned out, that particular story had a happy ending, since both their train and ours stopped in Osnabrück. After some frantic dashing from platform to platform, they were found, ashen-faced from the experience of getting into big trouble for attempting to cross the Dutch-German border without passports. They had freaked when they realised that the border guards were wearing guns.

The next year, I took a similar-sized group to our new exchange destination of Hamburg. Among the party was a boy who had been prone to epileptic fits. His parents were keen that this should not stop him from taking part in normal activities, so they enrolled him for the exchange. They assured me confidently that his medication meant that there was no danger that he would have a fit.

Slightly disorientated, no doubt, by his unfamiliar surroundings, he forgot to take his pills one day, and had a massive fit in the middle of McDonalds, hitting his head on the floor as he fell. Luckily, he was with some marvellous friends and was rushed to hospital. The first I heard was a phone call from the police. He was okay, but there was a further problem. It was the day before we were due to fly home. Would he be able to travel? And, if not, what was to be done? Whatever one did, rules of supervision would be broken in some way. If I stayed in Hamburg with him, the rest, accompanied by only one teacher, would be under-supervised. On the other hand, he couldn't be left on his own in a strange city.

No farewell party for me that year; it was spent making endless phone calls to the boy's parents, his British doctor and my Headmaster. Still, things looked as if they were going to work out. The German doctor said the boy could travel and that he would bring him to the airport the following morning.

At the last moment, they appeared, and the doctor took me aside. "Look," he said, "I'm afraid there's a good chance that he may fit again in the aeroplane. I've given him some medication in the form of a suppository which I'm afraid you'll have to administer if it should prove necessary."

Well, thanks a bunch. We had climbed into the air and the Fasten Seat Belts lights had been switched off when I asked the boy if I could have a look at the medication in order to read the instructions.

"Oh, that," he replied, "I put that in my suitcase."

The suitcase, needless to say, was in the hold with no means of access. My feelings on that flight and the joy felt when the wheels touched the ground may well be imagined.

There was one further upshot of this event. One or two parents saw fit to complain about some trifling aspects of that exchange over which the teacher in charge could have no control, such as inter-penfriend niggles. They clearly had no notion at all about the burdens of responsibility borne by teachers who sacrifice their holidays for the sake of their pupils. These teachers are involved, literally, in matters of life and death.

One particularly rewarding musical adventure came on a class trip to Luxembourg in 1983. Because I had been kind enough to spend an entire day accompanying a pupil to hospital rather than being out having fun with everybody else, my colleagues gave me the evening off to go and see Steve Winwood at the local theatre. Recently rejuvenated and at his very best with the comeback album

Talking Back To The Night, Winwood, with a crack team of American session musicians, was so sublime that I completely lost track of time. Suddenly remembering the Youth Hostel curfew, I ran all the way back in a pair of ill-fitting new trainers which caused agonising blisters. Of course I arrived too late and had to wake up the enraged hostel warden, much to the entertainment of the children, to whom we had been emphasising the importance of punctuality. Next day, one of my colleagues asked, "Anyway, Oliver, did you enjoy Stevie Woodwind?"

The exchange visits were always filled with drama and almost empty of music. Cloppenburg was a small, out-of-the-way town and probably the Camel In The Cowshed gig which I secretly went to with Birgit in 1976 was the last show they ever had there. The kids found it boring too, so I jumped at the chance of changing our destination to Hamburg. From then on, organisation was a breeze, because Gert, the German teacher who co-organised the exchanges with me, was efficient and keen and we agreed on all aspects of organisation.

Apart from that, though, we had absolutely nothing in common with one another, which often made the visits a trifle strained, especially as he and his family lived in Elmshorn, a tortuous journey from central Hamburg involving several changes of train. This was not conducive to gig-going.

On the very first day of the very first visit to Hamburg, in April 1984, the first thing I did was buy a copy of the local listings magazine. This told me that an American band I had heard good things about was playing at a club called Knust, in the centre of Hamburg, that very evening. I had a real "feeling" about this band from the tracks I had heard on the radio and also from reviews I had seen in the UK music papers. I believed it was essential for me to go and see them.

Not wanting to appear rude, I explained the situation to Gert and assured him that I would make my own travel arrangements. Also not wishing to appear rude, Gert would have nothing of it. In the over-hospitable manner that many Germans have, he absolutely insisted on driving me there and back.

"Well, thank you, but won't that be inconvenient? What will you do while I'm in the club?"

"I'll come in with you."

"Well, if you're really sure ..."

The Knust Club was a minuscule room, holding at most a hundred people. REM, it turned out, were doing two nights there and two sets each night, there being no support band. To get to the stage, they had to walk through the audience. This being a very long time before stadium rock status for REM, they were all dressed in black jeans and leather jackets, rather in the manner of The Ramones. They creaked as they pushed past me, Peter Buck apologising, "Excuse me, man, it's a bit hard to get through here." I've often thought it weird that I had the feeling of being in the presence of megastars before they had played a single note.

This understated but supremely atmospheric music was precisely what I needed to hear, but not Gert:

"It is not very good."

"I think it's great."

"No, I do not like them. They are terrible."

Well, it's impossible to enjoy any music when the person you're standing next to is hating it, so I deserted Gert and went to stand next to the stage, only returning in the interval (when he clearly hoped I would suggest leaving) and at the end. All the way home, he went on and on about how anyone could possibly like such alleged music. That band, he said, would never get anywhere. Our relationship had got off to a bad start, from which it would struggle to recover.

The next evening, I wanted to go again. I was confident that, this time, he wouldn't insist on accompanying me (not even ultra-keen hospitality could justify such a level of masochism) and, thank goodness, I was right. The second show was watched in circumstances which made enjoyment a lot simpler and I came back on the last train, unfortunately having to miss half the second set. A couple of years later, the *Observer Colour Supplement* ran a front page feature: "REM: The Greatest Rock and Roll Band In The World." I took immense pleasure in sending a copy to Gert.

During that week, I discovered that Horten, a big department store in the centre of Hamburg, was selling plastic personal stereos at a crazily cheap price. As I was working on a half-developed idea of using personal stereos in class to help pupils with their language learning, I bought thirty of these items, along with an extra travel bag to transport them in. It wasn't until arriving at customs in Harwich that it crossed my mind that I might get into trouble. If they opened my bag, they would at the very least assume that I was planning to re-sell them for a profit. I would be humiliated in full view of all my pupils.

Luckily, fate intervened:

"Look, Mr Gray, what a funny-looking man!"

It was true. Something resembling a scrawny crow with a blackened wasps' nest on his head had attracted the attention of the entire customs team. They were crowding round this figure, examining his luggage in microscopic detail. It was, of course, the unmistakable John Cooper Clarke, presumably en route from a tour of Germany, where one can't begin to imagine how he went down (as his speciality is anti-German jokes).

Well, isn't that just typical, I thought. Elizabeth from Hungerford's adage was as true as ever: It's not the trousers, it's what's inside them. They had picked on John Cooper Clarke because he looked so distinctive, while the real drug smugglers, not to mention smugglers of small electrical devices, are allowed to swan past with impunity. However, with grateful thanks to the Bard of Salford, I hastily ushered the gathered children through the green channel.

Yes, well, I always did think the best of people. Some years later, I read *Songs You Never Hear On The Radio*, James Young's mind-boggling biography of Nico, in which John Cooper Clarke's drug activities are described in gruesome detail. It seems likely that the customs officers' intelligence was all too accurate after all.

The last Hamburg exchange I did before packing them in (overwhelmed by the kind of responsibility detailed in the *Teachers Weekly* article) offered what seemed to be a good opportunity to repeat an REM-style experience. I phoned up and reserved a ticket to see The Fall, playing at *Grosse Freiheit 36*. I hadn't seen Mark E. Smith in action for a while, and I was keen to visit a venue I'd often seen but never entered. *Grosse Freiheit 36* is a dance hall situated over the Kaiserkeller, the Beatles' bread and butter gig in their Hamburg days.

Trouble was, when I innocently turned up at the door at 8 o'clock, I was informed that The Fall weren't due onstage until 1.30 am. This presented two problems: first, how to get back to Elmshorn afterwards, and second, what on earth to do in the interim. The first problem was solved reasonably quickly. I approached a taxi driver who agreed to take me back for a fixed fee, picking me up at 3 am. The other problem was less easy, because the Reeperbahn area is one of the least salubrious in Europe, being inhabited almost entirely by junkies, alcoholics and very large numbers of prostitutes.

I wandered the streets, getting lost on a number of occasions. Finally, I got the shock of my life. A terrifying-looking painted lady leapt out of a dark doorway and grabbed tightly hold of my arm.

"Come on," she said, "make up your mind. This is the fourth time you've walked past me in an hour. You know you want me!"

This was indeed an offer I could refuse. Shaking her off, I literally sprinted away in blind panic. There were many things I would do for rock and roll, but that wasn't one of them. I doubt if that old curmudgeon Mark E. Smith appreciated what I had been through for his sake, even though he does sing of "Bremen Nacht", which is probably not dissimilar to a "Hamburg Nacht".

Once again, I nearly died on the way home. The exhausted taxi driver kept falling asleep at the wheel on the Autobahn and I repeatedly had to poke him in the ribs and yell in his ear to keep him conscious. When he dropped me in Elmshorn, instead of going home, he pulled on to the verge and passed out.

VIII. Radio Head

I first became aware of the existence of BBC Radio Solent in a roundabout way. On the first day at Henry Beaufort School, I was handed my timetable and straight away spotted a mistake: I appeared to be teaching two classes of English.

"Therese, there's a mistake here."

"No mistake. You've been teaching English, so we thought you wouldn't mind."

"But that was English as a Foreign Language. I've no idea how to teach English to English people!"

"Never mind. I'm sure you'll manage."

I didn't. Despite the well-meaning efforts of the Head of English, I was cast adrift in a sea of mutual incomprehension, in which I didn't understand what I was doing and the children didn't understand what I was doing either. I would have been happy to teach grammar, but that was forbidden. It had to be Greek Myths and Legends, about which I knew nothing and wanted to know less.

So I requested some help, and soon was booked onto a course for new English teachers at a hotel in the New Forest. Like every other course I have ever attended, it was worse than useless. Far from practical help, we were subjected to ego-trips by grey-haired, grey-suited, grey-minded ex-teachers who had been promoted to the status of "advisers". I sulked the whole weekend.

Guest star billing on the Saturday night was reserved for a young man called Nick Girdler, who forced us to play embarrassing and pointless games. Apparently, he was a local personality who had his own radio show. What he was doing helping to run an English course remains a mystery. Probably he was getting paid.

His programme, which he plugged a lot, was called *Albert's Gang* and went out on Saturday afternoons. I noticed that he was very handsome and that he attracted the attention of several of the young female teachers on the course, who gathered round him admiringly. I decided to tune in to the programme the following weekend

It was great, a kind of radio *Tiswas*, an anarchic comedy extravaganza for children. But it was surrounded by lots of stuff which didn't interest me at all. No matter when I tuned on to Radio Solent, there didn't seem to be any music other than bland, middle of the road pop.

Knowing that BBC local radio was supposed to have the brief of catering for a wide range of minority tastes (folk and jazz both had their slots), I penned a "Disgusted of Tunbridge Wells" letter to the BBC in Southampton, enquiring why there was no "rock" music on Radio Solent.

Within a few days, I received an encouraging reply from someone called Gethyn Jones. Not at all as Welsh as he sounds, Gethyn protested that not only was there a rock programme, but that he was the presenter. The programme was called *Beat 'n' Track* (soon mercifully changed to *Solent Rock*) and it went out at 6.30 pm on a Saturday. Would I like to meet him and discuss a possible collaboration?

When we met, it didn't take long to establish what I would do. As live music was my passion, I would compile a gig guide, to be called the *Solent Rock Roundup*, and to generally cover any live rock music in the Solent area.

Great! But how was I to get my information? I knew about the venues in the immediate vicinity of Winchester (not many, to be sure), but Solent's slogan was "From Chichester to Weymouth, from Basingstoke to the Isle of Wight". This was quite an area to cover.

My trusty *NME* was a great help, because it had an "advance notice" section with details about forthcoming tours. This told me all I needed to know about concerts by established and semi-established acts. The big venues in the area were Poole Arts Centre, Southampton Gaumont and Portsmouth Guildhall, all of which were very active in promoting big shows. Almost any tour would stop off at one or other of these venues, and occasionally at all three. The respective publicity managers, when I contacted them, were friendly and interested (well, they would be). So that bit was easy.

Colleges were more of a problem. King Alfred's College, the teacher training college in Winchester, were surly and uncooperative (they had a hang-up about non-students invading their territory), the Art School was completely loopy, and the further outposts such as Basingstoke Tech and Bishop Otter College in Chichester held so few events that they were hardly worth contacting. Portsmouth Poly had such a rapid turnover of Social Secretaries that I soon gave up trying to keep track of them. Paul Crockford at Southampton University was wonderfully efficient and easy to work with, so it came as no surprise that he went on to manage Level 42 and become a major league music business manager.

The bread and butter of the Rock Roundup, however, was the surprisingly big maze of little pub and club venues scattered all over the South. Gethyn got me off to a good start because he was friends with a Portsmouth band called Smiling Hard, who in turn knew other local outfits such as Jumbo Route, Edward Bear and Arms and Legs (both the latter featuring Joe Jackson). A series of phone calls led me to a place called (appropriately) the John Peel in Gosport. There, the landlord John, who sounded a nice sort of chap, invited me over to visit his venue.

The John Peel turned out to be the most unlikely of places for live music. It was a characterless modern seventies pub situated slap bang in the middle of a housing estate. John turned out to be a huge but extremely affable ex-boxer with cauliflower ears, who permanently wore the same black leather waistcoat. He was passionate about music and seemed to relish the never-ending run-ins he had with neighbours, councils and licensing authorities about noise, misbehaviour, late-night van-loading and all the other problems so well-known to live music promoters.

Because he ruled the roost in that particular area, John had no problems about giving me the phone numbers of a whole series of other similar venues in the South, as long as they weren't too near Gosport. He also gave me contact numbers for a number of bands and agencies.

So began a regular Wednesday afternoon ritual which lasted, without a break, for three years. If I was off on a school trip or on holiday, I simply recorded three weeks' worth of "Roundups" before I left. The timing of the show moved about a lot but it was mainly broadcast on Friday or Saturday evenings, which wasn't too bad. But, because it was the only day I had a free period in the afternoon, the recording always had to be done on a Wednesday.

Although Radio Solent is based in Southampton, it has little satellite studios in each of the main towns it covers. The Winchester studio, from where I was to work, was (is, actually) tucked away, absolutely unbeknown to anybody, in a tiny cellar half way up the High Street, right in the middle of town. It took me ages even to find it. The only sign of its existence was a tiny brass plate beside the door.

Getting in was a bit of a rigmarole. As it was unmanned, I first had to go to the Castle, which is Hampshire County Council's administrative centre, further up the High Street. There, I had to engage in conversation with a uniformed jobsworth, who initially was very sceptical about handing over the key. Because the jobsworth would vary from week to week, I arranged for Gethyn to write me a note, explaining that I was allowed to use the studio.

After a few weeks, things settled down with the appointment of a regular jobsworth called Ron, who wasn't really a jobsworth at all. Whereas his predecessors had all had the attitude, "Who's this disreputable-looking sod? Let's obstruct him", Ron's attitude was, "This is a top media personality, maybe he's famous", so he was friendly almost to the point of obsequiousness. If anyone else on duty looked doubtful about my right to pick up the key, Ron would set their minds at rest:

"What? Don't you know Oliver? He works for Radio Solent. Oh yes, he's all right, old Oliver is."

Ron would quiz me about the presenters on the station, about whom I knew little. Gethyn, having worked his way up from being an assistant in the record library, had a steady if unsensational profile, but the star of the station was a lounge lizard type called Richard Cartridge. With his sexy tones and suggestive banter, he set the housewives' hearts a-flutter every day. Everyone knew Richard Cartridge, except me, of course, but I couldn't disappoint Ron.

"How's old Richard, then?" he would ask each Wednesday.

"Oh, he's fine," I would reply. "Great bloke, Richard."

"My wife loves him, she does."

"No wonder. What a guy!"

After a few months, I got fed up with this and nipped into Mr Minit and got my own key made, very much against the rules. Some time after that, I bumped into Ron in town.

"Haven't seen you for a while, Oliver. Don't you work for Solent any more?"

"Er ... no ... no, I'm doing something else now."

The following Wednesday, I was caught red-handed. As I turned the key in the lock, the door opened and there stood Ron, having obviously just carried out some job in the studio.

"Oh, er ... hi, Ron ... Guess what, Solent have given me my own key," I lied.

"Good on you, Oliver," he replied, with a wink which said, "I've got you sussed, matey."

Once in the cellar, I was in a little world of my own. There were two rooms, a desk with a telephone plus, of course, the studio itself. If times get really hard, I thought, I could move in here and nobody would notice. I also thought about ringing up all my friends in Germany for hours on end, but decided against it in case calls were monitored.

I did all the calling round of venues from the cellar, because I sure as heck wasn't going to incur any expenses. Yes, as the Solent Rock programme had no budget (Gethyn did it as a labour of love), presenting the *Rock Roundup* was an unpaid occupation, done, I guess, solely in order for me to be able to tell people casually that I was a part-time broadcaster. Stupid, stupid, stupid ... but sometimes fun as well.

The first thing to do was ring round the venues and find out what was on. This was a job with varying degrees of reward. Someone like John from the John Peel would be delighted to be rung up. We would natter about the latest gossip among the bands, plus, having an idea of public relations, he realised that the more mentions his pub got, the better. Other landlords could sometimes be unhelpful or unfriendly (it was obvious that I was disturbing their afternoon naps). I felt like telling them, "For crying out loud, you stupid bastards, all I'm doing is offering to publicise your shitty pub for free!" But I didn't, of course.

There were some good and interesting venues in the Solent area. The Pinecliff was a big pub in Boscombe, a suburb of Bournemouth. It had a proper stage with live bands most nights and it was run by a middle-aged couple called Mr and Mrs Shipway (Christian names not offered). They were committed to music despite not seeming to be at all interested in it. The Chequers was a little pub in a village near Sturminster Newton called Lytchett Matravers. Unlikely as it certainly sounds, this was a very active venue, whose landlord managed Joe Jackson's early bands, who would play there regularly. Another surprising band to play there came all the way from Wales. They were called Seventeen, and later became The Alarm.

The Brewers Arms in Poole was more problematic, in that it worked on a "self-promotion" basis, whereby bands would hire the room and take the door money. Thus, when you rang up, nobody could tell you who was on. This was particularly frustrating during the period when Poole bands briefly looked as if they would be the Next Big Thing. Luckily, I gleaned the phone number of Ronnie Mayor from Tours, the leading "Poole Sound" band, and he kept me up to date.

The Elm Tree in Ringwood was an extraordinary place in that the stage was a hay loft. You got a really sore neck from trying to watch the band. The DOCs would have gone down a storm there, having only ever played in a hay loft. The barman of the Elm Tree kindly insisted on giving me endless free drinks when he discovered that I was a media superstar.

The Old Mill in Holbury was the best venue, if also the strangest. Here, it was the sound engineer who was in the loft, while the band actually had a stage. Holbury is a hamlet near Fawley, which is where a large Esso refinery is situated. It was well-nigh impossible to find the Old Mill, and I got lost at every attempt, on the way home as well. Yet there was always a good crowd there, as it was also a restaurant. The landlord, Chris, was an obvious alcoholic but a loyal music fan. He suddenly disappeared in mysterious circumstances (bankruptcy was rumoured) and the Old Mill immediately closed its doors to music.

None of these places has bands any more. Indeed, apart from the famous Joiners Arms in Southampton, only one music venue survives from those days, the Royal Oak, near Petersfield. I never went there because the landlord seemed very pedantic in his tastes and most of his bands were pretty poor. The Larry Miller Band played there regularly in 1977 and The Larry Miller Band still play there regularly in 2000. Good luck to them.

One problem of *Rock Roundup* compilation was the huge range of bands which played at each of these places. Most of them seemed quite at home putting on heavy metal, hard rock, punk, covers bands, blues bands and middle-of-the-road duos. Presumably, confusion could occur if a chapter of Hells Angels were to turn up for Glenda 'n' Dave's Singalong Nite, while Glenda 'n' Dave's followers would doubtless not gain much from an evening with the Vomiting Rodents.

To maintain the purity of the *Rock Roundup*, I tried hard to weed out anything which might not be rockin'. Any duos were instantly banned, and names were shamelessly scrutinised for tell-tale clues about possible blandness, which would exclude them. Two bands which I included for years, but never saw, were called Mustard Pot and Mead. Both played three or four times a week and I was suspicious about their rock credentials but included them out of goodwill. A band called Mission Impossible seemed never to go home, playing virtually every day in the Poole area. They had a Sunday lunchtime residency at the Jolly Sailor on Poole Quay which ran for the entire three years that I did the Rock Roundup. Eventually we went there for a Sunday roast. They turned out to be doing rock and roll covers, and thus were quite kosher.

You couldn't always make correct assumptions on the basis of names, however. A gentleman called Squire William came highly recommended, but I omitted him on the basis that he was more of a comedian than a musician. On the other hand, Surfin' Dave was a new-wave poet and songwriter who gained much credibility and featured regularly in the indie charts. Jim and Dave, far from being a "resident duo", actually featured ex-Joe Jackson drummer Dave Houghton, who was damn good.

Gethyn Jones prided himself on his catholic tastes, as did I, but he tended more towards the older guard while I had become completely swept up in the punk/new wave ethic. It became apparent that there were some really good bands in the area and I was determined that Solent Rock should be their outlet. There was nowhere else they would get radio exposure, unless they had a single and could get John Peel to play it.

Examples of excellent Solent area groups were legion. The Martian Schoolgirls, for example, despite hailing from Sturminster Marshall, had a guitarist who had played with Joe Strummer in the 101ers. Eyes, from Portsmouth, had a great glam-rock image with oodles of make-up. Last Orders were a good new-wave group with a shaven-headed singer called Keith Wymark, while The Skavengers were a sub-Police ska trio but great at what they did. Two Portsmouth bands which both got record deals with major labels and put out good albums were The Planets and the Keys. The Planets held a big record company showcase gig at the John Peel, while The Keys' singer was Drew Barfield, who has spent his subsequent career collaborating with Paul Young.

Before I could invite any bands into the Winchester studio, I had to master the technology. First, I had to dial up the studio in Southampton and ask to be put through to the "Duty Op". Normally, the Duty Op had not been forewarned that I would ring, or had forgotten.

"Hi, this is Oliver Gray in the Winchester studio."

"Sorry, who?"

"Oliver Gray."

"Oh ... er, what do you want?"

"I'm ready to record."

"Record what?"

"The *Solent Rock Roundup*."

"What's that?"

"It's the Gig Guide for Solent Rock."

"What's Solent Rock?"

"It's a rock music programme. It goes out on Saturdays."

"Oh, does it? Hang on a minute."

(Click, whirr, buzz, frequently complete silence.)

"Okay, test for level and go."

It's a miracle that anything ever got recorded, but there I was, completely alone, intoning the listings into the beautiful old plinth-mounted Alvar Lidell-style BBC microphone. "Hi, and welcome to the *Solent Rock Roundup*. It's a busy old week, so let's start in Basingstoke ..."

One alleged qualification I had stressed to Gethyn was my skill with language labs. This meant that I was supposedly adept at spooling and splicing reel-to-reel tapes. This was important, in that Solent had no facility for playing cassettes and CDs hadn't been invented. If a band wanted its demo played, it had to entrust to me its treasured studio master tape. This was a risky thing to do, because the tape facility in the Winchester studio was so antiquated (the sort of thing Lord Haw Haw would have used), that it made the school language lab seem like the cutting edge of technology. On more than one occasion, priceless (to the bands) master tapes were turned to spaghetti and mercilessly chewed up by the tape deck.

Sometimes, too, tracks were faded out early if the recording quality or the quality of the performance was deemed to be too poor. This was because I was so determined to encourage young bands that I would interview virtually anyone who had a demo tape. A stream of scruffy young oiks passed through the portals of the cellar, causing much curiosity among the passers-by in the High Street, who did not suspect the rock and roll secret beneath the paving slabs.

Early bands which visited the cellar included The Ba, whose "Bus Garage Café" was faded out (boo) and Thieves Like Us, whose visit is documented elsewhere. The Time popped in, as did The Britz. This latter was a Salisbury band, notable for the fact that their front man, Andrew Golden, was a journalist who later came to specialise in tabloid exposés and whose by-line was to be found in the *Mirror* and the *News of the World*. Andy Golden, what a great name for a rock singer. Or a tabloid journalist, come to that.

We certainly were the first to give exposure to a number of bands which did well. Tours, from Poole, were briefly signed to Virgin and made some immortal singles. Titles like "Language School" and "Foreign Girls" rang a few Bournemouth bells, and they were classic two-minute pop songs. Tours later expanded into Biz Internationale, a very swinging seven-piece with a funky brass section. They got a deal with Warner Brothers and put out a beautifully sentimental single called "Stay True". With the right production and, above all, the right promotion, it could easily have been a chart hit.

In order to interview The Warm Jets, I took a tape recorder up to the Bridge House pub in Canning Town, where they were particularly popular. This was odd, in that the Bridge House was a centre for skinhead music, constantly plugged by the odious *Sounds* journalist

Garry Bushell. The Warm Jets, by contrast, were a very musical unit, fronted by a classically-trained musician called Milton Reame-James, who had previously been in Cockney Rebel. The connection with Solent was the drummer, Dave Cairns, who had been in a band with Joe Jackson.

Interfearance was a Mod band who played a great deal round the area. They mutated into The Jagz and had a big, and deserved, hit with "I've Got Your Number (Written On The Back Of My Hand)", before disappearing. My favourites, however, were a delightful bunch of yokel punks from Salisbury called The QTs. They arrived in the cellar having spent two hours in the pub and were so paralytic that the results were unbroadcastable. We remained on good terms, though, and their leader Colin Holton still puts on occasional hardcore shows at Salisbury Arts Centre. The only change is that he's now about ten stone heavier.

A final example of the kind of band we attracted was The Piranhas. A hard-working punk / comedy act from Brighton, their sound was very much in the "Portsmouth" mould, stripped-down guitars and upfront bass with reggae tendencies. They were plugging an indie single called "I Don't Want My Body ('Cos It's So Bloody Shoddy)", but their gimmick was that their singer, Boring Bob Grover, was purposely just that: Boring. So it didn't make for a gripping radio interview. Also, they were going through an identity crisis, because they no longer liked being seen as a comedy band. Just as they metamorphosed into a serious-minded, heavy dub-reggae bunch of musos, they finally got themselves signed to a major label (Sire, very appropriate), and found themselves in the Top Ten with the gimmicky instrumental "Tom Hark". Under these circumstances, what else could they be but one-hit wonders?

One day, after I had had a few weeks to get used to the tranquillity of my little subterranean kingdom, I was startled to hear a clattering sound by the front door. Cautiously, I peeped out of the studio into the gloom, to be confronted by a man who appeared to be armed - at least, he had a stick in his hand. Having briefly panicked, thinking I was about to be attacked, I realised that the man was, in fact, blind, which presumably was the reason he hadn't needed to switch the light on.

He pottered around, apparently unaware of my presence, and I wondered what to do. Not wanting to startle him too much, I quietly cleared my throat:

"Er ... hello, can I help you?"

"No thanks, I'm fine," he replied, unperturbed."I'm just going to send something down the line to Southampton."

"I hope I didn't startle you?"

"Not at all, I realised you were there."

This cheerful fellow, it turned out, was Peter White, a blind broadcaster from Winchester who often used this studio rather than having to travel down to Southampton. It was obvious even then that this was an unusually gifted individual, and it is no surprise at all that Peter, now the BBC's Chief Disability Correspondent, is one of the UK's most respected and loved radio personalities. From then on, we would frequently bump into each other (sometimes literally) in the cellar.

The sudden chart success of Joe Jackson briefly put South Coast music on the map, and Gethyn Jones, keen to capitalise on the new-found interest, hatched a plot for a series of programmes tracing the history of rock in the area. We met to divide up the tasks of tracing and interviewing the chief players.

Gethyn had already achieved the big scoop by interviewing Joe Jackson before his first record came out and playing the demos of songs like "Is She Really Going Out With Him?" This was fascinating, because they differed in hardly any way from the actual released versions. The follow-up interview for "Baked On The Premises" (the eventual title of the series) was a phone chat with Mark Andrews. Mark had been in Arms and Legs with Joe, in fact had been the lead singer, and now he, too, had just been signed by A & M. A charismatic character, Mark was exploding with optimism in his interview with Gethyn. To me, Mark was a true star and still is one, even though he has long since returned to playing in bread and butter covers bands on the cabaret circuit. His album "Big Boy" was notable for a crazy reggae version of "Born To Be Wild", but his career was ruined by brutal management difficulties.

Our search for further interviewees wasn't promising. Brian Eno had studied at the Art School, but his management let it be known that Brian had absolutely no wish to recall those days. The only other famous person ever to have come out of Winchester was Mike Batt, who had attended the local grammar school. We didn't really want to plug the Wombles, but there wasn't much choice. The only interesting thing that Gethyn extracted from him was that he occasionally returned to Winchester because there he could go out and get drunk without the fear of some journalist exposing the dissolute behaviour of the chief Womble.

For my part, I got the glamorous job of talking to Bob Young, road manager of Status Quo, who had grown up in Basingstoke. It was initially a tense meeting, because Bob had been under the false impression that the interview was intended to publicise his newly-published slim volume of poetry. Added to this was my snobby sniggering about Quo and my scornful slagging of Whitesnake. This was a poor tactic because I had forgotten that Bob Young had actually made an album with Micky Moody from Whitesnake, entitled "Young and Moody". Oh dear.

He soon warmed to the topic, however, and before long came up with a useful collection of anecdotes. Chief among these was how he had seen John Mayall's Bluesbreakers with Eric Clapton backing Sonny Boy Williamson in an upstairs room at Basingstoke Town Hall. Oh, to have been there.

Then Gethyn got an unexpected boost. Having tentatively enquired as to whether Robert Fripp would be prepared to be interviewed, he received an enthusiastic phone call from the man himself. In stark contrast to his reported "difficult" persona, he was delighted to talk at length about his roots in the Bournemouth area. The result was by far the most candid and entertaining interview of the entire series, a veritable onslaught of sustained name-dropping. Music archaeologists might be interested in the following nuggets:

Giles, Giles and Fripp, he revealed, had originally gone to London in order to back The Flowerpot Men (of "Let's Go To San Francisco" infamy), but instead ended up backing a cabaret singer in an Italian restaurant. When looking for a singer for King Crimson, they had an unsuspected encounter:

"I turned Ferry down, you know. Brian Ferry auditioned for Crimson in December 1970. I'm probably one of the few people who've heard Brian Ferry sing 'In The Court Of The Crimson King' and '21st Century Schizoid Man'. And I also met Hendrix. He was one of the most luminous men I've ever met. Crimson were playing at the Revolution Club in Mayfair. He came up to me after the first set, dressed completely in white and with his right arm in a sling. Remarkable smile! He said, 'Shake my left hand man, it's nearer to my heart.' A quite remarkable man."

That sort of thing was hard to beat, but I was determined to try. The two victims I was delegated to track down were Reg Presley and Andy Summers. Reg, as was well known, came from Andover (his priceless tones familiar to everyone from the infamous Troggs Tapes) and Andy was a native of Bournemouth, having worked with various local groups before teaming up with Zoot Money in Dantalion's Chariot and eventually straddling the world (in his mid-thirties, but looking like a fifteen year old) in the Police.

Locating Reg Presley was surprisingly easy. I simply got the number of Page One Records from Directory Enquiries, rang them up and they gave me Reg's home phone number. Just like that! And so I rang him and asked him if he'd be willing to talk to me about his "roots". Of course he was more than happy to do so, and invited me and Birgit over to Andover the following week. I borrowed the reel-to-reel tape recorder from my classroom, since to get hold of a portable BBC Uher would have entailed a round trip to Southampton, a complicated signing-out procedure and the necessity to drop it back the same evening.

Having heard the Troggs Tapes and knowing Reg's Sexy Wild Man Of Rock image, I was ill-prepared for the sweet domestic scene which awaited us. I kind of expected a Rock Star Mansion (which I believe Reg, post "Love Is All Around", now possesses). Instead, it was an unostentatious modern estate residence, but warm and welcoming. As we entered, it was clear that some kind of family disagreement was just coming to a close. Reg and his wife had clearly been having words with their teenage daughter about her plan to go out to the Country Bumpkin, the dodgy night club in Andover. Obviously, they had just relented.

"Thanks, Mum, thanks, Dad."

"Yaas, well, don't be late now, and don't you go talking to no strangers."

"Don't worry, Dad. See you later."

While Mrs Presley (well, actually, Mrs Ball, I suppose) made tea, I set up the Tandberg on the coffee table and recorded the story which Reg must have told a thousand times, but which to me was pure historical magic:

"I was working on a job in Andover, on a building site, and I was finishing a gable, and on the other scaffolding was a painter from some other town, who didn't know me or anything, and we'd recorded "Wild Thing", and he had a little transistor radio on the scaffold while he was painting the eaves, you know, the top part of a house, and all of a sudden "Wild Thing" came on. Now I knew the week before it was Number 43 or something in the chart, you know, and I carried on bricklaying and all of a sudden this guy shouted over, and he said to me, he said, 'Cor', he said, 'have you heard this record?' he said, 'It's great, I'm sure it's gonna be Number One.' And after the guy had finished playing it, he said, 'And that's Number Eleven in the charts this week, The Troggs.' And I thought, 'What am I doing here?', you know. I threw down my trowel, I walked down and they'd just stopped for lunch, and I just said, 'Share me tools out, I'm not working any more!'"

And not a single "fuck" or "cunt" to edit. What a triumph! And when, twenty years later, Reg came to the Tower Arts Centre to lecture fascinatingly on crop circles and UFOs, he claimed to remember our encounter. Wild Man Of Rock And Roll, tish!

Andy Summers was a completely different proposition, however. Admittedly, we were aiming high, because the Police at that time were the biggest act in the world. So, Poirot-like, I set out to track him down. After a while, a possible contact appeared. Jim, of Jimz Music in Bournemouth, knew someone whose wife knew Zoot Money's wife. Zoot Money's wife, in turn, knew Andy Summers' wife. A lengthy series of phone calls to all these people eventually produced the response that Andy would, indeed, be prepared to be interviewed backstage at the Southampton Gaumont, where the Police were to play the following week. On this basis, I secured a backstage pass from the concert promoters and, Uher in hand, nervously ventured past the security at the end of the show.

Backstage was a scene of complete bedlam, akin, I guess, to what Beatlemania must have been like. The theatre was besieged by screaming teenagers, some shinning up the wastepipe, others attempting to batter down the stage door. I moved towards a window to get a better look at the minor riot going on in the side alley, and a massive scream went up. I stepped back and it stopped. I tried again, and up went the scream again. Bloody hell, they were screaming at me! Except that they weren't, they were screaming at who they thought I possibly might be and who they thought I might be associated with. So that's how ugly roadies get to sleep with groupies.

The interview was just awful, a humbling, humiliating experience. Even though the Tour Manager was well informed, Andy Summers claimed not to know that it was due to take place, but reluctantly agreed to give me five minutes. Just enough time to put me in my place.

I suppose the unsmiling posters should have given me the clue. Summers was supremely condescending, quite uninterested in delving into his past, and of course I helped him by nervously asking stupid, naive, ill-phrased questions. Here is the grisly encounter in full:

Summers: I did actually grow up in Bouremouth, but I left there early on and went to London. I played around Bournemouth for a short while. I used to know Robert Fripp and Mike Giles. I went to London and played with a guy called Zoot Money, who first came to prominence with the Big Roll Band. We did play in Bournemouth and Southampton a couple of times but in those days we played every night of the week, year in, year out.

Gray: Were you in any local bands before moving to London?

Summers: No, I wasn't, I went to London fairly early on. The band was pretty popular, we were on TV a lot and we made quite a lot of money out of it, actually. So I've always felt I was destined for great things, frankly.

Gray: And then you worked with Kevin Ayers?

Summers: Well actually, Zoot and I were in the Animals for a while. I stayed in America for about five years. Eventually Zoot and I ended up in the same band again, playing with Kevin Coyne, and then we also both went on to play with Kevin Ayers. So we've had quite a lot of karma.

Gray: Looking at the scenes here tonight, you're obviously at the very top of the tree, aren't you?

Summers: Well, I'm afraid I am.

Gray: Do you have any regrets?

Summers: Absolutely none. I mean, it would be dishonest to say one goes entirely through life with no regrets at all. I certainly regret buying a pair of Y-fronts from Woolworths the other day. I'm feeling the pinch a bit right now. No, I've always enjoyed my life in music, and it's very gratifying to be at this point. Of course, really, when you take everything into consideration, it was inevitable.

Gray: Any hankerings for returning to your home town?

Summers: No. I do go down to Bournemouth once in a while and feel fairly nauseous, and then I return to London and feel better.

Actually, now I re-listen to it, it's quite funny. Anyway, the interview safely in the can, Birgit and I escaped by walking out of the front door of the Gaumont (since the mayhem was concentrated on the stage door). The next evening, I dropped the tape off at Radio Solent headquarters in Southampton. I knew where Gethyn's desk was, so I left the tape on it, clearly labelled. It wasn't much of an interview, but Andy Summers was the trump card in the *Baked On The Premises* pack and I certainly wanted it to be broadcast.

A couple of days later, I got a call from Gethyn:

"Hi, Oliver. Did you manage to get the Andy Summers interview?"

"Of course I did! You've got it!"

"I haven't. You never gave it to me."

"But I left it on your desk on Friday night."

"What? Don't you know that they come round every Saturday morning and pick up all the tapes? Anything left out on a desk is wiped ready for re-use!"

"How the hell was I supposed to know that?"

"Sorry, I thought you realised."

I don't know if I'd had a premonition, but I'd made a cassette copy, through a microphone, before delivering the tape. In the end, we decided to use it, even though it sounded more like a couple of Daleks than a conversation. To complete the humiliation, Gethyn had to make a public apology for the poor quality of the recording.

There was another unwelcome postscript to the Andy Summers encounter. A week or two afterwards, Blondie played a warm-up date at the Village Bowl in Bournemouth and I wangled Birgit and me on to the guest list. As we queued, I realised that the diminutive peroxide figure in front of us was none other than Andy Summers himself. Eager to impress my girlfriend, I tapped him on the shoulder.

"Hi, Andy, how are you?"

"I'm sorry," he replied, witheringly, "I don't believe I've had the pleasure."

For the last few months of Rock Roundups, I found things increasingly difficult. Maybe there was stress at school, but the cellar seemed to be becoming more and more claustrophobic. Panic-like symptoms, quite similar to the driving phobia, began to appear. The basis was the same: nowhere to run. Although it wasn't going out live, it effectively was live, since I knew that it was going straight to tape and likely to be broadcast in full. I started to think about things too much. Instead of just getting on with it, I worried about making mistakes, which in turn made mistakes more likely. I suffered from nausea and breathlessness, which, although people assured me it wasn't obvious, I thought everyone could hear.

The final straw came when I at last got to interview my old hero from Camel, Peter Bardens. In a scenario which was really depressing, in view of what I considered to have been an illustrious career with Them, Camel and Van Morrison, Bardens was without a record deal and was trying to plug a misconceived single on his own label. The interview took place on a grotty industrial estate, in the "office" (warehouse) of a small-time manager. We rambled for over fifteen minutes and parts of the interview were quite interesting, such as an illuminating insight into the volatile character of Van Morrison. But we were frequently interrupted by loud bangs and crashes from the industrial activity around us, plus I made a number of fluffs. "Don't worry, that'll be edited out," I reassured Peter, on tape, on several occasions, but sure enough, the entire tape was broadcast, complete with the "Don't worrys".

Nobody complained because, quite obviously, hardly anyone was listening. It was rare to get any feedback, apart from one girl in Bournemouth, who tried to seduce me by claiming she loved the way I said "White Buck" in the gig guide. I doubt if she was bright enough to appreciate the Cockney Rhyming Slang implications of this, but I resisted on the grounds that I was spoken for. It was time to quit.

It was good to be broadcasting during the only musical "purple patch" the area has ever had. But the BBC never paid me a single penny, and apart from the blessed weekly credit in the Radio Times (not everyone can claim that, I suppose), never acknowledged my existence, or, indeed, my absence. The *Rock Roundup*, and, not long afterwards, *Solent Rock* itself, just stopped and have never been replaced.

There is, however, a strange but quite pleasing postscript to my fumbling non-career in radio presenting and that is the number of my ex-pupils who have, in stark contrast to their teacher, gone on to have successful careers in broadcasting.

John Roder was a quiet boy who was overshadowed at school by his younger brother David, who was the most outrageous punk the school ever had: blue spiky hair and the cheekiest grin you ever saw. David's speciality was spooking the tourists by leering at them from the Butter Cross in Winchester High Street. Both he and John would talk to me for hours between lessons, either about music (John wrote several reviews for my *Hampshire Chronicle* column) or, more often, about the traumatic marriage break-up which their parents were going through. John, also, would set out to me his unshakeable ambition to be a radio presenter.

Unshakeable ambition normally pays dividends, and, sure enough, John Roder is now a sports presenter on BBC Radio Five Live.

A cherubic little boy called Simon Vigar, who also used to quiz me about getting into radio, did rather well too. Working his way up through commercial radio, he became a newsreader for Independent Radio News before breaking into TV, where he now expertly presents the Nightly News on Channel 5. His predecessor Kirsty Young transferred to another channel for over a million pounds, so the boy can be said to have done good.

My classroom was next to the gymnasium, and there could be found a diminutive PE teacher called Helen Grindley. In quiet moments, we would chat in the corridor and one day, she asked if I knew anyone at Solent, since she fancied the idea of doing some sports reporting. I gave her the name of one of the sports presenters and they immediately took a liking to her, commissioning her to phone in reports on local hockey matches.

At the end of the year, Helen applied for and got a job as a sports presenter for BBC radio in Wales, from where it was a meteoric rise until, as Helen Rollason, she captured the nation's imagination with her personality, and then its heart with her warmth and courage as she publicly moved towards death from cancer. So, what with Helen, Reg Presley and Peter White, my radio "career" allowed me to meet a number of people I was proud to know.

IX. Jaded Hack (2)

As a teacher, I made quite a reasonable journalist. What I should have done, of course, was leave school after O-levels and enrol on a training course. As that didn't happen, all my journalism has had to be carried out as a pastime and the career has had a depressing "almost but not quite" feel to it. I only ever wanted to be a famous rock writer, but I had to settle for being an obscure one.

Having said that, if there was an entry in the *Guinness Book of Records* for the Longest-Running Rock Column Written By The Same Person, I would be in it. The *Hampshire Chronicle* Rock Column began in January 1977 and it's still going strong in the year 2000. That's a claim to fame of sorts.

At the beginning of 1997, the Rock Column reached its twentieth anniversary. Here's what the paper had to say:

Oliver's Column Still Rocking After All These Years

The first Hampshire Chronicle Rock Column appeared on January 21st 1977, which means that the feature celebrates its 20th anniversary this week.

This may not seem a particularly big deal nowadays, when analysis of rock and pop music is a regular feature of all respectable broadsheet newspapers, both national and local. Back in 1977, however, such items were positively revolutionary. In retrospect, the Chronicle, *or, to be more precise, its then editor, Monica Woodhouse, can be seen to have been well ahead of its time. The paper's readership caught its breath, blinked slightly, but soon grew to accept and possibly even welcome this upstart new companion to Eric and Joan Wood's "Music Diary".*

Newly arrived in Winchester from Germany, and with music journalism already in his blood, Oliver Gray set about covering the live music scene in Winchester, Southampton and Portsmouth with enthusiasm bordering on the unhealthy. That very first column featured Dr. Feelgood, Kiki Dee, Steeleye Span, Caravan, Manfred Mann's Earth Band and Jess Roden, but the world was just adapting to the arrival of punk and the new fashion in journalism was the stream-of-consciousness mode of Ian Penman and Paul Morley, which Gray espoused with alacrity. Before long, Chronicle *readers were being asked to believe that "The Blue Aeroplanes skitter, claw, chase and tease like a basketful of kittens", and to accept that the music of the Fall was an "itchy, beaty, unsophisticated but highly potent Molotov".*

The readers accepted this self-indulgence with their customary sang-froid.

As was the trend at the time, Gray had little time for the Heavy Metal fraternity, and would lay into them in merciless fashion: "It's tempting to see Chinatown as pedestrian, but compared to this band, most pedestrians are positively graceful". Such opinionated stuff would occasionally provoke a furious reaction in the correspondence columns. Undeterred, Gray would go on to see his work published in magazines such as Night Out, Due South, Sounds, Record Mirror, Musicians Only, Musicians Weekly, Soundmaker, NME, Sound Info, Insomnia, Mojo and Blueprint.

The Rock Column is regarded with bemused affection by Chronicle readers, many of whom read it for the jokes and don't actually understand very much of it at all. Gray has made a couple of attempts to retire, once when having young children made it difficult to spend evenings in homely dives like the Joiners Arms, and once when running his publishing business was becoming too time-consuming. But somehow, the addiction to the noise was just too strong, and he always returned.

A flick back through the years reveals that there have been 289 Rock Columns, which have written about a grand total of 763 bands. Covering an area containing a number of small venues, the column has a good track record of finding future world stars before they have been heard of. Occasionally, wild predictions for success have proved hopelessly inaccurate (remember The Primary or The Templemeads?), while regal slaggings have failed to damage the careers of certain bands: Supergrass: "Deeply unattractive, bog standard punk rock"; Oasis: "Marginally less interesting than a slumbering lugworm". A number of acts destined for fame have received their first-ever live reviews in the Chronicle. Examples include The Hoax, Black Grape and Automatic Dlamini (featuring P.J. Harvey).

There are certain oddities about the Rock Column. At one stage in the early Eighties, it reached enormous proportions, sometimes filling up to a third of a broadsheet page, yet for some reason it has seldom featured photographs. The column has never appeared on a regular weekly or fortnightly basis, since it is only written when there is something to write about. There have been times of little action, although at the moment it would be possible to attend local gigs every night of the week. One major disappointment for Gray has been the lack of quality music in the city of Winchester itself (or emanating from it).

Whatever else his motive may be, Gray isn't in it for the money. The Rock Column fee increased from £5 to £7 in 1989 and has remained static ever *since. Not that it matters, because half the time the accounts department manages to forget the payment altogether!*

Overlooking jibes about attending gigs supported by a Zimmer frame (which he plans to do), Gray has no intention of hanging up his earplugs. "Music has never been more exciting," he says. "Why should age have any bearing on what kind of music you enjoy?"

What do you mean, it's obvious I wrote it myself? The fact is that no one else on the paper could possibly have written it, because the Hampshire Chronicle, even today, with its colour photos and property supplement, is a satisfyingly old-fashioned broadsheet, full of local news and opinions. Apart from my column, the main other "regulars" are columns about Classical Music, Farming, Shipping and Wine Tasting.

Twenty-three years isn't really that long, but, looking back to the way things were done then, it seems a completely different world. Monica Woodhouse, the elderly proprietor and editor, was an absolutely amazing woman, dispensing what now seems to be almost unbelievable kindness to this maniac who was submitting semi-incomprehensible copy about bands that none of her readers had ever heard of. Here is an early example, from March 1977, encouraging me to send in more material:

"If you would consider letting us have a feature along the lines of your first column, perhaps monthly or every five weeks, we should be more than happy to receive this. Your views covering recent rock events would be most acceptable."

Don't you just yearn for the days when people had the courtesy to communicate with each other properly? Here is an extract from just one of the many letters Mrs Woodhouse wrote to me over the years:

"We owe you sincere apologies. Your Rock Column has been in type since you first sent it in, but I'm afraid it is not possible to promise next week, as so much has been held over. We are quite at our wits' end at the moment, as our production will only go to 24 pages, but we are in the process of installing new machinery to increase this. We are trying to keep our regulars happy, but the time around Michaelmas has always been marked by increased advertising, still a rural characteristic. I am sorry to burden you with our worries, but do deeply regret not printing your appreciated notes, and hope that the forgoing may help you to understand, if not to forgive." (October 1979)

If you contrast that with what happens when you submit things to newspapers today (i.e. no reply at all), you can see why it has been such a pleasure working for the *Chronicle*. Even in times of adversity, they have always been supportive way beyond the call of duty. Take this exchange of letters between Monica Woodhouse and a pompous Entertainments Manager at a local college:

Pompous Ents Manager:

"This Union does not consider itself a facility for all and sundry, nor does it consider itself a charity. Therefore, your reporter's assumption that he has a right to enter our event free, simply because he wants to exercise his journalese upon the matter, shows only his arrogance.

Your reporter evidently wishes to raise our credibility; I feel that we have managed quite well without him so far, and will continue to do so long after he has become a jaded and rather seedy hack.

Your reporter's review shows more a sense of peevish indignation at not being treated as a demi-god by the members of the Union, than a sensitive and critical attitude towards the band and the audience ... It is not for your reporter to question us, it is for him to write a sensible and critical piece of journalism. Once he has mastered that art, he may be worthy of more respect.

Until then, he should not submit his pathetic pseudo-witticisms for print, and the Chronicle itself should cease to encourage and employ such "Grub Street" writers."

Monica Woodhouse:

"Thank you for your letter and your derogatory remarks about my 'Grub Street' writer. It may interest you to know that Mr Gray is a valued and knowledgeable contributor, who is a schoolmaster, a distinguished German linguist, who regularly broadcasts on Radio Solent in a programme dedicated to Rock music. He is therefore more highly educated than most students at your college, who should learn to treat him with some respect, especially when he is representing a newspaper such as my own."

That put him in his place! And even today, the editor, Alan Cleaver, is happy to stand up in defence of his ageing contributor. After a jokey feature I wrote about the Creamfields Festival in 1998, the paper printed a riposte from an ex-pupil with a grudge:

"I have long thought that the Hampshire Chronicle *is out of touch with young people in the area, and Oliver Gray's Creamfields diary confirmed this.*

I am not aware of exactly how many years Mr Gray has been writing his 'critiques' for the paper, but he appears to have little or no understanding of musical genres beyond his own favoured style of faded rock.

The hope that, for this special event at least, the Chronicle *might have sent a more appropriate reporter to the festival was, unsurprisingly, disappointed. Rather than writing an account of the varied performances on offer, or creating an idea of the atmosphere, your reporter chose to write a little story about what he did at the festival, and not exactly a rivetting one at that."*

Ouch! She actually had a good point, although the article had been intended to provoke a reaction. The following year, the same girl wrote in and asked if she could cover the festival instead of me. No thanks, said the Editor, we'll stick with our own correspondent.

Over the years, when things occasionally got overwhelming, I made several attempts to hand over the column. For some of my band managing days, the Rock Column was taken over by a fine local music writer called Baz Mort, and various staffers helped out with reviews: Alison Glanville (nice, but an unhealthy obsession with Budgie, unfortunately), Johnny Morris (nice, but prone to grammatical errors, unfortunately) and Lizzy Millar (very nice, but a slightly restricted knowledge of music, unfortunately). But the reasons I have stuck with the *Chronicle* are the fair treatment, the regular outlet and the small but welcome payments.

One unexpected spin-off from music journalism is the minor deluge of freebies which you receive. The pay being either very low or completely non-existent, I never objected to gifts like this, although most of the free records weren't really worth having. The Magnet label kept sending me terrible records by people like Chris Rea and Bad Manners. One valuable trophy which I prize to this day is a mint copy of "If You Don't Want To Fuck Me, Fuck Off", by Wayne County and the Electric Chairs, pressed on dung-coloured vinyl. Besides being a really good record, it offers the hope that it might one day be worth hundreds of pounds.

As a live music junkie, I was really only interested in free admission tickets or backstage passes, although the latter aren't much use for anything except wearing prominently on your jacket in order to make people jealous. At a Jam concert one night, I spotted a couple of dangerous-looking Mods eyeing up my backstage pass and suddenly realised that such an artefact might well make me a target for mugging, and that prominently wearing your pass was the musical equivalent of walking round with your wallet sticking out of your back pocket. From then on, I have always kept my pass in my pocket, just bringing it out to flash at the security.

Not that I have often had either the desire or the necessity to go backstage. This, however, does not apply at Glastonbury, where backstage toilet facilities, though not particularly smart (unless you're a Manic Street Preacher, of course), are at least normally marginally better than the hell outside. Personally, I'm not unwilling to piss in the bushes, but my family of girls certainly are. Luckily, in all the years we have been attending Glastonbury (every single one since 1983, when Annabel was 0 years old), I have always had access to Birgit's medical pass.

The joys of Glastonbury: Björk asks Lucy and Annabel for their autographs.

Birgit is one of the trusty team of midwives who deliver the festival's occasional babies. Her pass is, strictly speaking, not transferable, but for a quick nip to the loo it's okay. I always return it as soon as possible in the fear that I might be called upon to administer first aid to someone.

I have covered every one of these festivals for the press, but have seldom received either a press pass or a free ticket. Nowadays, I work for the frantic on-site-produced "Official" *Glastonbury Live* paper, but not even they have passes to spare. Luckily, I made the discovery that, while the organisers may be parsimonious in their handing out of passes, the security people are dozy in their checking of them. If you approach with sufficiently confident stride, it doesn't matter what you wave at them. In 1997, for instance, I discovered that a receipt for a Cornish pastie and a pint of Palmers Bitter (from the Ilchester Arms in Symondsbury) gave me unlimited access to the VIP zone. No wonder you never recognise anyone there.

There's nothing wrong with a bit of ambition, is there? My journalistic downfall is that I keep achieving my ambitions and failing to follow them up. I don't understand why this is. If they print one piece, you'd think they would print another. But it doesn't work that way.

An early example of this phenomenon was the first review I ever submitted to *Sounds*. It was a piece about The Lesser Known Tunisians at the Old Mill, and they printed it. The band was ecstatic and so was I. What a breeze! Without really trying, I was a *Sounds* journalist. Except that I wasn't, because, despite all my efforts, they never printed anything else.

Musicians Only was a much more positive story. Richard Newton, a stringer for the paper who lived locally, suggested I contact them and ask if they needed a correspondent to cover the South coast. Indeed they did, and my spell with them lasted a whole year.

Musicians Only was a good music paper, and it was a proper one, published by IPC alongside *Melody Maker* and *NME*. Its Deputy Editor was Chris Welch, a well-known music writer. I didn't actually like his style very much (he tended to make in-jokes and had an annoying habit of measuring all drummers against John Bonham), but his was a good name to drop.

One really good feature of M.O. was that every live review had to be accompanied by a comprehensive run-down of all the band's equipment. This meant that it wasn't normally possible to lurk at the back of the room and write a hatchet job. You actually had to make contact with the band.

Throughout 1980, I wrote live reviews for *Musicians Only* on an almost weekly basis. This was a dream come true, because it was a relatively well-known national paper and bands would often get in touch, asking for some coverage. What's more, the pay was regular and reliable. Among the major bands I wrote about were Blondie, UB40 , Orchestral Manoeuvres In The Dark and, on its last legs, The Enid. In the case of the last three, I cheated by getting the sound crew to list the gear, thus being able to slag the performance after all.

With small local bands, I was always supportive, and I made some good friends. The Limos' Mark Easton went on to form a record company with Chris Stonor after Thieves Like Us split up, while Paul Dominy, the manager of The Time, became and has remained my closest friend after we met when I approached him for gear information. And I finally got to plug my friend Tim Holt from the Freshly Layed Band by reviewing a gig by his new band The Outsiders.

Someone else I wrote about was Richard Mazda, another refugee from Bournemouth days, who had been in a latter version of Tours. His band Cosmetics briefly featured Richard Furter, the bassist from The Freshly Layed Band. Cosmetics were a great little band, funky and serious-minded, which was signed to Virgin, and my association with Richard Mazda enabled me later to put him in touch with John Parish, a connection which I like to think had a positive effect on John's future career.

By late 1980, Mazda was working in Germany, producing an album for Tom Robinson. After that, he started working with a German diva by the name of Ingeburg Thomsen, producing an album by her called "Weisse Sklavin". Richard got a bee in his bonnet about translating the lyrics into English for a possible American release of the album. Would I be prepared to translate the songs? Phonogram would pay handsomely, he assured me. For hours I struggled with those damn lyrics, the translations of which, of course, turned out to be gibberish:

Golden French Fries
and salad green
Yellow sauce
The cheese is cream
For Culinary Colour
Come to the Bürger King.

With onions and grease
Meat balls round
Tomatoes and peas
Deep-fry browned
For Culinary Cost
Come to the Bürger King.

Jesus! I should have got some kind of literary award. Richard got into the habit of ringing up from late-night recording sessions in Hamburg. Doped out of his brain, and thus friendly but incoherent, he never considered that incomprehensible phone calls at 3 am were hardly convenient for someone due to teach the next morning. And, needless to say, despite repeated submission of modest invoices, Phonogram denied all knowledge of any commitment to pay me.

Another good reason for working for *Musicians Only* was the opportunity to do proper features. I did interviews with several young bands from the Southampton and Bournemouth areas, and there was also a huge four-page spread, which took ages to research, about the "Bournemouth Music Scene". This gave me a good opportunity to mention Ronnie Mayor's new band, Dabiz.

An old friend called Paul Brown conveniently chose this time to start putting on gigs at a club called Knights, at the Crown Hotel, Eastleigh. Not so conveniently for Paul, this was the tail end of punk, and he had endless trouble with people gobbing, pogoing and scuffling, not to mention many of the shows being seriously under-attended. The Piranhas had a particularly rowdy set of followers, but one of the most memorable evenings starred the Nips. Even then, Shane McGowan looked as if he was likely to drop dead at any moment. Paul Brown wisely decided that music promotion wasn't for him, but at least "Beastly Eastleigh" received probably its only ever mentions in the music press.

For years, Birgit and I had been attending the Reading Festival, partly because it was nearby and partly because we got in free on account of the *Chronicle* being considered "local". It was normally quite fun, because we were also given backstage passes. We could wander around looking at all the smacked-out hard rockers with their poodle cuts and their over made-up girlfriends, all (male and female) wearing what we called "Reading Trousers" (skin-tight latex, fine if you have a trim bottom, not fine if you don't). Schmoozing with the stars wasn't an option, because clearly no one had ever heard of the *Hampshire Chronicle*.

1980 was different, however, because this year I was going to be covering the festival for *Musicians Only* and, what was more, the piece was to be co-written with Chris Welch. I thought that meant that we would co-operate, but in the event he was most unfriendly and wanted nothing to do with me. The previous year's festival with The Cure, The Police, Peter Gabriel and The Ramones had actually been quite good, but 1980's line-up was a hideous collection of preposterous heavy metal acts such as Samson, Def Leppard and Whitesnake. The audience threw bottles and other missiles at any acts they didn't like (which invariably were the ones I did like) so the "VIP Area" in front of the stage was by far the most dangerous possible place to be. I hated every moment, and luckily so did Chris Welch, because the two-page feature was headed "Reading Slayed", a reference to the fact that Slade had been the only non-heavy metal band to win over the hostile fans.

Musicians Only disappointingly closed down at the end of the year, but from then on, it always seemed that new outlets would miraculously appear from nowhere. From October, I started getting reviews published in *Record Mirror*, which gave me an opportunity to plug The Time. I took a terrible dislike to Rick Wakeman and slagged him off something awful ("music which wouldn't intrude on a TV documentary about the emotional life of snails"), but enjoyed the end of the year show by Tom Robinson at the Marquee. Tom was by now using Cosmetics from Bournemouth as his backing band.

Record Mirror work fizzled out after a while, and was followed by a spell with a short-lived Brighton listings mag called *Night Out*. It was June 1982 before another national outlet presented itself. This was a strange paper which was trying to step into the shoes of *Musicians Only*. Called *Musicians Weekly*, it was published by Northern and Shell. Once again, they seemed to welcome my contributions and paid reliably.

I don't know what got into me in 1982, but I was horribly negative about almost every gig. My affair with Camel was finally over. They were promoting a weak album called *The Single Factor*, meaning that Andy Latimer was the only original member left. Then I was nasty about Joe Jackson, quite unreasonably in view of the fact that all he was trying to do was expand his horizons and was, in fact, at his best. Gethyn Jones read the article and rang me up to complain. He was right.

Musicians Weekly mutated into a bigger enterprise called *Soundmaker*, designed, this time, to challenge *Melody Maker*. But the staff and publisher were essentially the same as before. Now I could really get my teeth into attacking the heavy metal bands I had grown to hate, and *Soundmaker* gave me my platform, complete with gratifyingly big photos and headlines: Whitesnake ("A Bite To Sicken"); Gillan ("Bathing In Safe Water").

A steady flow of reviews continued for the rest of the year, including two gigs which we hoped would give our unborn child a good sense of rhythm: swing band Roman Holliday in Redhill and our old friend Tom Robinson at Salisbury Arts Centre. The support act here was a bone-shakingly bass-heavy dub reggae sound system. On both occasions, Birgit spent most of the time in the toilet throwing up.

Soundmaker inevitably collapsed before the end of the year (are you beginning to see a pattern emerging here?) but I already had another outlet to run alongside the *Chronicle*. A new magazine called *Due South* opened in early 1983 and somehow managed to keep going for the best part of a decade, mainly in conditions of total chaos and financial ruin which belied the fact that it was actually quite good. Everyone who ever worked for it, including me, ended up out of pocket, because they couldn't pay their bills, moving from one slum-like set of premises to the next. But I have fond memories of it.

Early on, I attended for *Due South* a couple of gigs by Annabel Lamb. This was a singer in whom A & M had invested a lot of money, and who had a minor hit with a version of "Riders On The Storm", going on to be, naturally, Big In Germany. She was married to a record producer called Wally Brill and was touched when we decided to call our first daughter after her. Well, not exactly after her, but she gave us the idea.

Due South, out of chance, not intent, was a hotbed for developing hot new journalistic talent. I had great respect for its unspellable editor, Sally O'Shaughnessy, for her dedication in the face of permanent catastrophe. One if its music editors was a small person by the name of John Aizlewood, who later moved to London to join a pop magazine called *Number One*. Soon he graduated to the new glossy magazine *Q*, which changed the face of rock journalism, and rose to a high position there. I, by contrast, merely received a letter of rejection when I wrote to *Q's* editor Mark Ellen in July 1987.

In November 1987, I set out to see a local band called Flik Spatula playing in a pub called the Dolphin, in the village of Botley, near Southampton. I had a "feeling" about them, and so took along my friend Paul Dominy, the ex-manager of The Time. On the way, I played him REM's "Murmur", which he was entranced by. Flik Spatula turned out to be a fantastic band, and as I wrote my review, I was frustrated by the thought that the band deserved a much wider audience than I could offer.

I thought of the *NME*. Naturally, I'd sent them stuff before, but to no avail. All I'd ever had in the *NME* were letters, of course complete with smart arse replies from the letters editor. One was about Udo Lindenberg (gratifyingly, the Great Man wrote a thank-you letter the following week) and the other one attacked a smug piece by David Quantick, who had said negative things about children at Glastonbury. But, just for the heck of it, I sent the Flik Spatula review to the *NME*. Amazingly, they printed it.

This turned out to be an exact replay of the *Sounds* incident five years earlier. The post of Reviews Editor was in the process of being changed over and some miscalculation had been made of how much space there was to fill. I had sent the review in under my *Due South* pseudonym of Gary Revilo, so they wouldn't associate my name with inferior music papers of the past. Wow! I thought, now I'm an *NME* journalist. Except that I wasn't. They never printed anything of mine ever again.

The *Chronicle* and *Due South* ticked over comfortably. Staff at *Due South* came and went, including, at different times, Adam Green and Richard Williams, who had both been in a Henry Beaufort school band called I Am Seven. Both of them went on to have sporadically successful musical careers. A regular music writer on the magazine was a large rugby player called Mark Sutherland. In time, he would go on to work at the *NME* and eventually to become editor of *Melody Maker*.

On the occasions when I met him, Sutherland was unfailingly unfriendly and uncommunicative. These traits seem to be essential qualifications for success in music journalism.

I think the motivation for all the years of unpaid writing I did for

Due South was a sentimental desire to support the local music scene. I couldn't bear the thought of Winchester never having a successful band, so whenever a likely one came along, such as Trip, I would support it. In early 1988, I decided the time had come to do a "Winchester Music Down The Ages" feature and was shocked to find that it ran to two whole pages. I received a delighted phone call from the landlady of the Willow Tree, the city's "alternative" pub:

"You'll never guess what," she said, "what with your article, we've sold double the number of copies of *Due South* that we normally sell!"

"That's fantastic," I replied. "How many copies exactly?"

"Well, we normally sell two copies but this month we've sold four."

At around the same time, I made a contact which would be very useful for the future. A Portsmouth indie label called "Bite Back" sent in a cassette to review by a band called the Psylons. I thought it was rotten, and I said so. Bite Back's boss Ian Binnington was enraged, looked up my phone number and rang me, berating me for several minutes. This has never happened to me before or since, and I was shocked. My attitude was that, if you submit something for review, you have to take the risk that it might get a negative response. Lord knows, I've had enough experience of being on the receiving end. Ian, however, considered that I was being unfair to the band.

This all had a happy ending. The lines of communication between us had now been opened and I discovered in Ian a fellow music obsessive. In Ian's partner, Claire Davies, I discovered a fellow enthusiastic language teacher. I have a massive amount of time and respect for both of them and, now that Ian has switched from running a record company to promoting live shows at a number of venues in the South, we have the simplest and most civilised of arrangements: I provide Claire with free language teaching materials, they provide me with free tickets to gigs. Good, eh?

From the early to the mid-eighties, I wrote a series of articles on language-related matters for the *Times Educational Supplement*. Because I was still teaching but also by now publishing language teaching materials myself, I wanted the freedom to make comments without being suspected of having a conflict of interests. For that reason, I invented yet another pseudonym, this time Gary Shawford, after a nearby village. These articles went down quite well, with the added advantage that I was able to overhear people saying what they thought of them, not realising I was the writer!

Another person who, like Ian Binnington, has an extraordinary talent for spotting the Next Big Thing is a gentle, quiet soul called David Burston, but known to everyone simply as "Mint". In 1991, he started promoting gigs at a down-at-heel pub called the Joiners Arms in the back streets of Southampton. He boldly called the promotions Next Big Thing, and over the next decade, he demonstrated his uncanny ability to book bands about to be worldwide stars, just at that vital moment before they got too big to play in this tiny pub. The current Joiners Arms promotional postcard lists a few of the bands which played there in the nineties:

Super Furry Animals, Space, Asian Dub Foundation, Sneaker Pimps, Mansun, Reef, PJ Harvey, Suede, Skunk Anansie, Catatonia, The Verve, Oasis, Manic Street Preachers, Radiohead ...

I can't claim to have been at all these gigs, but I've certainly been at a good chunk of them. For several years, Mint (who had, for a time, been music editor at *Due South*) also ran a good little Joiners house magazine called *Sound Info*, for which I was happy to write in return for free admission to Next Big Thing shows. I feel privileged to have experienced so much great music at such close quarters in such a warm, friendly atmosphere. In his own unassuming way, I consider Mint to be some kind of genius.

Since 1992 (bloody hell, this is beginning to sound like a curriculum vitae!) I have contributed reviews and features to a small circulation blues magazine called *Blueprint*. This isn't easy, because I know next to nothing about blues. I was put on to Blueprint by an enthusiast called Mick Meech, who ran a rustic blues bar called the Boar's Head, somewhere in the back lanes of Hampshire. He hoped to raise the profile of his venue by getting some of the shows reviewed in the magazine.

The first show I wrote about was a complete revelation to me. A white American blues guitarist called John Campbell, of whom I hadn't heard, completely blew me away with the gut-wrenching, voodoo-inspired power of his performance. It was almost as if he felt he didn't have long to live and wanted to express a lifetime's

The Joiners Arms, everybody's favourite front room.

emotion in one evening. It was quite shattering and opened my ears to a whole area of music which, while it can plumb quite awful depths of banality, can also be uniquely expressive. Within a year, poor John Campbell was, indeed, dead, but he showed me the possibilities of blues and I'm trying hard to learn. *Blueprint* has put up with me quite tolerantly, allowing me to write big features on my two favourite UK blues bands, The Producers and, more particularly, a brilliant blues-rock amalgam called The Hoax.

My final diversion was probably stupid, in that I thought I could change the unchangeable. I was aware that there was a listings magazine in Portsmouth called *Venue*. For a start, I couldn't understand how they got away with that name, considering that there was a considerably longer-established magazine in Bristol with the same title. On the odd occasion that I had read the Portsmouth *Venue*, I had been appalled. All the articles were badly written, badly-spelt paeans of praise to the kind of act I hate most: crummy hard rock bands playing bad cover versions in pubs. On no account would I ever consider writing for such a publication.

Then, in June 1996, I received a phone call from my old sparring partner Greg Watkins, the ex-pupil with whom I had had a disagreement following his failure to disown prog-rock. Greg, now living in Portsmouth, had actually bought the rights to *Venue* magazine and was now intent on both improving it and broadening its scope. Would I be interested in helping out? Depends, I said.

In the next post came a CD for me to review. By a band called Stone Cold, it was called (you'll have to believe this) *Harsh Parsnip*. I duly gave this offensive artifact the drubbing it richly deserved, and it was published, along with a disclaimer from the editor, dissociating the magazine from the content of the review. It was not an auspicious start.

I thought it was worth persevering, however, and in a way it was. For a couple of years, articles by Charlie Rowsell (another ludicrous pseudonym, provenance unimportant) stood alone in a sea of pub rock. Not that I'm claiming superior quality of writing, since Greg kept his promise and considerably improved the standard of literacy in the magazine. In employing me, he had also extended its scope, but *Venue's* essential character remained intact: a tribute to small-town musical mediocrity. Poor Greg. He made a real effort, but eventually he sold *Venue* and moved away. Now it's even worse than before he took it over.

Some time in 1996, I wrote, just for fun, a kind of mini version of this book. The theme was: mad old git can't rid himself of his enslavement to pop music. It wasn't written for publication, but nonetheless, I sent it to *Mojo* magazine. This wonderful publication, from the same stable as *Q*, was designed for music obsessives like myself. Although there was clearly no room in its format for the article (*Mojo* consists of learned and meticulously-researched articles about music and musicians), I thought the content of the piece might ring a few bells among the staff and at least give them a laugh.

I was sweeping up leaves in the garden when I got the call:

"It's Mat Snow."

"Who?"

"Mat Snow, editor of *Mojo*. We love your article and we want to publish it."

It turned out that there was room in their format after all, in the form of a last page feature called "Identity Crisis". I couldn't believe it. This was the greatest compliment I had ever received, or could ever receive. The pages of *Mojo* were more than I could ever have aspired to. And when it appeared, it was even better: full colour, not sub-edited, not a hint of a misprint. I instantly started getting phone calls from all over the country, and even a letter from Trevor, the excellently-smoothed sociology student from UEA (who turned out not to have been a sociology student at all). Now living in Maine, USA, he was a subscriber to *Mojo*.

In the afterglow of this success, I made the mistake of being over-eager. I had noticed that another contributor of an "Identity Crisis" page, called Dave di Martino, had started having articles regularly published in *Mojo*, and I hoped to do the same. My mistake was in being ignorant of the fact that, in contrast to me, Dave di Martino was a hot shot journalist in America.

I developed a few ideas which I wrongly thought were good ones and rang Jim Irvin, the deputy editor. He was consistent in rejecting everything I suggested. That was okay, but I wasn't so sure about the tone of voice at the end of the phone. It reminded me of all the sour-faced music journalists I had met over the years, in particular the disinterested creatures at the fateful Thieves Like Us gig at the

Moonlight Club, whom we shall meet in the next chapter. I could hear him thinking, okay, we'll put you in as a joke on the last page, but take you seriously? No chance.

And so it proved. *Mojo* had a page called "It's Your Round", in which contributions from readers were invited. There were prizes in the form of bottles of Jack Daniels for anything published, or a complete case of Jack Daniels for the "Lead Letter". I had one of each: Firstly the Sandy Denny "Fuck off" story, and then the story of how I fruitlessly attempted to woo Birgit with a Camel record, which, in print, received the "Best Letter" accolade. Of any Jack Daniels, however, there was not a sniff, and, despite phone calls, faxes, letters, e-mails and threats of "Watchdog", there has been not a sniff to this day. I call that deception, what do you call it? Never buy double glazing from a representative of EMAP Metro.

One story sums up just how widely read a magazine like *Mojo* can be. In order to understand it, you have to have read the article for which the alleged prize was (not) awarded:

It all happened such a long time ago that I hope they won't now come round and arrest me. So here's the fact: In 1973, I fell in love with one of my pupils. Well, here's nothing you can do about these things, they just happen. In the first lesson of the first day of my first teaching job, at a secondary school in Bremen, Germany, I was bowled over, never to recover.

Naturally, I fought the instinct fiercely. It was out of the question to pursue it. But resistance was futile. So, as we both used to catch the same tram into town after school, I devised a way in which I thought I could express my feelings. It being the height of the prog-rock era, I took to carrying under my arm a copy of the second album by the subsequently much-maligned but actually rather good Camel (whose echoes you can today hear in everybody from Grandaddy to Gorkys Zygotic Mynci). One epic track on this record is entitled "Lady Fantasy" and rejoices in the chorus, "Oh my laydee fantaseee, ah luuurve yew."

Feigning indifference, I asked whether the object of my desire would like to borrow said vinyl. Before handing it over, I had added a large felt-tip asterisk next to the vital title. Then I waited.

When handing it back, she made no comment. But the transaction paid off in that conversation had been broached. A relationship was formed which survived two clandestine years of illegality and, to date, has lasted for twenty-two years.

And the tattered album sleeve still bears the crucial ink-mark. Crucial, except that, when I subsequently asked about my sure-fire seduction record, she revealed that she had never even noticed it.

In the line of business, I had just negotiated selling a substantial amount of English language resources to a large comprehensive school in London. I was feeling quite smug about this, when I suddenly received an upsetting phone call from the Headmaster of that school:

"Is that Mr Gray? I'm afraid I'm calling to cancel my order."

"Oh dear, I'm sorry to hear that. What's the reason?"

"Well, I'm a subscriber to *Mojo* magazine and I've just read your piece. I'm sorry to say that I can't allow my school to be associated with such disgusting behaviour."

I went cold. How could this be coming back to haunt me after all these years?

"But ... but it was such a long time ago. Surely it isn't of any relevance today. We've been happily married for nearly twenty years."

"Yes, but I'm not talking about having an affair with a pupil. I'm just shocked at the thought that you're prepared to admit to owning a Camel album."

The rapid alteration of *Mojo* from being my favourite to my least favourite magazine (not really) had a stinging postscript. In mid 1997, I returned home one day to find a note from Birgit. It came as no surprise (her handwriting being terrible and her telephone technique unreliable) that it made absolutely no sense.

"Sylvia Sims rang about the levers," it read. "Please call her at home."

This was shocking. Sylvia Sims was a British film star of the Sixties. It was unlikely that she would want me to ring her, and certainly not at home. And, despite the fact that we were by now running a small business, we definitely didn't sell levers. I decided to dial the number.

"Is that Sylvia Sims?"

"Nearly. It's Sylvie Simmons."

Christ! Sylvie Simmons! This was one of the most respected music journalists in the world. She had run *Sounds'* US Bureau for years and had written for all the world's best music magazines. And I was talking to her.

"It's like this ..."

Sylvie explained that she had just taken over as reviews editor of *Mojo* and that she would like me to review the latest album by the Levellers. Apparently, Mat Snow had said that I would be the ideal person to do this. I was speechless. Why should this be? I'd once seen the Levellers busking in Winchester High Street, and Scott, from Flik Spatula, had played percussion with them, but I actually hadn't taken any interest in them at all. But of course, I breathlessly accepted the invitation. Sylvie's last words were, "Welcome aboard *Mojo*, Oliver. We're looking forward to working with you!"

The album was nothing special, but I did my best to pen a fair and objective review, keeping precisely to the suggested word limit. It was duly published, I received a cheque (it's still on the kitchen wall) and from then on, I was a *Mojo* journalist. Except that I wasn't. I never got another call from Sylvia Sims (to me, she'll forever be Sylvia Sims), and I have never again appeared in *Mojo*.

Never mind, because another adventure was just around the corner. As a change from taking the *Observer*, we started ordering the *Independent On Sunday*, in which I was startled to find something very much like the *Chronicle* Rock Column. Written by Nicholas Barber, it followed exactly the same format: reviews of two or three live acts per week. No other national paper had a column like that, so I wrote to Nicholas and complimented him on it. No ulterior motive was involved at all, so it was a genuine surprise to receive a call from Joanna de Lisle, the editor of the Culture section of the *IOS*.

"Nick Barber is moving house. He suggested you might like to do his column this week."

This was perfect, because I'd just fixed up to cover the Acoustic Stage for *Glastonbury Live!*, the free paper they give away to everyone attending the festival. It would be simple to double up. Of course I'd do it!

Only after doing the job did I realise that someone like Nick Barber has a far, far higher readership than any of my precious music press journalists. I got calls from all over the place, most notably from colleagues and friends not remotely interested in music. I was allowed to do the following week's column too, covering the Meltdown Festival and the Capital Radio "Party In The Park" (ahem). I took Lucy to that one and it was quite an experience. I got to stand behind David Frost in a queue, while Lucy shook hands with Prince Charles and got David Duchovny's autograph. The Truth was Out There. I then was allowed to do yet another week, in which I was able to take my friend Trevor, a huge Ian Dury fan, to see Ian and the Blockheads at Dingwalls in London.

I don't know why they never called me again. I was really proud of those three articles, but every time Nick Barber has been on holiday since, they have employed other staffers to sit in. Maybe my expenses (train to and from Winchester) were too high, maybe the couple of errors which a sub-editor inserted while I was dictating my copy on a mobile phone from Bournemouth beach were to blame; maybe they found out my age.

At any event, I would be prepared to give serious consideration to any enquiries the *Independent On Sunday* may make regarding the serialisation rights to this book.

X. Daylight Robbery

A surprising thing happened in 1978. I bought a house.

This certainly wasn't anything I had intended to do. House buying was something rare in Germany, and I was still in a German mindset. But we were finally being asked to leave the House Share From Hell, because the owners were returning from abroad. Not knowing what to do, I looked at some modern terraced houses which were being built at Badger Farm, just on the edge of Winchester. Today, it's a massive estate, complete with its own out-of-town superstore, but then it was just one half-built row in a mud bath of a building site. A smooth-talking lady in a Portacabin said that if I gave her £100, she would reserve one for me. Easy!

A town planner called Bill Blincoe had moved into the old house share when the nymphomaniac music teacher left. Bill and I got on great because he was a big fan of the Clash and the Buzzcocks, so he moved in to one of the three bedrooms. Birgit, now training in Basingstoke, moved in as well, and before long, 107 Maytree Close became the headquarters (and dormitory) for my band-managing operations.

It was during this time that Birgit and I were putting on the gigs at the Riverside. One day, I was slightly miffed to spot in the *Chronicle* an advert which said that a band called Thieves Like Us would be playing there on a Tuesday night. What must have happened was that they had seen it was being used as a venue, rung up the landlord and booked themselves in independently.

I would have gone along anyway, but they rang me up and invited me down. I presumed that they wanted a *Chronicle* review or an interview with Solent, but they actually had other plans. Thieves Like Us needed a manager.

It was not surprising that this band caught my imagination. I was in a state of musical schizophrenia, still listening to my Camel and Caravan albums while being entranced by punk bands like The Clash and The Damned and being really proud of local punk heroes The Ba. TLU were an amalgam of the two styles.

The bulk of their set consisted of hilarious cod-punk songs with titles like "Sex and Violence", "Rabid", "Repellent" and "Life Is A

Downer", played with enormous skill and at breakneck speed and with a uniquely flamboyant stage manner involving costume changes, masks and much shouting and charging around. But in between, there were a few slow, Genesis-style ballads such as "Mogadon", and there were even a couple of instrumentals. Crucially, even the two-minute punk thrashes always had an ear-catching keyboard riff of some kind. I thought this band was just wonderful.

Any sensible, experienced manager would immediately have spotted a fatal lack of defined direction and declined to become involved. But I was a stupid, inexperienced manager and thought that there must be masses of people like me who would welcome the kind of "punked up-Camel" crossover which the band skilfully represented. They were very good, and they were unique.

The original Thieves Like Us spot a stain on the Grays' living room ceiling.
L-R: Chris Stonor, Mark Meredith, Tim Barron, Tony Oxley, Paul Bringloe

They looked right, too. The singer, Tim Barron, was just in the process of joining the band, who had met him at a gig at UEA, where Tim had been studying, many years later than me. Tim was good-looking and tall, with an almost operatic voice and a cheerful willingness to carry out any daft theatrical ideas which came up. On bass was Mark Meredith, a heart-throb with a golden voice for backing vocals and a bass-playing skill which was acknowledged by all musicians to be second to none. These two were the easy ones, the reliable, unflappable bedrock which any band needs in order to survive.

The drummer was a youngster from Winchester called Paul Bringloe. He attracted attention from other drummers because he had such highly-developed technique. His role models were drummers like Bill Bruford and his style was extremely ornate, some would say flashy. I was impressed, particularly as this kind of drumming was a rarity in the punk era. He was also handsome, but oddly nervous. Paul was a well-known figure in Winchester and spent a lot of time round the pubs, drinking pints of bitter.

Tony Oxley couldn't have been more different. To look at him, you'd never have imagined that he was a conservative sort of chap with a public school background. His parents owned an antique bookshop in Alresford, and it was here that the band rehearsed. Tony's father had a Volvo Estate which was used to transport the band's equipment. Tony was as thin as a stick, had a perm and liked to dress up in skin-tight red PVC trousers, as he tossed off his lead guitar lines in a casual way that belied the speed and skill involved. Tony had a penchant for Jimi Hendrix which would emerge at frequent opportunities.

The other Volvo belonged to the family of the band's main songwriter, Chris Stonor. Chris had a little stack of keyboards including a Korg synthesiser which he sometimes wore round his neck for forays into the audience. Chris, too, was prone to dress up in day-glo outfits, normally involving teeth-grinding clashes of colour. He attracted attention because of his attacking style of playing. He looked completely "out of it", but wasn't, of course. Chris was mild-mannered and totally committed to the success of the band. His supportive mother was also a crucial element, bailing the band out of financial crises on a number of occasions.

I was flummoxed, on first meeting the band, by their "niceness". This was a rock & roll attitude which I hadn't come across before. I was also unnerved by the plummy public school accents which abounded, all the more peculiar because, in fact, only Tony and Chris had been to public school. My own awful schooling had led me to be a lifetime opponent of elitist education systems, so this was quite important. However, I also felt that a public school background hadn't hindered Genesis or Joe Strummer, and today it hasn't done Radiohead much harm either. So I decided to say yes when they asked me to be their manager.

The public-school joshing which went on between Tony and Chris could sometimes be hilarious, as was demonstrated in an early interview on Radio Solent:

Chris: Our approach is very theatrical. We have quite a few props, ranging from catapults and masks to a fly with detachable wings and legs.

Tony: Not to mention the make-up, of course, to cover up our spots.

Chris: And my synthesiser, my mini-Korg, I have a strap over it so I can do my Angus of AC/DC and go whizzing around the venue.

Tony: He's absolutely lethal on stage, my God!

Chris: And obviously, I've got lots of other ideas, like I always had this idea of learning the tightrope or being shot out of a cannon ...

Tony: You're far too fat!

On the face of it, managing Thieves was a piece of cake. As the live act was so strong, we all agreed that the band's policy should be to gig, gig, gig, in the hope of attracting attention and building up a following that way. They were in a uniquely strong position for a young band, in that they not only had transport but also a P.A. system, an unusual but quite effective Bose set-up which Tony had bought. It was light and easy to transport, also small enough to be set up almost anywhere. And it could be used for recording demo tracks.

I, also, was ideally positioned to get work for the band, in that each week I was ringing up all the venues in the South for the gig guide on Radio Solent. I don't think I abused my position exactly, but it was quite simple to throw in, "Oh, by the way, I know a really good band you might like to consider booking." Gigs started to roll in, but first there was the little matter of Jonx.

Jonx was Chris Stonor's elder brother, and he had so far been standing in as caretaker manager. He had a policy which, while being quite clever, I considered to be disastrous for a band trying to break into the mainstream. He was booking the band into public schools. The thinking behind this was that public schools had a captive audience and also had money. Therefore the gigs were always successful and always paid well. When Jonx came to hand over the paperwork to me, he was proudly clutching a sheaf of testimonials which he thought I would find useful. Some of them were almost beyond belief:

"I am not personally au fait with the world of this type of music, but from the people I spoke to who were there and who do know something about it, I understand that the group were, as well as entertaining, of a high musical calibre. It was thoroughly enjoyed by all the girls." Bet it was.

My favourite came from the headmistress of a school in Sussex:

"We found them most friendly and easy people to work with, people who understood how to entertain happily and sensibly some two hundred enthusiastic young girls. I am not competent to offer any comment upon their music, but numerous members of School and younger members of staff assure me they were very good."

Bless her! But I assured Jonx that this was not a policy I planned to continue, and I steadfastly refused to attend any of the small number of school gigs I inherited.

The first few months were a honeymoon time and my happiest period of working with the band. I set to work feverishly, trying to build up a regular and reasonably-paid circuit of gigs on the basis of the good local venues I knew. This worked a treat, because the band was always invited back for better money wherever they went. The Old Mill in Holbury became a regular haunt, as did the Pinecliff in Bournemouth and the minuscule Magnums Wine Bar in Basingstoke, where the band had to play to a brick wall.

We worked our socks off for the whole of 1979. Audiences loved the band because of their theatricality, venue managers loved them because they pulled in crowds and, although punky, were musically good enough to impress the most beard-tugging of critical musos. The Bose P.A. was clear and not offensively loud. For the first few gigs, ex-vocalist Gary Carter had the mixing desk out front, doing what we called then "mime mixing", and would now no doubt be called "virtual mixing", i.e. hovering above the knobs and looking authoritative without having the slightest idea what he was doing. From then on, Tony mostly mixed the sound from the stage, which almost always meant that his own guitar playing could hardly be heard, which frustrated me greatly. My job was to operate a small set of stage lights, which I did quite well when sober and less well when drunk, which was most evenings.

The lyrics weren't easy to discern, and perhaps that was just as well. Lyrics were never TLU's strong point. To get a flavour of the kind of thing Tim was singing, peruse the following examples:

"I don't want your nine to five,
I don't want your talking jive,
I don't want your Aristotle,
I wanna get lost in a bottle."
("Life Is A Downer".)

"Well your socks they're running away,
While the lice come out to play,
Yeah you pick your nose with your tongue,
As the sulphate collapses your lung."
("Repellent")

The - er - questionable nature of these words didn't matter much. Firstly, the lyrics were very much "of their time", and secondly, people were entranced by the stage act. The band would start up as a four-piece, with Tony singing Hendrix's "Can You See Me?", before Tim came bursting onto the stage, dressed as a naughty schoolboy, firing boiled sweets dangerously into the audience with a catapult and threatening all and sundry in a rowdy song called "Bully Boy". Then came a few uncostumed songs, including the rocking "Strike Out" and "Touch Your Love", a slow interlude with the unfortunately-titled but atmospheric "Mogadon", a pointless instrumental called "Samba" and the grand finale, "Murder In New York", in which Chris for some reason donned a horror mask and disappeared into the audience for a long and spectacular solo on his Korg.

Audiences were invariably gobsmacked by this performance, ten times better and more interesting than any pub rock they had encountered before. The gigs piled up and I inaugurated a policy of placing box adverts in the *NME* on a regular basis. The advertisement manager was a helpful guy called Brian B., who gave us a discount for bulk advertising. I invented spurious titles for tours, such as the "Nuts In May" tour and the "Loon In June" tour. This had the intended effect of raising the perceived importance of the band, and in return, the music papers listed all the shows in their gig guides and forthcoming tours sections. "I saw you in the

NME" would become a familiar phrase.

An entire book could be written just about that year's gigs, but here are a few highlights. The White Horse, Rogate, was a tiny pub in a village near Petersfield, where Paul Bringloe fancied the landlady. The first gig went excellently, but during the second, drummer Paul did something he would do ever more frequently: disappear off stage for a piss in the middle of the set. He had a weak bladder, to be sure, but he made things worse by calming his nerves with several pints of bitter before going on. At the third White Horse gig there was a tense atmosphere caused by the arrival of a gang of skinheads, and the fourth was a disaster because Tony had a romance problem. But that's another story.

Through Robyn Hitchcock, I got a prestigious show supporting The Soft Boys at Alex Wood Hall in Cambridge. This was a high-profile home-town gig for The Soft Boys, but more importantly, lots of industry people were present on account of the other band on the bill, Dolly Mixture, a trio of young girls being chased by the record companies. Paul was going out with a woman much older that him who was a member of the middle of the road Eurovision group Guys and Dolls. Somehow, she got talking to the ultra-cool Robyn Hitchcock, who operates in a different sphere of existence from the rest of humanity. I nearly died of embarrassment as I overheard her saying, "I do so hate drinking wine out of plastic glasses, don't you agree?"

Hitchcock's reply was not recorded, because onstage something awful was happening. Mid-set, drummer Paul disappeared through the back curtain in search of a toilet but, in the unfamiliar surroundings, he couldn't find one. The interlude lasted five minutes, as the band at first stood around looking embarrassed and then played an aimless drum-free instrumental. Not for the last time, an important gig had been blown.

At the Royal Oak, Passfield, someone in the crowd poured a pint of lager over Chris as he writhed on the floor during "Murder In New York". For a second, the unworthy thought entered my head that we might get some publicity if Chris, like Les Harvey, were to be electrocuted on stage, but on balance it felt as if it would be better if he remained alive. At the aptly-named Nowhere Club outside Bicester, the only people in the audience were two Scorpions fans who left after three numbers, and at the Plume in Hungerford, someone (it had to happen eventually) took exception to the spoof abuse meted out by Tim during "Bully Boy", stood up and nutted him on the nose. The trusty instrumental swung into action as Birgit administered first aid in the kitchen. The offending punter was shown the door and Tim completed the show with a handkerchief clutched to his highly swollen nose. But, beggaring belief, both these latter venues requested return bookings. We declined.

The most important thing to do was get gigs in London so that record company scouts could see the band in action. Unfortunately, the main London venues such as the Nashville and the Hope and Anchor were in the stranglehold of the Albion agency. No amount of phone calls to its boss Dan Silver would persuade him to try us out. It was rumoured that these venues operated a "pay to play" policy, but I couldn't possibly comment. At any rate, you had to know the right people in the industry, and we didn't.

Our break came courtesy of the Lesser Known Tunisians, who owed me a favour after I wrote a review of them in *Sounds*. They introduced me to Bob Keene, a small-time London agent who ran two venues, the Swan in Hammersmith and the Windsor Castle in Harrow Road. The Swan was the "try out" gig and the Windsor Castle the real one, although we always found the Swan better. He offered us a "try out" and we mobilised every fan we could think of. Since the Swan was packed, we were at last into some sort of regular London work.

The dressing room at the Swan was upstairs, so Tim's "Bully Boy" grand entrance was even more spectacular as he bounded down the staircase. The method of payment at the Swan was a convoluted percentage of the bar takings, worked out by the landlord on the back of a beer mat. I was always too drunk to comprehend, but Birgit kept her beady eye on the situation, and we always came away with a good wad of cash. My personal contribution to this success was to lay a trail of tantalising posters leading from the exit of the nearby Hammersmith Odeon, through the subway and all the way to the Swan. In this way, at about ten thirty, the place would get packed with concert goers who emerged from the Odeon, desperate for a drink. Birgit was also in charge of selling badges, a job which, being so pretty and approachable, she performed with great success. My job was to stick stickers on people. In theory, people might have taken exception to this, but in practice they never did.

The Windsor Castle, by contrast, despite having a higher profile, was a dive, normally full of disinterested and mildly aggressive drunks. It also paid well, however, on the basis of door money. As it had a late licence, we worked out a good strategy whereby, if the band played early enough, they could be offstage by the time the late-night boozers arrived from the other local pubs, and yet still profit from their entrance fees. It was the only venue where it was actually better to support than to headline.

College gigs in London were less successful. One at the South Bank Poly was booked by a student who had seen the band in Bournemouth. However, she had over-estimated the band's pulling power in London and there was practically no one in the large hall. She was embarrassed and expressed this by being unfriendly.

Worse still was the London School of Economics. As we arrived, the snobby social secretary immediately came up to me and demanded, "Let's get this sexist song weeded out." He had heard that part of the act entailed Tim leafing though a copy of *Playboy*. In a variation on the "Pictures Of Lily" idea, the song was called "Get Down And Love Me", and it was obvious to any cretin that it was intended ironically. Not to this cretin, though. To make life easy, we agreed not to play the song, but once again there were few people there and at the end of the evening they refused to pay, claiming that Paul Bringloe had knocked over a can of heating oil in the "dressing room". Although he denied it, I suspected he probably had, but my tail was up and I wasn't having this treatment. A hilarious exchange of solicitors' letters followed:

"We would point out that the Contract specified that the Students' Union would provide dressing room facilities for the Group, and it can hardly be said that a boiler room full of oil cans qualifies as such. Furthermore, we understand that the boiler room which was provided as a so-called dressing room gave on to a corridor which was much used by persons unknown to our clients and that furthermore, members of the Students' Union and other persons freely used the boiler room to talk to the Group and so on, so that there is absolutely no evidence that our clients were responsible for the spillage which you allege, and furthermore, our clients strenuously deny any such charge..." (etc., etc., ad infinitum).

All the while, we were searching for a record deal. The band was undoubtedly good enough, but I now realise we went about it in entirely the wrong way, sending out a demo tape designed to demonstrate their versatility. Versatility is the last thing record companies are looking for; they want a "direction". But, as it happened, negotiations were already under way when I met the band.

By a coincidence so strange that I interpreted it (wrongly) as a "sign", the band was already talking to a record company three doors down from us at Badger Farm. Well, the record company, Ember, was based in Brighton, where Chris Stonor had approached them, but Ember's scout lived in Winchester. His name was Chris Denning.

Now anyone who, like me, had kept a close eye on the music business for a number of years, would know about Chris Denning. He was one of the original Radio One DJs, and a very good one at that. If you remember the famous photo of the Radio One DJs outside Broadcasting House, you could probably say what became of most of them. Some, like Mike Raven and Kenny Everett, are dead, some are on other radio stations, and one, John Peel, is still with Radio One. But Chris Denning just disappeared.

So what was a big shot DJ doing living in a tiny house on an obscure estate in Winchester? I knew what had happened. He had been sacked from Radio One because of an indiscreet remark he had made on air: "This morning I woke up feeling like a sixteen-year-old boy. But where do you find a sixteen-year-old boy?" His alleged keen interest in male youngsters had led to his being disgraced. Certainly, a stream of young lads, some of them pupils at my school, frequented Chris's house. Should I say something, I sometimes wondered? But nobody ever complained or seemed less than cheerful, so I decided to be a good neighbour and avoid making possibly false judgements.

In the interim, Chris had worked with the likes of Gary Glitter (gulp) at Bell Records (remember that name) and now worked in A & R for Ember while also running his own printing business in Winchester. Chris was a very kind and friendly neighbour. His passion was cats, of which he had a smelly houseful on account of the sexual appetite of his un-neutered black and white tom. This creature twice impregnated our female cat Harry and she had two litters of lovely kittens. Chris helped us to rear them when Harry was run over just after having had the second litter.

Chris Denning had a plan for Thieves Like Us, but it was not a good one. Ember had what they laughably considered was a good song with which to jump onto the punk bandwagon, and they were looking for a band to record it. Ever eager to please, Thieves had made a demo of it in Tony's shop. The song, called "I'm Dead", wasn't exactly promising:

I'm dead, I'm dead,
Bored out of my head,
I find that I'm
Bored out of my mind.

Of course, what was needed was a sneering, Johnny Rotten style vocalist for these gripping lyrics, but Tim's dulcet tones sounded completely un-threatening as well as completely un-bored. Any other record company would have sent a curt rejection or simply not written at all. To demonstrate just what a fine chap Chris Denning was, here is what he wrote:

"A problem arose in that I originally found Thieves Like Us when I was looking for a band to record a one-off single and, although their demo of the song is more than competent, two thoughts kept haunting me. Firstly, the song I wanted to record required a basically moronic approach and I think Thieves Like Us are, both intellectually and musically, a little too intelligent to get the right feel and image across. Secondly, I felt that the group would really be at their best if given a chance to develop as an album-orientated act, recording their own material. Having been unable to find support for this within the company, I must reluctantly opt out of any further discussions with the band."

To be rejected for not being moronic enough was a backhanded sort of compliment, but a rejection it was, nonetheless. As were the letters we received from all the other record companies we approached. In those days, record companies actually wrote polite (if patronising) letters of rejection rather than just ignoring you:

Arista: *"After a careful evaluation, I am sorry to say that I do not hear the commercial potential so necessary to effectively launch a new artist's career."*

Jet: *"Although enjoying the stage act tremendously, I feel that the material is not directly commercial enough to consider the band for Jet Records."*

Warner Brothers: *"While there is some merit in the work, we feel it does* *not meet the needs and requirements of Warner Bros Records."*

A & M: "After listening, I don't feel strongly enough about the group to express any interest at this time."

Polydor: "Although the time and effort spent on this project are greatly appreciated, we do not hear the commercial potential so necessary for launching a new band's career." (Do you think he used to work for Arista?)

Criminal: "Thank you for sending us your tape, but on this occasion we feel we must pass."

Phonogram: "Unfortunately, after careful consideration by the A & R Committee, it was decided that the material was not viable for us and therefore I am sorry to say that we pass."

Ariola: "After careful consideration, I have to advise that we do not feel the material is suitable for Ariola at the present time."

Only one company sent us a duplicated rejection slip. It was RCA (boo). So, in the fine tradition of then and ever since, it was time to do our own Indie Single.

For this, it was over to Jonx, who was providing the finance in the vain hope that the record would make a profit. Only the best for Jonx, who booked the band into Surrey Sound, the very studio where the first two Police albums were recorded, and with the same producer, Nigel Gray. God knows what it must have cost him, but inevitably, there wasn't enough money to complete the job and we ended up putting out a record on which only the title track had been mixed down, and even that in a cursory way. The quality of the record was terrible, although not from a performance point of view.

The title track was a committee decision, taken because nobody could agree which song to do. "Do It" was a collection of different tunes and time signatures which appeared to have been thrown together haphazardly. As a choice for a single it was absolutely the wrong song, but I didn't feel qualified to argue against it. The lyrical drift was "don't get stuck in a dead end job" and it started:

I'm pedalling along unending roads to work,
I try to be late,
Rank on rank of faceless men,
I hate them but then again they're my mates.

Pardon? It was that old lyrics problem again. Track 2 was "Touch Your Love", a "new-wavish" song which would have been my choice for lead track, plus "Murder In New York", for people buying at gigs who wanted a souvenir of a stage favourite.

Never mind that the recording was obviously inadequate, there was also an amazing palaver with the sleeve. Rather than employ someone who had experience in making record sleeves, a printing firm was chosen which used a quite unnecessary laminating procedure, managed to put the hole in the wrong side of the sleeve so that the record kept falling out, and also used too much glue, so that a good percentage of singles had sticky blobs of glue all over them, rendering them unplayable. Apart from that, everything was great.

In actual fact, many benefits flowed from this record. Because most people had heard of the band, we managed to get a couple of

The first single, complete with trick sleeve and free added glue.

distributors to buy quite a lot of stock to be sent out to indie record stores, plus masses were sold at gigs. There are a few still in the shed today, but eventually, we sold the bulk of the 5000 pressed. But, far more importantly, what would the industry think?

The reaction, as it was to everything that TLU did, was mixed, but we couldn't possibly have got off to a worse start. With entirely well-meaning intent, I sent an advance copy to Gethyn Jones, to be played on his Saturday morning show, which had a New Release section with a panel of local critics. Obviously, I requested that he shouldn't mention that I had a connection with the station. As we tuned in with bated breath, this is what we heard:

John Thompson: *I don't like this. I think it's an attempt to be a bit clever musically and electronically. It just hasn't come off, if you'll pardon the expression. I don't think very much of that at all and it certainly won't see the light of day.*

Pete Cross: *I think that's the worst we've played today. This is really too bad to make it. There's nothing going for it at all.*

Frantic Fran: *I thought it was rubbish. Come from Winchester? They should stay there. Being released next week? I don't know why, 'cos it's a waste of time. Thieves and who are they called? Rubbish! It'll never do nothing.*

(Voted a unanimous "miss".)

Luckily, a more cheerful response was just around the corner, as a journalist called Simon Tebbutt made the record "Single Of The Week" in *Record Mirror.* Such recognition in the national music press was all we had dreamed: "Tempering raw, brash energy with a deep respect for melody and musical dexterity, they exude an irresistible and enigmatic quality." Blimey! Couldn't have put it better myself, although, purely objectively, not even I would have claimed it was worthy of Single Of The Week.

It couldn't last, of course. The local press were very kind, keen for a star act to emerge from their neck of the woods. " 'Do It' will be listened to and appreciated for the excellent song it is," said Steve Keenan in the *Evening Echo,* while Graham Garnett in the *Basingstoke Gazette* rather oddly called the band "stimulating and tongue-tingling through your electronic voice box in the living room". In the *Bournemouth Bugle,* Barry Lane, a cheerful bloke who adored the band, noted that the single had "more hooks than a fisherman's tackle box". Yes, Barry, that's the problem.

Not all the national papers were beastly, and we were thrilled when Chris Difford from Squeeze, a songwriter we all liked, called it "good and eventful" in *Smash Hits*. In *Superpop*, a readers' panel declared, "I can't believe anything as awful as this has made it to the studio", and Sandy Robertson of *Sounds*, of whom we had had high hopes, talked of "much sincerity and thrashing to no purpose". The *NME* ignored the single completely, and John Peel played it once, without commenting. That meant he didn't like it.

It was becoming clear that the band was polarising opinion. You either loved them or hated them. An example of how essentially the same performance could be interpreted in two completely different ways can be seen in the contrasting reactions to the live show of two different reviewers. A character called RAB saw the band for *Sounds* at Crockers in Bristol, while Simon Tebbutt of *Record Mirror* attended a show at, guess where, the Windsor Castle:

Record Mirror: *They are as intriguing to watch as they are exciting to listen to.*

Sounds: It's the same old shallow thrash they've been hawking round the country for nine months.

Record Mirror: *They provide something completely different, incorporating wit, entertainment and drama in a first class set.*

Sounds: When it gets caught up in the singer's ham acting and the shallow, easy shot lyrics, not to mention the cheapo cheapo props, the whole exercise becomes nigh on unbearable.

Record Mirror: *The songs are powerful and compelling, abrasive new wave energy and strong melodies. "Do It" is the most notable.*

Sounds: A more shapeless, forgettable meander than "Do It" I have yet to bump into.

Record Mirror: *They're not some cheap cabaret act. They've got intelligence and artistry and what's more, they aren't afraid to use it.*

Sounds: The music is grab bag rock. They can play two bars of just about anything.

So you paid your money and you took your choice. Let's just say that all the best bands cause differences of opinion.

Meanwhile, trouble was brewing in the ranks. Paul Bringloe was continuing to be unreliable and there was an unpleasant incident after a gig we did as a favour to some guys who used to run a pub called the Fighting Cocks in Winchester. They had taken over a country hotel near Petersfield and wanted the band to play for a party. Against my wishes (it seemed a pointless gig), they rehearsed a set of covers and played the gig. Paul then got uncontrollably drunk and on the way home was yelling obscene abuse at passers-by out of the car window. Not long after that, he was attacked by someone in the street one evening in Winchester. He valiantly played on with his broken jaw wired up, and even got a mention in *NME*, but it was somehow symptomatic. Paul was the kind of guy people liked to hit.

By August, for a whole variety of reasons, Paul had left the band, but finding a replacement was easy. From a huge list of applicants (maybe reflecting the minor "buzz" that was around), it was obvious that John Parish was the drummer we needed. Only nineteen, John was intelligent, keen, serious-minded, reliable and, above all, not a show-off. He was keen on the band and we knew immediately that we wanted him.

After a few weeks of rehearsal, the band was interviewed for a lengthy feature in *Musicians Only*, written by Richard Newton. To my surprise, he started off the article with something which had never crossed my mind:

"It seems to be a growing habit for bands to enjoy an amazingly casual relationship with their management. Take Winchester band Thieves Like Us, for instance. Their manager is a reasonable chap called Oliver Gray. He fulfils his function admirably, after all, the band are playing an average of fifteen gigs a month. But ask what percentage he's on, or even if there's a signed management contract, and he'll merely reply that they don't work like that. They prefer a more relaxed set-up. It certainly seemed relaxed. When I arrived to interview the band at Oliver's abode, he was still in bed. One or two Thieves were sunning themselves in his lounge, drinking his coffee and nicking his fruit (presumably living up to their name)."

Gosh! But it went on to be a well-written analysis of our situation. Having made a point of mentioning the public school connection (huh!), Newton went to the heart of things:

"Comparisons are difficult because every song seems to shoot off at a

tangent. It is this lack of continuity which is their main weakness. They seem to be exploring various avenues but are reluctant to make a decision about which to pursue. Perhaps this is why that magic recording contract remains just beyond their grasp." Yes, well.

None of this seemed to matter too much, because, in November, Tony Oxley left the band. There isn't too much to say about this, because it was very simple: His girlfriend made him leave. Now, Tony says he deeply regrets what happened, but we all know how it is when you're in love. The girl in question, a highly possessive person called Vanessa, who worked as a waitress in a Winchester Burger Bar called Alice's Restaurant, simply said, "It's the band or me", and Tony had no choice. He did, however, give notice. The tense last few gigs, during which Vanessa would insist that Tony stayed outside in the car with her except when physically required to be on stage, culminated in an emotional farewell at the Swan, Hammersmith. The relationship didn't last and it was years before Tony would look me in the eye again, because his departure meant the beginning of the end of the band.

But before that, there were lots more traumas to be experienced. In went the advert to the *Melody Maker*, back came a stream of applications, and into the St. John's Rooms in Winchester we went to audition a select few. There were instant thumbs-downs for Norman from Potters Bar, who had a long beard and shoulder-length hair, and for a member of another South Coast new wave band, who arrived in a state of cocaine-induced confusion and was incapable of playing.

The job went to Barry Mizen. He was by far the best choice from the available options, because he was a good, individual-sounding player, he had experience and he looked great: feather-cut hair, tight trousers and, like the rest of the band, not averse to a spot of make-up. The band said yes, but there was something about him which I found untrustworthy. Also, I knew that his background in Cockney R & B bands meant that he wouldn't fit in socially. This was a fact rather than a value judgement. I was all for placing another advert, but I was out-voted. Things were urgent because (cue celestial choir) we had got our record deal.

I still think it's a great story. In August, we were doing a run-of-the-mill show at (guess where?) the Windsor Castle. It had been a very trying gig because a couple of drunks, in an attempt to provoke me, had been fiddling with my lighting board all evening. I was therefore in no mood for what I assumed was a tramp, when an old bloke in a brown raincoat came over to me and started talking in what I thought was a spoof American accent. He was the president of a record company, he said, and he was interested in signing the band. Yeah, sure. I thought if I ignored him, he would go away. After a while, he pressed a business card into my hand and told me to ring him if I was interested.

It wasn't until we were packing up that I thought to look at the card. What I saw was quite a shock: Private Stock Records, New York. Private Stock was a name I recognised from conversations with Chris Denning. After quitting Bell Records (yes, Bay City Rollers, Gary Glitter et al), Private Stock was the label that boss Larry Uttal had set up in its wake. And what was more, it was the label which had discovered Blondie. I made a mental note to quiz Chris Denning about it the following day.

In fact, Larry rang me at 9 o'clock the next morning. He definitely wanted to open negotiations with the band, he said. When could he come and see them again? I suggested a forthcoming gig at Salisbury City Hall. In the meantime, I consulted Chris Denning, who was equivocal. On the one hand, he said, we'd be unlikely to get a good deal; Larry would drive a hard bargain. On the other hand, as his track record demonstrated, he was damn good. Chris counselled that we should be careful, take good advice, but certainly not reject Larry's advances out of hand.

Larry took the train down to Salisbury shortly before Tony left the band. Unfortunately, I had chosen an awful gig to invite him to. For a start, Vanessa virtually held us to ransom over Tony, refusing to let him play. We spent much of the day chasing the pair of them round the lanes of Hampshire. A local promoter had hired the cavernous City Hall and of course there were only about twenty people there, one of them a stoned punk who lay in the middle of the floor and slept throughout the performance. Larry's enthusiasm was un-dampened, however, and he had a point. If the band could put in a good performance in such circumstances (which they did), they could obviously handle any adversity. Me, I had to handle some adversity that very night, because of course the promoter couldn't pay us. We had a contract and, more to the point, an obligation to pay the cost of the large P.A. we had hired in an attempt to fill the big hall. Frantic negotiations took place in a dark alley at the back of the hall as the hapless promoter emptied his pockets of every penny he had. Things, I hoped, could only get better.

Just for a brief while, they did. Larry wooed the band, sometimes ringing me up several times a day. We hired a lawyer who claimed to understand music business contracts (he didn't) and eventually, in Larry's suite in central London, the contract was signed. I remember the day because my car broke down in Twickenham and Larry was offended because we were late. For some reason, he had prepared some scrambled eggs and was upset that they were spoilt.

The contract was no use to us, we very soon found out, because the percentage to the band was far too low, and because it obligated Larry to do nothing at all other then to make recordings and then promote them. But TLU were a live band, and, what was more, a live band without a P.A. or transport, now that Tony had left. Chris found a solution to the problem of transporting the gear by buying an ancient left-hand drive German post van. Luckily, I had found the perfect P.A. company in the form of One-Two P.A. Hire, run from Bournemouth by a languid Welshman called Tommy Winstone. Tommy had worked with the Freshly Layed Band and its various offshoots, and was the best sound engineer any of us had

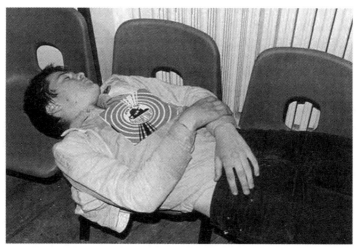

He shouldn't have sniffed the sleeve. Salisbury City Hall, 23.11.79.

encountered. He was also a mine of salacious stories about his past, which I won't dwell on, on account of the fact that he is now married to a barrister. He took a liking to TLU, but he cost money.

It is unfair to be completely negative about what Larry Uttal did for the band. Everything about the single (well, everything apart from the sleeve) was superb. The band was whisked into a smart London studio called Marcus Music and recorded with a young engineer called Mark Wallace, who created a very bright, sparkling production of a perfect song for the job, "Mind Made".

This song, with its chugging pace, its ear-catching but not embarrassing lyrics, its strong chorus and false ending, was a true high point of the band's career. In its way, it is a minor classic, in that it wasn't just "of its time", it still sounds good today. This song was representative of the new maturity that John Parish had introduced to the band. Many miles from being "just the drummer", John was immediately influential in all areas of TLU, notably the songwriting. By the time the record deal was signed, the live set had some marvellous new songs, such as the crazy echo-fest of "Trampoline" and the almost-funky "Golden Handshake". John had a strong influence on all these, and a whole lot more too.

When Larry visited the recording session, he caused some consternation by questioning some of the lyrics:

"Guys, I'm not sure about the Pig Farm."

"The Pig Farm?"

"The line which goes 'She's got a pig farm'."

"No, Larry, the line is 'She's got opaque form'."

"Oh? Well, I still don't like it."

I believe that, if things had gone right at that stage, Thieves Like Us could have made the transition into being a "serious" band. This was, rightly in my opinion, the direction that John wanted to take them in, and Tim and Mark were in agreement. Chris, I think, saw John as a threat, likely to take his band and change its character. And the audience, well, the audience wanted the band to stay as it had been, complete with "Bully Boy" and "Murder In New York". So all that happened was that the live set became an even more incongruous set of inappropriate contrasts than it had been before.

Barry Mizen, like Larry Uttal, was a double-edged sword. Although his brief spell with the band was a disaster, his playing was crucial to the quality of the single. The guitar figure he played characterised the whole of the A-side, while his solo on the B-side, "Strike Out" is brilliant, a model of brevity, taste and attack. But that was about it. As we continued gigging, Barry turned out to be hopelessly unreliable. In fact, he missed more gigs than he actually played. When he did play, as at the opening gig at John Parish's alma mater, Yeovil Technical College, he looked and sounded great. But, more often then not, he subjected the band to the humiliation of having to play as a four-piece with Tim on guitar.

The end of this brief and unhappy spell came with a horrible, horrible evening at Kings College Hospital in London. This was by far the most violent gig the band ever did. Extraordinarily, considering that it really was a hospital, there seemed to be some kind of gang warfare going on. Whatever else the audience wanted, it certainly wasn't Thieves Like Us. From my position on the balcony, wielding a spotlight, I could look down on the vicious brawl taking place below. Our poor London P.A. man, hired because Tommy was unavailable, was hauled from his mixing desk and beaten up.

As I made my weary way backstage, the first thing I saw was Barry and some other band members, gathered interestedly round some chopped-out lines of coke on a mirror. I immediately assumed that Barry must have been responsible for the introduction of this new pastime.

"What the fuck are you doing?"

"Mind your own business, you public school creep."

No words could have provoked me more.

"It is my fucking business. I'm not going to let you destroy my band!"

He wanted to hit me. I almost hoped he would, because Barry is the only person in my life that I would have really been keen to hit back. But we were both restrained and that was that. Appropriately, the corridor to the exit was literally flowing with blood. Barry was out, and so, I decided, must I soon be. At this stage, I was managing the band, writing for the *Chronicle*, writing for *Musicians Only*, doing the Solent gig guide, organising school exchanges and holding down a full-time teaching job. Something had to give.

Chris Stonor: "Who threw that lager?" *Tim Barron: "Oy you, yeah, you!"*

John Parish: "How do you spell Dlamini?"

Craig Whipsnade: Should he have joined Blue Zoo?

Mark Meredith: "Uh-oh, Boy's Own Rock."

Tommy Winstone: "The water pump's fucked."

By the time the single was launched, we had a new guitar player, recruited by the trusty *MM* advert. Norman from Potters Bar applied again, but we didn't call him for audition. Instead, we did this time find the perfect person in the form of Craig Whipsnade. This was the ear-catching stage name of David Hubbard, a tiny, thin man who played the right style of guitar, wrote good songs and had contacts in the business. Craig had previously been in Screeens, a band we had supported in Salisbury. He had even had a Christmas solo single out, called "It Looks Like Rain, Dear" under the name The Antlers. What more could we want?

This was a strange period indeed. Craig was joining a band whose single was about to be released although he hadn't played on it. Indeed, Craig's second gig was the Grand Single Launch, held at the Tower Arts Centre in Winchester. As Larry was unwilling to help in any way (he didn't even attend the show), poor Mrs Stonor had to stump up for the food and drink. The show was great, but I felt out of my depth. Larry had hired a new press agent called Howard Harding, who was next to useless. I couldn't believe how little press coverage a paid agent gained compared to what I had managed, unpaid, with the previous single.

One thing Howard did do was persuade a trendy journalist from The Face called Neil Norman to follow the band around for a while and document it, in theory, for the *Observer* magazine. We doubted whether this would ever come to anything, and indeed it didn't. It did, however, encourage me to keep a diary of events and send it to him. Here, then, is the diary that Neil Norman never used, starting with a reference to a dire and misconceived "showcase" gig supporting Doll By Doll at the Moonlight Club in West Hampstead.

"Dear Neil,

We last saw you on Monday, the night of the Moonlight gig. As you know, Chris's van with the equipment in it broke down on the way to London, and we only just managed to get there. Actually, his exhaust pipe had also fallen off, but we decided not to tell him that, as he has been getting so depressed about the van.

Doll By Doll did a ninety-minute "sound check" (actually a rehearsal), which left us with five minutes in front of an incoming audience and only a few square inches of stage space. Still, the omens didn't seem bad. It was fairly full and we'd worked with the sound people before, though it turned out they knew who they were working for tonight. Things which were totally impossible for us, such as a bit of echo on the vocals and putting the drums through the foldback, magically appeared during Doll By Doll's set. But we know all about the support band blues, and the band played superbly, not putting a note wrong and getting quite healthy applause from an audience consisting entirely of press and business people, plus fans in Doll By Doll T-shirts (who later didn't even ask Doll By Doll for an encore).

Anyway, the band came off feeling really happy and were instantly thrown into depression by people such as Howard Harding and yourself coming up and saying, "You weren't as good as on such and such an occasion". Nobody has yet put a finger on why the general reaction wasn't very positive, so we'll just have to call it "one of those things". As we left the gig, the van packed up completely a mile down the road. It was totally knackered, so we eventually left Craig and Chris to sort it out. For them, this entailed getting the AA, who couldn't do anything, getting two hours' sleep in the van, finally being towed to a ripoff garage and hiring another van, thus incurring huge bills which none of us has the wherewithal to pay. On Tuesday, I'm going to have another go at getting some money out of Larry (which will no doubt be as unsuccessful as other attempts.)

Meanwhile, John and I got to Winchester at 4.30 am, and I was up at seven to go to school, not in the best of moods (it's exam season). At break, I gave Larry a call and was very nearly rude to him when he stated that the band had played badly and would have to try harder (!), which I thought was pretty clever of him, considering he hadn't been there. It turned out that Dan Silver of MAM didn't like the band. Well, he's never liked them right from the days when he was with Albion, and if I'd known Larry was going to invite him, I'd have told him not to bother. We had a slightly strained conversation.

Wednesday at the Greyhound and it looked like nightmare time was approaching again. Through a series of misfortunes too boring to relate, we had to support an unknown band but still use our hired P.A. Inevitably, Tommy broke down somewhere near Southampton, so no P.A. materialised. (Tommy rang to say "The water pump is fucked!") There was a prevailing mood of "blow it out", which really got my blood up, as it's so bloody difficult to get these gigs in the first place. I said we were going to do the gig even if it was acoustic! It turned out there was a house P.A of sorts, normally used for the disco, and the manager was really helpful, conjuring up some mikes and stands from a friend down the road, so the show went on. Thieves always rise to a challenge, and really won over the smallish audience to the extent of a real encore. So strange: This time the reaction from the business people was very enthusiastic, despite several mistakes and an appalling sound. PAN agency now seem interested, as are Bron. Brian Harrigan was impressed and will, I think, give us a good write up. Howard Harding was happy again. I don't think he liked being surrounded by hundreds of rather uninterested Record Mirror staff at the Moonlight.

Thursday was newspaper day, and we were all amused to see Record Mirror call it a lightweight pop song, while New Music News called it heavy and doom-laden. My pal on the Evening Echo did us proud with a huge piece and an interview with John, including this gem: "Having Neil Norman in the dressing room is a bit strange"! The Brighton Evening Argus reveals that "Brighton-born Chris Stonor is set to follow in the wake of David Cassidy and Gary Glitter"! We never did have much credibility, but that's ridiculous!

Distinctly unglittering were Friday's and Saturday's gigs. On Friday, we depped for The Limos at Southampton Rugby Club. This was an all-ticket affair in something resembling a scout hut, but sadly not many people had wanted to see the Limos. They were rather over-awed when we appeared, having all read the Echo and thinking we were superstars. Some of them zoomed round various pubs telling people TLU were at the Rugby Club, but nobody believed them! Saturday was at Bognor Regis College, again a last-minute thing organised too late for me to send them any publicity. Now this is a teacher training college and Saturday was the second day of half term, which hadn't struck the social secretary as a disadvantage. Naturally, anyone with any sense had hightailed it out of Bognor the day before. However, despite small audiences, both gigs were very good, double encore jobs, and the band has a zappy new short set for maximum impact. The week was ironically quite good for pulling everyone together. Craig is now really part of the band (he stamped TLU on his guitar case on Saturday), and we work very well with Andy and Tommy (P.A.Hire). They are really involved now, and not only because their fee is always 90 percent of the gig money.

During my half term, I spent a few days in London acquiring a distinct distaste for the business side of things. For this reason, I have been encouraging the band to get involved with a management company which is interested in them. They have a sort of sentimental attitude that I should stay as manager, but I think they are now aware that I don't have the experience or desire to get involved in the business and couldn't possibly *do justice to them. Also, Larry wants to work with an established company, although he's going to get a shock when people start to stand up to him! Anyway, back to the diary:*

June 3,4,5: *The whole band was doing session work in Southampton in order to pay a few of the debts ...*

6th: *Windsor Castle. A good gig. Larry came and his faith was reaffirmed despite the venue being less than pleasant to be in. The promised journalists did not appear.*

7th: *We spent the day in London, sorting out the details of the journey to Bremen. This is the sort of thing a management company would sort out. Details too boring to relate. The Swan in the evening was a goodie as usual. The TV people were there working out their cues and tactics. The promised journalists did not appear.*

8th: *A lovely little gig in Southampton overcomes P.A. problems and is a big success, showing that local support hasn't waned.*

9, 10, 11: *By all accounts, the trip went well. The arrangements worked, the TV show went down a storm (3 encores). It's been sold to several companies in various countries already. I missed the next three gigs, being on a school trip, so will relate reports.*

15th: *A big disappointment. Returning to their favourite venue (the Pinecliff in Bournemouth), they found that noise problems have made its future dodgy. They are too loud and the management is very annoyed (i.e. "Don't come back!")*

18th: *I thought this one was likely to be a repeat of the Moonlight fiasco, supporting Supercharge at the Venue. But no, the band went down excellently. The promised journalists did not appear, but PAN agency did, and said they have decided to sign the band.*

A major problem is going to be the following: PAN have several acts going out in the Autumn for which TLU would be a good support, but it is now standard practice for large sums of money to change hands in order to secure support slots. Larry has laid it on the line that he will not put up money for anything other than the record side of things, and isn't interested in live performance at all. And we certainly haven't got any money.

21st: *Goodbye to another old favourite gig, the Cellar Vino in Weymouth. Now that the band is so scattered and we have to hire a P.A., we lose on all these small gigs. Tim's props case was stolen at this gig, causing him much* *fury, but giving me a chance to zap out a press release.*

28th: *Gig at the John Peel, Gosport, almost had to be called off when the P.A. people broke down, but I managed to get hold of a substitute at the last minute. A potential disaster turned into a minor triumph.*

30th: *Keep quiet about this one. I sweated blood to get this gig (supporting Kokomo at the Thomas A'Beckett in London), but the turnout was poor and the promoter, Jazz Summers, sneaked off without paying either band. We daren't make an issue out of it because he runs several other venues in London. Understand why I want out of the business side?*

4th: *Windsor Castle. A fairly standard gig.*

5th: *The Swan. Ditto. A prevailing feeling of not being any further than a year ago. I have no more gigs lined up, because we expected an agent to have stepped in by now, and there had been the hope that the single might just take off. John and Tim have got themselves jobs for the summer, as the crock of gold seems a way off yet and we can't do much more than wait and see what happens."*

The reviews of the Moonlight gig could hardly have been less helpful. Here's an example, from Chris Westwood in *Record Mirror*:

"Thieves Like Us are the sort of cabaret stock-rock I thought had become extinct years ago. They attempt to stab and parody rock and roll rigmarole, showbiz, theatre pop, all that stuff, but look like nothing more than a symptom of the problem, whatever it is they're poking at."

New Music News was at least entertaining in its comments, comparing the gig to watching open-heart surgery on a teddy bear. Ouch! On the other hand, we were still happy with the single. Although it only got one play on Radio One (courtesy of a DJ called Adrian Juste), it was released in a variety of picture sleeves all over Europe. Larry also kept his promise of a live TV special in Bremen. I nearly died with frustration at not being able to go with them to my old stamping ground, but at least made sure that all my old friends and ex-pupils went along, together with Birgit's brother Harald. That programme was sold all over Europe as well.

But the band was broke. I had a sad conversation in Weymouth with Craig, in which he explained that, unless something happened, he wouldn't be able to afford to stay on. I made various begging phone calls to Larry until he eventually said he would consider it if

I wrote a detailed request. Remember that most bands at this stage would have had at least some kind of recoupable cash advance. We had nothing. Not one penny. The list I sent to Larry was completely ignored, but here, for the record, it is:

1. *The purchase of a small P.A. system, in order to reduce the present crippling cost of hiring a P.A. for each performance and each rehearsal.*

2. *The purchase of a satisfactory drum kit for John Parish, whose present "mongrel" kit tends to collapse at every gig.*

3. *The purchase of new stage clothing for the entire band, in order to avoid their present gear falling from their bodies any moment now.*

4. *The repayment of debts incurred from promotional material production, P.A. hire, rehearsal room hire, petrol and travelling expenses, telephone bills and sundry other band expenses incurred by begging and borrowing, mostly from Oliver's angry bank manager.*

The one thing Larry didn't mind paying for was recording, and so it was that the band went into Park Gate Studios near Hastings in order to record the "album for release in Europe". Even this was unsatisfactory. We all wanted Mark Wallace, who had done such a great job on the single, to produce the album, but for some reason, Larry didn't. He tried to inflict Andy Scott from The Sweet on us, but we eventually settled for Steve James, whose doubtful claim to fame was that he'd worked with Peter Skellern.

Birgit and I drove down in our very unreliable VW van to visit the recording sessions. In the garden, we found John Parish and Mark Meredith busy re-writing the lyrics to one of Chris's songs, "Three Day Week". The way they were being changed showed just how the power structure and attitudes within the band had shifted. Re-arranged musically in such a way as to be almost unrecognisable, the song was just as good in its way, but very different:

This was how Verse One had started out:

"The idea was good,
The Government said,
Three days in the week,
The working man's dead,
Computers and robots are here."

And this is what it became:

"My front door is red,
It serves as a warning,
Don't trespass at breakfast,
I'm worst in the morning,
Time's leaving me poorer today."

Entering the studio, my eyes were immediately attracted to tell-tale razor blades and rolled-up banknotes on the mixing console. Maybe the band was using them, maybe it was the studio staff. I didn't care. Either way, this wasn't the sort of environment I wanted either the band or me to be in, so Birgit and I simply drove back home.

The "album", with whose recording quality I personally was less than satisfied, was, of course, never released. It had some good parts and even a prospective single in the form of a cover of Todd Rundgren's "I Saw The Light", which was recorded at Marcus Music. Larry was keen on the idea of a cover version, but nothing ever came of it. I'd love to release the album on CD, but of course we don't own the rights to the recordings.

I tried desperately to fix up a support tour of the UK with Fischer-Z. This band, "Big In Germany", seemed perfectly compatible with Thieves, but a "buy-on" was required, along with accommodation and transport costs. Larry refused to offer any money and, in any case, Chris Stonor said that he wasn't willing to do the tour. There were tensions between him and John and his band had changed almost beyond recognition. It was over.

In 1998, eighteen years after they split up, Thieves Like Us reunited for my fiftieth birthday party: John, Mark, Tim, Tony (back in the fold and wishing, ironically, that he'd never left in the first place), plus Mark's brother Guy on keyboards because Chris hadn't felt he could do it. The audience, few of whom had ever heard of the band, was as amazed at their power as people had been back in 1978. Several of them came up to me afterwards and suggested that I should consider managing them.

I told them I'd give it some thought.

Thieves Like Us "Where Are They Now?

John Parish has a flourishing career as a record producer. He is renowned worldwide for his work with PJ Harvey.

Tony Oxley runs the family bookshop and picture framing business.

Mark Meredith is a successful graphic designer in Reading.

Tim Barron has spent the entire interim as a professional actor, with TV credits and lengthy spells in the West End.

Chris Stonor has had massive success in Japan and the USA with his albums of ambient relaxation music.

David Hubbard (Craig Whipsnade) is a prolific producer of TV jingles and library music.

Paul Bringloe, now teetotal, works for an advertising agency in London and still plays drums.

Barry Mizen was last heard of as sound engineer on Channel 4's "The Word".

Tommy Winstone is one of the UK's leading tour managers, currently working with Mansun and Cast.

XI. Automatic For The People

After an experience like that, it was obvious that I would never get involved with bands ever again. Like heck. Like an alcoholic, a musiholic is full of good intentions until caught off guard.

The phone call was unexpected:

"Hello, Oliver, it's Tony Oxley."

"Hi! What do you want?"

"Well, I woke up and realised that I'd just written sixteen songs."

"Congratulations. What do you want me to do about it?"

"Not only that, but I've formed a band as well."

In view of the way he had quit Thieves Like Us, this really was a bombshell.

"You've what?"

"I've formed a band. Would you like to manage us?"

Oh God. And yet I didn't dismiss the idea out of hand, because it perhaps offered the opportunity to go back to the most rewarding time of my involvement in music, that of working with a band which was a big fish in a small pond. I could easily get local gigs, we wouldn't have to hire a P.A., and we wouldn't have to travel far. Maybe it could actually be enjoyable.

But first, I had to find out a great deal more about the band.

"What are you called?"

"It's a secret."

"What's the use of that?"

"No, that's the name of the band. A Secret."

"Don't you mean The Secret?"

"Whatever. We're having a practice on Sunday. Why don't you come over?"

"Who else is in the band?"

"Well, there's Paul Bringloe ..."

"What? Have you taken leave of your senses?"

"No, no, he's fine. He's stopped drinking and he's completely changed."

"Oh yeah? And who else?"

"A young lad from Winchester, called Stuart Knowler. Do you know him?"

"Of course I know him. He's one of my pupils!"

Stuart, I knew, was somewhat of a prodigy on bass, having just turned sixteen. And if Paul Bringloe really had turned over a new leaf ...

The Secret demonstrate how to get lots of press before actually playing a gig.
L-R: Stuart Knowler, Paul Bringloe, Tony Oxley

A group of German ex-pupils from Bremen happened to be staying with us at the time, so I took them all over to Kings Worthy Village Hall, where The Secret were going to "audition", in other words, try to tempt me back into management mode. And they were good, in muso-speak, "tight", a zippy little trio, very precisely rehearsed with a clean, uncomplicated sound. Tony's new songs were indeed not bad, far more poppy and commercial that anything Thieves had done recently. I didn't hear anything that would suggest any possibility of fame or record deals, but I did hear something which theoretically ought to go down okay in the local venues. And a trio with its own P.A. ... gosh, it might even be an economic proposition.

As they would have said on the farm, Olly, you're daft as a fucking brush. The Germans were impressed and clapped each new song (there was about an hour's worth of material), and before I knew it, I was managing another band. It seemed so easy, but the ease of it caused me to make a fatal error. How could we get work? Easy, exploit the goodwill which TLU had built up in the area. And so, unforgivably, I made some posters declaring: "The Secret: Ex-Thieves Like Us".

The rewards for this policy were instantly apparent. Gigs poured in ("Ex-TLU, eh? Well, they certainly ought to be worth a try out"). Tony had just bought a good camera and took some super band photos, while I cooked up a press release emphasising the band's gimmick: They were all teetotal. It was an Entertainment Editor's dream: a good quality free photo and an angle. Almost before the band had played a single gig, we had a healthy collection of press cuttings. In its own sweet little way, it was a hype. Initially, it worked, but as soon as The Secret started playing live, the exact nature of the double-edged sword became clear. To me, "Ex-TLU" meant that two out of the three members had been in that band. No way was it a case of false pretences. But to the audiences responding to the posters, "Ex-TLU" meant that they should expect extravagant keyboards and spectacular theatrics. Things which The Secret, as a power pop trio, were not equipped to provide.

At one of the earliest shows, at the Majestic Hotel in Bournemouth, the problem became quickly obvious. Sure the songs were fine, but the limitations of the line-up were manifest. As a frontman, Tony was actually quite shy, and certainly insufficiently communicative. Also, his singing voice was limited and lacking in variation. If you'd come along expecting a pop trio, fine, but if you'd expected a show, disappointment was inevitable.

In the foyer of one of our old haunts, Jumpers Tavern at Christchurch, I was berated by a couple of girls who had followed the original Thieves around:

"We want our money back."

"Why?"

"Because it says 'Ex-Thieves Like Us'."

"They are 'Ex-Thieves Like Us'."

"But we expected Tim or John. We've never seen any of this lot before."

There was never any chance of the band lasting any length of time. Paul decided to leave after just a few gigs, having received a better offer from a promising Winchester band called Zip Code. In a coup worthy of a football transfer, we managed to fix it that Zip Code's drummer John Jeffery simply swapped bands and took Paul's place in The Secret. But unfortunately, Stuart, being so youthful, turned out to be hideously unreliable, as shown in this undelivered missive which I have found, still sealed, in the shed:

"Dear Stuart,

When you come in, you might like to spare a moment or two to ring up and explain why you failed to turn up tonight to a gig which you have known about in advance for upwards of two months. I recommend that your explanation should be a good one.

I have devoted a large amount of energy and effort in the last few months, for no reward whatsoever, with the sole motive of helping, advancing and publicising YOUR interests. As a result of your total selfishness, my reputation has suffered badly in an area where I have spent five years building up a reputation for reliability.

Quite obviously, any relationship of trust which we had is now over, but the very least I expect is an apology."

I'm sure Stuart won't mind reading his rebuke after all these years. He was only sixteen, after all, so I'm glad it was never delivered. He subsequently started a successful DJing set-up with Wendy May from the Boothill Foot Tappers, whom he also married. They now live a blissful existence in Devon. Tony Oxley decided that being a rock star wasn't a sensible option after all (although he still has hankerings). Paul Bringloe stayed with Zip Code, who became Four People I Have Known.

Since then, I have been tempted by far better bands than the Secret, but having young children made it hard to give the necessary commitment. Besides, young children are much nicer and more rewarding than bands.

Before the Secret disbanded, they were instrumental in helping Birgit and me to get married. I asked her after a gig by The Time at the Joiners Arms (although Greg Watkins claims that I used to propose to her on a regular basis whenever I got drunk, then withdraw the suggestion the next day). Wanting to avoid the hassle connected with conventional weddings, we didn't tell anyone except the two witnesses until the night before, when the news was announced from the stage at a gig at the Victory in Southampton, where the Secret were supporting The Time. At the registry office the next day, Tony Oxley took the photos and we drank champagne from plastic beakers ("I do so hate plastic glasses, don't you?"). And in the evening, shame of shames, horror of horrors, blushes upon blushes, we went out to a gig. Kind of inevitable, I guess.

Meanwhile, as happens when bands split up, the other ex-Thieves were all busily getting on with new projects. Craig Whipsnade teamed up with someone called Derek Green and recorded a twelve-inch single for A & M called "Show Me The Way" under the name Any Day Now. Tim Barron rather incongrously also formed a duo. It was with an ex-member of Suzi Quatro's band called Jamie Crompton, who worked for Gibson guitars, and then for Fender.They named themselves Odeon, but didn't get beyond the demo-making stage. Chris Stonor was perhaps more adventurous, joining up with Mark Easton, late of the Limos and Mark Andrews and the Gents. The two of them set up an optimistic record label called Shout Records. Their claim to fame was that they put out an album by an Icelandic band called Peyr. This band garnered lots of press because there was some sinister-sounding connection with Jaz Coleman of Killing Joke, and because their unlistenable album had a very explicit cover. Various members of Peyr went on to form the Sugarcubes, one of whose singers was Björk.

John Parish, after the demise of Thieves, wasted little time before finding a new direction to explore. Far from being demoralised by the way the business had chewed us up, he became more determined than ever to plough his own furrow and never again to work on anything but his own terms. The way that he carried his ideals through to eventual fruition is a story which is not only fascinating but inspiring.

John almost immediately returned to where he had grown up, in Yeovil, Somerset. For a good number of years, he earned his living by teaching drums and guitar, both privately and in local schools. One of his earliest drum pupils was to become a long-term musical collaborator. Rob Ellis, known to all simply as Rabid, was a slight, open-faced young man with a disconcerting resemblance to Nigel Mansell, and an unfussy drummer of great precision and insistence. He was a part of John's first post-Thieves band, The Headless Horsemen.

The bulk of The Headless Horsemen's repertoire consisted of the kind of quirky, jerking, oddly-worded songs which John had been introducing into Thieves. "Love Smarts" was a good example of this style, a pun-based song with a tuneful hook and several time changes. The Headless Horsemen were a trio as well, but very much John's band. Dressed in a Spiderman pullover (reflecting his interest in that particular super-hero), John had suddenly moved from behind the drums to lead vocals and guitar.

The first sign that John was going to delve further into the avant garde and away from the mainstream was the song which, in an extraordinarily bold move for the time, he made the lead track on The Headless Horsemen's first demo. "Hopeless" was a desolate-sounding, funereally slow offering based around a sparse single-note bass line and a lonely swishing cymbal. In characteristic Parish lyrical style, each line was stuffed with too many words to actually fit in:

I thought that I was immunised against it,
What in Heaven's name is love?
'Love is' not our future plans,
I'm hopeless,
When I'm in love I say,
Do your own thing, it's always the same.

In a contrast which could scarcely have been more pronounced, the next track was a punked-up version of The Beatles' "Drive My Car", which was viewed either as extremely clever or as an absolute disgrace, depending on the listener's attitude to the Fab Four. As far as I was concerned, these two tracks were clear evidence that John was on his way to doing something really special. We booked the trio into the Railway, and also the rather unsuitable Cathedral Hotel in Salisbury, where the same gang of German visitors who had encouraged the Secret ensured that there was at least a modicum of applause.

It was around this time that I had a series of regular confrontations with John about music. He was a real young firebrand and almost reminded me of my father in the inflexible nature of his views. We had countless conversations along the following lines:

Oliver: I know Camel aren't much good now, but they used to be quite a good band.

John: No, they weren't. They were crap.

Oliver: Oh, come on. Parts of the Snow Goose are quite inventive ...

John: No, It's crap.

Oliver: But you have to admit that Peter Bardens is quite a good keyboard player ...

John: No, he isn't. He's crap.

During the course of the conversation, John's bushy eyebrows would narrow as his frown got more and more intense. I was convinced that his eyes were gradually turning red, as Christopher Lee's did in the Hammer Dracula movies. This condition came to be known as "eye-blazing", but our disagreements never led to any really friendship-threatening confrontations. But John's pet hate, as is mine, is when bands "bland out" for the sake of commerciality. Among bands he will never forgive are the Thompson Twins, REM and even Pavement.

After the free transfer from the Secret, Paul Bringloe's new band Zip Code changed its name to Four People I Have Known. Enigmatic, arty and with a hint of glam, this quartet (of course it was) specialised in heavily-flanged guitars and Kraftwerk-sounding keyboards. Importantly, they had a mysterious-looking frontman called Jack Burnaby, who was a bit of a local heart throb. They were viewed by many as being pretentious, but for me they had that factor vital to any band: They didn't sound like anyone else.

Bands are like London buses. Big, red, smelly, ugly and always late. No, actually, you wait years for one and then three come along at once. In this most purple-hued of purple patches, yet another fantastic band popped up, even better than the other two.

It was another of my "feelings". Birgit was away somewhere and I was desperate for a gig to review for *Musicians Only*. I saw that a band called The Time was going to play at a pub called the Plough in a village called Durrington, which the map told me was somewhere in the middle of Salisbury Plain. Promising it certainly wasn't, but I climbed into the VW van and set off.

The Time truly had everything. Sounding like The Beatles on speed, they had punky energy, wild harmonies, sparkling songs, a brilliant spiky-haired guitarist and an angelic-looking yet sneeringly provocative singer. It seemed crazy that such a top-notch band, which should clearly be able to command big stages, should be playing in such a dive. Not even Thieves had played in such a woebegone venue.

I had to approach the engineer on the mixing desk to get the compulsory equipment list. They obviously had their own P.A. and the peroxide-headed young man, who introduced himself as the Time's manager, Paul Dominy, wrote out copious details in impeccably neat handwriting. I am pleased to say that Paul has been one of my closest friends ever since that day. What a great way to meet.

The Time had a bit of the appeal of Thieves, in that all the band members were mild-mannered, polite, academic under-achievers. They had been together at grammar school in Gosport, where they'd formed a band called Virginia Doesn't, which had risen to the heady heights of a John Peel session. The Time specialised in careering round the stage like dodgem cars. The guitarist was a tiny, cheeky-faced man with the nickname "Tweets", who had a semi-mohican and played a pretend Flying V guitar which had been specially built for him by a Gosport guitar maker called Melvyn Hiscock, who later went on to write a best-selling book about guitar construction. Tweets would roll around the floor like a demented hedgehog, while blasting out ridiculously speedy heavy-metal solos which were inoffensive because, placed as they were in the context of humorous new-wave style songs, they were obviously a piss-take.

The other main focus of The Time was the singer, Kevin Robinson. This golden-voiced character was, even then, clearly destined for greater things, in that his between-song patter was laden with mimickry and improvisational flair. He was a master of the one-line put-down and obviously had a very bright, quick mind. He also had the essential streak of arrogance, which not everyone took to. This apparently cheery individual, prodigiously talented, could also, on occasion, be "difficult".

If stand-up comedy had been around then, Kevin would probably never have been in a band at all. Nowadays, under the name Kevin Eldon, he is one of the UK's leading stand-ups, and a stalwart of TV comedy series like "Big Train". My friend Richard Williams, who had been an early fan of The Time, spotted Kevin twenty years later at the 1999 Edinburgh Festival, ligging with various other luminaries of the comedy world. Slightly the worse for drink, Richard marched up to Kevin and announced:

"Kevin. The Time. Top band!"

Kevin looked astounded.

"Fuck ... fuck ... fuck ... fuck ... You're right! Bloody hell, you're right! We were a top band!"

Birgit and I had a period of following The Time around. It could be a dangerous business, because the band, completely against their will and in stark contrast to their true nature, had picked up an evil following of Portsmouth football supporters. One of The Time's many wittily-worded songs was a ditty called "Roughies and Toughies":

The roughies and the toughies don't bother me,
Just 'cos they're bigger and meaner than me,
Just 'cos they wear big nasty boots,
I don't care, I don't give a hoot.
Just 'cos they've really only got one eyebrow,
Just 'cos they've got little dinky brains,
Just 'cos they like making people bleed,
They don't bother me,
They don't bother me.

The irony of this song was completely wasted on the meatheads in their audience, who liked nothing better than to start riots, often by purposely excessively rumbustuous pogoing near the front of the stage. On one early occasion, we drove up to the Royal Hotel in Guildford for a Sunday lunchtime show. A huge but gentle bouncer employed by the venue was attacked by a gang of Pompey supporters when he tried to stop people climbing onto the stage, and the car park swiftly became a battlefield. Most unbecoming on the Sabbath.

Something similar happened when The Time played at the Joiners Arms in Southampton. It was a Saturday night and Southampton football fans emerging from the Dell got wind that there was a roomful of "up for it" Portsmouth supporters waiting for them, and sought out the venue. Again, the band was completely innocent as the entire street played host to a re-enactment of the Battle of Little Big Horn.

Having no allegiances, we were able to cower in corners and avoid involvement, but not when The Time played at the Railway in Winchester at a party to celebrate the birthday of my fellow *Chronicle* rock writer Baz Mort. Birgit found a man in the process of stealing her handbag, and he reacted badly to her intervention. When I heard the kerfuffle and came running over, merely interested in finding out what was going on and certainly not acting in any aggressive manner, he went for me.

As the world's least courageous man, I retreated under a table and crawled, crab-like, under several more, until I reached the stage, where the band was lined-up, each brandishing a mike stand to repel boarders. I hid behind the drum kit while Birgit drove her mini up to the stage door, so that I could jump straight in without touching the floor. As we drove off, the friends of my attacker hammered on the roof of the car, while he himself was being physically sat upon by several sympathisers of mine. So, whenever I see Kevin Eldon on TV, I think, thanks, mate, you helped to save me from serious injury.

So there we had it: three bands, all brilliant in their ways, none of them with recording contracts, all of them too clever, individual and idiosyncratic to have any hope of a record deal. All of them gigged a lot but had no "product" to sell. They also all came from the same part of the country, and I thought I sensed the possibility of a "buzz", such as different geographical areas throw up from time to time. It seemed unjust that they weren't getting the attention they deserved. What could be done?

Ideally, I'd have liked to put out a vinyl compilation album, but such artefacts had been more or less discredited by often being patchy and incoherent; besides, there was a little matter of not having any money. In the end, I decided to copy the idea of a successful Southampton-based label called Stick It In Your Ear and make it a cassette-only release. This is how "Burnt Offerings" came about.

Don't ask where the title came from, I've no idea. The format was to include three tracks by each band, so that listeners could build up a really good impression of each of them. The remaining space on Side Two was filled with three well-recorded Thieves Like Us live tracks, because, obviously, any studio recordings were the property of Larry Uttal. I wanted to include Thieves because I still felt they hadn't had a fair crack of the whip with regard to general availability of their material. Also, I felt guilty about my silly misappropriation of their name in order to attract attention to the Secret.

The mechanics of "Burnt Offerings" were simple. I had recently bought, from Comet, a Sharp stereo system with a double tape deck. I bought a load of TDK C46 cassettes from a wholesaler and literally hand-recorded each tape. Although laborious, this did at least ensure good sound quality and no waste. The cover was designed by another good neighbour, Jenny Rosser, the partner of our trusty printer Tony Hill, who, not surprisingly, also printed it. It depicted an overdone chicken being removed from an oven. The significance of this? Absolutely none.

As a totally non profit-making exercise, "Burnt Offerings" worked surprisingly well. The bands each bought a supply from me at cost price and then sold them at gigs and to friends for a bit of a profit. The rest were sold by me by mail order after a range of press coverage almost out of all proportion to the actual product. In order to achieve this, I put the experience gained from the Secret into action, and supplied the papers with good photographs, user-friendly quotes and angles, plus contact numbers for interviews.

The compilation thus got big splashes in all the Southern press and, very gratifyingly, mentions in the music papers too. If that can be achieved on a budget of nought pence, it's easy to see how any crummy old band can be hyped into the public consciousness if enough money is spent on the operation. At any rate, a healthy number of "Burnt Offerings" tapes was sold, with the help of one small classified ad in the "For Sale" section of the NME, which brought in orders from all manner of collectors of obscurities.

This particular adventure was climaxed by a Burnt Offerings live showcase at the Tower Arts Centre, with great performances from all three bands. Needless to say, no "South Coast Sound" movement resulted. This was partly because, as bands do, they all started falling apart anyway. Four People were the first to go, principally because they were intelligent young men with good, sensible careers ahead of them. Paul Bringloe was still hard to work with and Jack Burnaby was pretty insufferable too.

The Time lasted much longer, and had plenty of chances to prove their worth on big stages with support slots for the Jam and Joe Jackson, among others. Eventually, they "did a Thieves" by coming over all serious and putting out a beautifully-presented cassette E.P. full of songs which didn't represent them at all, thus alienating most of their original fans. Then Paul accused Kevin of having a fling with his girlfriend Alison (True? Who knows?), and Paul resigned. The Time did something very sweet at that stage. Deciding they were unlikely to hit the big time in their current form, and with a big debt to pay off for the P.A. they had purchased, they metamorphosed into a Sixties covers band, with the twist being that they played the songs in outrageously raucous punk versions. This allowed Kevin's humour a freer rein than before and Gerry Hackett and the Fringes ("The Fareham Creek Beat") were a fantastically entertaining act, which played when Birgit became pregnant and we held a "Quick Before It's Too Late" party at the Railway. Just for a change, nobody tried to beat me up.

So what happened to John Parish? Becoming less and less musically conventional by the moment, he founded Automatic Dlamini, a much-misspelt band which he was to maintain for close on ten years, a band which was a spawning ground for a whole collection of successful musicians. Any serious attempt at documenting the complete ins, outs, ups and downs of this extraordinary band will have to wait until I am commissioned to write John's official biography. For now, edited highlights will have to do.

The first, and longest-lasting, Dlamini was yet another trio, but not at all a conventional one. They lived in a succession of freezing, like really, really freezing farm cottages in the countryside around Yeovil (getting it together in the country again, yippee!), where Birgit and I would visit them regularly. As ever, I was attracted by music which was different and good, and this band was certainly those things. For a start, they had hardly any instruments. Rabid played drums, Jamie Anderson (another ex-pupil of John's) played bass and John (now re-christened Scott Tracey on account of an alleged resemblance to said puppet) commanded the front of the stage, leering, singing lead vocals and thrashing away at a crazy collection of percussion instruments. A few of these were actually originally intended as such, but most of them were agricultural instruments of various sorts: a ploughshare, a pig trough and a mercilessly battered Castrol can. All three members sang in startlingly complicated harmony, and, oh dear, all three of them sported headset microphones and dressed either in yellow Devo-style boiler suits or in track-suit bottoms held up by braces.

This was the state of Automatic Dlamini when we first encountered them in the skittle alley of the Antelope Hotel, Sherborne. It sort of worked, in that the frenzied percussion (Rabid by name, rabid by nature) was almost frightening and the unusual nature of the line-up was appealing. But they couldn't help looking self-conscious. Still, it was a start and, in this form, Automatic Dlamini made a whole collection of demos and also ended up on a West Country compilation album which I reviewed (in a disgracefully biased way) for Soundmaker.

From the start, I was keen to help this band in any way I could, but logistical considerations, plus the fact that Annabel was born not long after they formed, made any thought of managing them a non-starter. Nonetheless, I was known to knock out an occasional press release for them, and sometimes I wonder whether having a manager (which they never did) could have led to greater recognition for them. Over the coming years, they went through untold numbers of personnel changes, publishing deals, videos, record contracts, near misses, crises and triumphs, but they never approached achieving their true commercial potential.

We tried to support any version of Dlamini. I even did some "mime mixing" at a sticky-carpeted venue called the Bristol Bridge Inn, while the infant Annabel very nearly froze to death in the sub-zero flat they inhabited at the time. We put them on several times at the Railway in Winchester and even at my school, in an afternoon gig following which they were chased round Winchester by a gang of nubile fifteen year-old girls. I got into trouble over this when a senior member of staff got annoyed by my playing the band's E.P. at great volume in the school dining room and called me a "selfish bastard". The day after that gig, we cooked up the idea that I should put them in touch with Richard Mazda, who by now was a successful record producer. They immediately hit it off, a relationship which led directly to John's working with Wall of Voodoo, which in turn led to connections with further American musical collaborators.

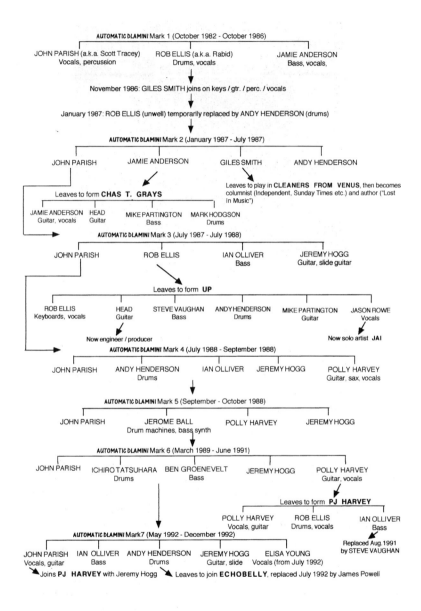

AUTOMATIC DLAMINI Mark 1 (October 1982 - October 1986)

JOHN PARISH (a.k.a. Scott Tracey)
Vocals, percussion

ROB ELLIS (a.k.a. Rabid)
Drums, vocals

JAMIE ANDERSON
Bass, vocals,

November 1986: GILES SMITH joins on keys / gtr. / perc. / vocals

January 1987: ROB ELLIS (unwell) temporarily replaced by ANDY HENDERSON (drums)

AUTOMATIC DLAMINI Mark 2 (January 1987 - July 1987)

JOHN PARISH   JAMIE ANDERSON   GILES SMITH   ANDY HENDERSON

Leaves to form CHAS T. GRAYS

Leaves to play in CLEANERS FROM VENUS, then becomes columnist (Independent, Sunday Times etc.) and author ("Lost In Music")

JAMIE ANDERSON
Guitar, vocals

HEAD
Guitar

MIKE PARTINGTON
Bass

MARK HODGSON
Drums

AUTOMATIC DLAMINI Mark 3 (July 1987 - July 1988)

JOHN PARISH   ROB ELLIS   IAN OLLIVER
Bass

JEREMY HOGG
Guitar, slide guitar

Leaves to form UP

ROB ELLIS
Keyboards, vocals

HEAD
Guitar

STEVE VAUGHAN
Bass

ANDY HENDERSON
Drums

MIKE PARTINGTON
Guitar

JASON ROWE
Vocals

Now engineer / producer

Now solo artist JAI

AUTOMATIC DLAMINI Mark 4 (July 1988 - September 1988)

JOHN PARISH   ANDY HENDERSON
Drums

IAN OLLIVER   JEREMY HOGG   POLLY HARVEY
Guitar, sax, vocals

AUTOMATIC DLAMINI Mark 5 (September - October 1988)

JOHN PARISH   JEROME BALL
Drum machines, bass synth

POLLY HARVEY   JEREMY HOGG

AUTOMATIC DLAMINI Mark 6 (March 1989 - June 1991)

JOHN PARISH   ICHIRO TATSUHARA
Drums

BEN GROENEVELT
Bass

JEREMY HOGG   POLLY HARVEY
Guitar, vocals

Leaves to form PJ HARVEY

POLLY HARVEY
Vocals, guitar

ROB ELLIS
Drums, vocals

IAN OLLIVER
Bass

Replaced Aug.1991
by STEVE VAUGHAN

AUTOMATIC DLAMINI Mark7 (May 1992 - December 1992)

JOHN PARISH
Vocals, guitar

IAN OLLIVER
Bass

ANDY HENDERSON
Drums

JEREMY HOGG
Guitar, slide

ELISA YOUNG
Vocals (from July 1992)

Joins PJ HARVEY with Jeremy Hogg   Leaves to join ECHOBELLY, replaced July 1992 by James Powell

Dlamini Family Tree

Automatic Dlamini: the Graffiti is still there today

Every incarnation of Automatic Dlamini was controlled by John, who wrote all the songs and led all the bands. I won't say John was a control freak, but he was a control freak. That is, until one day he announced that his treasured trio, which had by then issued several singles and also an album ("The D Is For Drum") on the Idea label, was now a five-piece.

This was the Automatic Dlamini whose memory I will forever treasure. Ranking as among the most intriguing and exciting groups I have ever seen, this version of the band featured an almost unbelievably shy but brilliant slide guitarist (Jeremy Hogg, previously of Bristol band Grape), a crazy Japanese drummer called Ichiro Tatsuhara, who had permanent work permit problems, and, "oh, a girl we've found who plays saxophone". When I first heard about this, I dreaded the possible scenario: the percussion-led trio with some mad woman wailing improvised sax over the top. It wasn't beyond John, and I feared the parting of the ways at last.

By the time I finally got to see this Automatic Dlamini vintage, they'd done a character-building tour of Poland and East Germany and recorded demo versions of what would become their unreleased but magnificent album "Here Catch, Shouted His Father". "Giraffe In Warszawa", in which John contrived to rhyme "banker" with "Casablanca" and "pretence" with "ignorance" (*quoi?*) reflected their Polish experiences, but by far the most memorable track was a shockingly commercial song called "Johnny Pineapple". The extended dance mix of this song was like Fatboy Slim a decade before he'd been heard of, but the familiar succession of imploding record companies ensured that it didn't see the light of day. What a crime.

The mad saxophone lady turned out to be someone rather special, whom we first saw when we promoted the band at the Railway. Hiding from the twenty-strong audience at the back of the stage, almost as shyly as Jeremy on the other side, was someone who, without apparently trying, attracted everyone's attention. A slight, unobtrusive person, who only sang lead on two songs and spent the rest of the time strumming a semi-acoustic guitar in the shadows. So why did Paul Dominy sidle up to me and ask:

"Have you seen the girl?"

"Yes, what is it about her?"

"I don't know, but there's something ..."

Paul even went so far as to say that, if he didn't now have other commitments, he would ask the girl to consider a solo career and that he would offer to manage her. And I went so far as to say that, if I also didn't have other commitments, I would do the same. Isn't that extraordinary? A star is a star, and that's all there is to it. Neither of us had ever seen her before or had any prior knowledge of her, but both of us instantly knew that PJ Harvey had whatever it is that such people have.

I was now convinced that Automatic Dlamini were going to be major stars. The next gig was at the Joiners in Southampton, and I took along my newly-acquired second-hand video camera. This was a mind-bogglingly good performance, which I certainly won't forget. Walking gingerly backwards in order to try and get a wider angle, I inadvertently leant against the bar of the emergency exit, which burst open, leaving me lying on my back like a beached whale in the alley beside the pub. The normally slow-moving promoter, Mint, mindful of the noise and the neighbours, sprang across and slammed the door shut, unaware of my predicament. If it hadn't been for the felt-tip mark on my hand, I'd have had to pay again in order to get back in.

The next time I heard of Polly Harvey was in a routine phone call to Mint, to arrange tickets for a gig by the West Country band the Family Cat.

"And, as you know, PJ Harvey is supporting."

"Who?"

"You know, the girl from Automatic Dlamini. She's got her own band now."

I didn't know. Things had moved on so fast. The industry frenzy was already beginning, the first single was already out, and most people in attendance that evening were there for the support band. Again, I had good reason to remember that night, not just because of the breathtakingly good performance by the tiny, leather jacketed, black-bunned schoolma'am on stage, but also because I was very nearly killed (again). The Joiners was being renovated and there was a scaffolding tower rigged up in the hall to enable the builders to reach the ceiling. As the dancing reached a crescendo during "Sheela-na-Gig", one of the heavy iron bolts which hold bits of scaffolding together rolled off the platform and missed my cranium by a millimetre. After the show, Birgit engaged Rob Ellis (no longer called Rabid) in conversation about his newly-born baby, and we cooed over some photos. Very rock and roll, I'm sure.

During the well-documented rise of PJ Harvey, John was working at Yeovil Technical College as an associate lecturer, teaching what was an innovative prototype of the now common Music Technology courses. By now, I had started my language publishing business and, after recording some incidental music with Chris Stonor in Brighton, I signed on to a production course which John was runnning in a slum-like studio in Street, Somerset. Despite his well-meant teaching techniques, I understood nary a word. John also kindly recorded ILA, a school band from Winchester. This happened in another Yeovil studio called the Icehouse, where the first PJ

Harvey album was recorded. John had established himself as an in-demand producer for West Country bands like the Chesterfields and the Brilliant Corners, both of whom had indie hit singles. All John's clients were attracted by his relaxed and totally un-muso approach to production.

Automatic Dlamini had by now recorded a second album, called, probably explicably in some way, "From A Diva To A Diver", and it was cracking. Polly was to be heard on several tracks and the crucial difference as far as I was concerned was that I now, in stark contrast to ever before, had the contacts and even the finance, with difficulty, to manufacture a CD. John, in turn, had access to distribution facilities and vinyl production. At long bloody last, and just for a moment, I was going to be a "proper" record company.

Everything to do with *From A Diva To A Diver* was a pleasurable experience. It even made a proft, for goodness' sake. I had no inhibitions at all about plugging it for all I was worth, because I knew it was a superb record. We purposely soft-pedalled on the "featuring PJ Harvey" angle, because the music was strong enough not to need it. The distribution was arranged through a band from Street called the Tony Head Experience, who for some reason had the requisite music business contacts. The reviews were mixed but never bad, and a few thousand were sold. It was great to be associated with a success story, particularly when it featured a band I'd been willing to do well for a good number of years.

Very oddly, the version of Automatic Dlamini that promoted the album was a conventional four-piece line-up. The makeshift percussion had more or less disappeared and John now played guitar. A succession of drummers had been and gone (Rob Ellis now being a firm part of the PJ Harvey band). One notable drummer was Andy Henderson, later of Echobelly, and the one who went out on the road was James Powell, the son of Georgie Fame and, yes, an ex-pupil of John's. It was this version of Automatic Dlamini that I travelled to see at the Bier Keller in Bristol, supporting PJ Harvey.

There is a bit of a tale to this. The night before, we had seen PJ Harvey at the Pyramids in Portsmouth. I was desperate to go to the Bristol show, not least because I wanted to hand out flyers advertising "From A Diva To A Diver", but family responsibility really did mean that it wasn't fair to go out two nights running. We planned to spend the day at Lulworth Cove in Dorset, but it rained so heavily that we were about to head for home.

"Of course," I said to Birgit, "we could go and see Automatic Dlamini in Bristol."

"Hmm ... How far away is Bristol?"

"Oh, it's, er, quite near."

PORTSMOUTH VENUE CAMPAIGN
PRESENTS
WEDNESDAY 27TH MAY

PJ HARVEY

moonshake

PYRAMIDS CENTRE
PORTSMOUTH
7.30 pm
TICKETS £5.00 ADVANCE / £5.50 DOOR
AVAILABLE FROM
PYRAMIDS CENTRE BOX OFFICE
(0705) 877895
PORTSMOUTH POLYTECHNIC STUDENTS UNION
(0705) 819141

"How far is it to Bristol?"

Three hours later, I had to pacify them all by agreeing to put them up in a posh hotel while I headed for the Bier Keller. Luckily, the Holiday Inn was being renovated and did us a cheap deal.

This was quite an event, because it was at the height of PJ Harvey fever and the place was pouring with sweat. At the end of the evening, I was trawling round the tables, retrieving any abandoned "Diva" flyers for possible future use, when I became aware that Polly Harvey was standing, all alone, in the middle of the room, looking a bit lost. It took me a moment to realise who she was, because when she's on stage you don't really notice how tiny she is.

I think she recognised me from the Railway, but this meeting was a re-run of my encounter with Steve Winwood nearly thirty years earlier, in that I found myself completely tongue-tied. The only words which came into my head were, "I think you're wonderful", but I didn't utter them. Instead, I just said, "Hello" and literally scuttled for the door.

It's hard to explain my attitude to PJ Harvey, other than to say that I am simply an abject fan. I have never admired any other musician as much as I admire Polly. This isn't a sexual thing, because she's not actually "my type" in that respect, and, despite what critics see as the explicitly sexual nature of many of her lyrics, I don't actually listen to them. Or if I do, I don't see them as necessarily being confessional or, indeed, either my business or anyone else's. I just admire her, in the same way as I admire anyone who dumbfounds me with their brilliance or single-mindedness, such as, oh, I don't know, people like Tony Benn, Peter Gabriel, John Lennon.

As a result, I have crumbled ignominiously every time I have met her. At Glastonbury, in the pink catsuit era, I was so nervous that I gushed pathetically about what I saw as the derivation of her water-related lyrics, while I could see that she felt she didn't really need to be told this. Bumping into her and John on the Dorset coast one afternoon when out jogging, I said something, I can't remember what, that she clearly disagreed with. It looked as though she'd been taking eye-blazing lessons from John, so I rapidly made my excuses and left. We met them again, almost in the same place, on Boxing Day 1998. On that occasion, I was so terrified that I walked up the cliffs to avoid having to attempt to make conversation, leaving Birgit and Lucy to talk turkey (sic).

John and Polly gave me the best day of my life. After the end of Automatic Dlamini, John had teamed up with Polly as her musical collaborator for the "To Bring You My Love" album. They then made a record together, called "Dance Hall At Louse Point", which is, after much consideration, my favourite album of all time. They did a few dates to promote it, for which they warmed up in a minuscule wine-bar in Bridport called the Cavity.

We decided to make this a family day out, and booked ourselves into a Fawlty Towers-style hotel called The Bull, directly opposite the Cavity. First, we went for a walk at Eype, a secret, mystical pebbly beach nearby, and then, tired from the fresh air, all four of us, Lucy,

The best day of my life: John Parish and Polly Harvey at The Cavity in Bridport

Annabel, Birgit and I, fell asleep in the hotel room. We were woken from our slumbers in late afternoon by the strains of "Jesus, save me...", wafting across the road from the soundcheck at great volume, stopping the shoppers on the market in their tracks. Magical.

Thousands of people would have given anything to have been there, and we were. What a gift for John to have given us. In the band were Jeremy Hogg, Rob Ellis, John, Polly and the brilliant Eric Drew Feldman from Captain Beefheart's Magic Band. They took up more than half the room. We were crammed right up against the band, people were climbing in through the windows, and afterwards, all we had to do was stagger back across the road to bed. That evening had absolutely everything: It was a world debut, it was the best music I had heard in my life, it summed up what John had attained by proving he had reached world-class status after all the years of struggle. And Polly, defying the industry rumours about her alleged state of health, sang like an angel. It couldn't have been better.

For some unknown reason, I have had an adventure on almost all the many occasions I have ventured out to see PJ Harvey (normally with the kind assistance of free tickets from John). At the Shepherd's Bush Empire, we took along a French friend who was mad about the band, but there was a mix-up with the tickets and he initially couldn't get in. Birgit was compelled to try, in succession, pleading, threatening and eventually eyelid-fluttering, before the security man finally gave in. Then I got in a state because of an incident at the after-show reception. I approached some members of a band called Breed, whom I had seen, and liked, at the Joiners Arms, but the drummer was incredibly obnoxious, taking the piss out of me because of my age. This hateful person shortly afterwards joined Placebo, a band so terrible that he fits in perfectly.

Then my friend David Eno kindly drove me up to London for a show at the Kentish Town Forum. We almost missed it, because, having heard about road works on the M3, David decided to take an alternative route. In a moment of absent-mindedness, we got ourselves on to the M4, heading towards Bristol rather than London, with thirty-odd miles before the next available exit.

At the Olympia Theatre, in Dublin, I took along my Irish pal Brendan, a wonderful man, so full of good-natured bullshit that he must have shagged the Blarney Stone rather than kissing it. Half way through the show, Brendan tugged at my sleeve:

"Look, up there on the balcony, there's yer man."

Crikey! Brendan was right. Sitting in one of the gilded boxes was none other than Bono, accompanied by his manager (and Polly Harvey's) Paul McGuinness. This gave Brendan a characteristic idea, as, after the show, he tried to blag himself and me into an exclusive nightclub on the grounds that "Mr McGuinness is inside waiting for us". Needless to say, this cut little ice with the security staff.

In the meantime, back in Winchester, another of my ex-pupils had been making headway as a musician. Richard Williams had been an unobtrusive, rather chubby little boy, who liked to come up at the end of lessons and chat about music. I had noticed that he was coming on very fast as a guitar player, and he even joined me in the Weeke Jokes Mark Two for a leavers' party. Then, as on many subsequent occasions, he was so shy that he wouldn't face the front of the stage. Richard went through a succession of no-hope bands and I had virtually given up on him, when he suddenly blossomed into a real hero.

What happened was that he met a musical catalyst in the form of a laid-back but charismatic young Asian singer called Cave Samrai, who arrived, out of nowhere, in Winchester. Their mutual enthusiasm for The Clash and for the rock and roll lifestyle in general, led to their forming an excellent post-punk energy-ball called, inspirationally, Trip. It was fantastic to watch this band, complete with a re-born Richard, now a trim guitar hero, hurling himself round the stage and no longer afraid of his audience, very nearly make it. They got to tour the major circuit, they were signed to a major label, they even had a song on the soundtrack of Terry Gilliam's *Fisher King* movie, but, guess what, they were shafted by the record industry and corrupt management. Well, there's a surprise.

Richard and I became close friends, despite the great difference in our ages, because of our mutual interest in music. For almost a year, I had regular guitar lessons from Richard, to little avail, since, despite his Job-like patience, I was a hopeless case. In the dying days of Trip, they recorded some demos in Street with John Parish producing, which led to the preposterous idea that I might collaborate musically with Richard. In the meantime, there were other things going on in my life which needed attention.

Our language teaching resources were blossoming, and for every set of tapes, we needed introductory snatches of music. Richard was a supremely talented musician. I was a useless musician, but I liked writing. Maybe I could write songs? Maybe, if it worked, we might be able to record some songs together, perhaps even with the help of John. After all, John sort of owed me a favour after I had helped with the *Diva* album, and Richard, well, he owed me favours for hundreds of reasons, mainly gushingly supportive (and sincerely meant) articles about Trip. But how do you write songs?

Every morning, I set off along the muddy banks of the River Itchen in my jogging outfit and waited for inspiration to strike. One song came about as a result of my being surrounded by a threatening herd of angry swans, and another one, called "Don't Ask Me" was based on the tendency of an increasing number of my colleagues to treat me as an all-purpose sounding board for their problems, never for a moment imagining that I might have any of my own. And, just for a while, I did.

What had happened was that Birgit's father had died. To me, this wasn't a huge surprise, because he had had a series of heart problems, but to her, as a dedicatedly family-orientated person, it was completely devastating. I contributed to her depression by reacting in an insensitive way, although I was convinced that I was

Trip: They could have been big

being kind. All the things I said, which were meant to help her over it, merely made things worse:

"Everybody has to die some time."

"Surely you realised it was bound to happen sooner or later."

"It could have been worse. At least he didn't suffer."

These were not things she wanted to hear and they weren't things that helped her. It was too rational in an emotional situation. My own father having reached a ripe old age, and in any case not having had a warm relationship with me, meant that I wasn't equipped to deal with this period in a sensitive way. So she was angry with me, which I perceived as being unfair. Two songs presented themselves to me on the canal bank, one called "It's Got To Come Out Some Day", the other called "Please Don't Be Mean". For me, this exercise was a little cathartic, but the complete reconciliation would have to wait a while.

Armed with these songs, Richard and I headed down to Somerset, where, with John producing and drumming, we recorded all four of them at Small World Studios in Yeovil. This in itself was a fantastic thrill, because John and Polly had just completed "Dance Hall At Louse Point" in the same studio, and there had even been a publicity shot in Melody Maker that week, showing them sitting on the leather sofa in the control room. Poor John, talk about the sublime to the ridiculous. Richard played all the other instruments with great skill, but my voice was weak and characterless and the songs were just plain poor, despite all the effort which had gone into them. But there we were. I even sent a copy to Creation Records, the only possible record company for a mad forty-eight year old ex-teacher. They even had the courtesy to send a personal, hand-written rejection note: "Quite fun, but the lyrics are shite". Yes, well.

A few months later, we held a party at Twyford Parish Hall to celebrate Birgit's fortieth birthday. I felt an overpowering need to clear the air by demonstrating my love and support for her in front of all our friends, so Richard and I rehearsed a short acoustic set of significant songs, with me singing and Richard on guitar. Feeling sick with terror, I mounted the stage for what was one of the most emotional moments of my life. We did REM's "The One I Love" (only three chords, folks) and a slow version of "Stay", my old favourite Hollies song. Those cheesy old lyrics resonated with me in so many ways: my musical non-relationship with my father, my early admiration for The Hollies, my feelings for my wife and my children, and my inability to give up on rock and roll:

Well your Mama don't mind,
And your Papa don't mind,
If we have another dance, oh yeah,
Just one more time.
Oh won't you stay, just a little bit longer,
Oh let me hear you say you will.

First encore: Radio Head 2

"WIN 107.2, from the heart of the Brooks Shopping Centre, Winchester!" You really can't get much more obscure, yet here I am in the year 2000, still desperate to be involved.

Richard Williams is now the Publicity Manager of the Tower Arts Centre. He has skilfully negotiated a deal whereby the Tower pays an unspecified sum a year to WIN 107.2 ("Best Music, Breaking News for the Heart of Hampshire"). In return, WIN 107.2 (note the appellation, because if you get it wrong there's hell to pay) agree to allow me and Richard to have an "alternative music" slot between 9 and 10 pm on a Friday evening, the very time at which, uncannily, BBC TV runs one of its most popular programmes, "Have I Got News For You". Anyone not watching that will be out at the pub.

Richard is thrilled and so am I, because the unfeasibly young station director has said that we can just say what we like and play what we like. This we of course do with alacrity, playing the most obscure tracks we can think of, wittering away to our hearts' content with liberal spatterings of incomprehensible in-jokes and elitist references. All of it is broadcast, but none of my friends or acquaintances ever mention it to me at all. It is obvious that not a soul listens to us.

Richard has a theory. He claims that WIN 107.2 has a contract with the Radio Authority which compels it to ensure that a proportion of its output is "speech-based" and that this is why they not only tolerate us but actually seem to encourage us. This, says Richard, is because they like what we do.

I know better. As far as I can see, the only reason we are permitted to polish our egos by pontificating about music on WIN 107.2 (that's WIN 107.2) is that the Tower Arts Centre is PAYING for it.

"Pay to Play", remember that? It's been a long journey, but somehow I don't seem to have travelled very far.

Queen Elizabeth Hall
General Manager John Denison CBE

The Moody Blues
Saturday 29 June 1968
7.45 pm

Management: Harold Davison Ltd.

Rear Stalls
10/6   Row   Seat
           00   26★

Sonsabend,
3. November 69,
3 Uhr

RUST-
ERCK-
ALLE

TEN YEARS AFTER
& CHICKEN SHACK

RECHTS A

DM 11.—

Mittwoch, 31. Oktober 1973 - 20 Uhr
Stadthalle Bremen - Halle 2

MAMA CONCERTS
PRESENTS

RORY
GALLAGHER

TOUR 73
guests: Steidee

Vorverkauf: 12,— DM
Abendkasse: 13,— DM

STADTHALLE BREMEN
HALLE II

THE SWEET
+ Guests
IN CONCERT

unbestuhlt

16.   19.00
          EINLASS

DM   12,60 Vorverkauf
     14,00 Abendkasse

BREMEN

Örtliche Durchführung
KPS-Programme Bremen
Klaus Peter Schulenberg

Lippmann + Rau present
THE ROLLING STONES
+ Opening Act

Dienstag   4. Mai 1976   21 Uhr

Stadthalle   DM 20,—
              + Vorverkaufsgebühr, incl. 5,5 % MWSt.

Bitte Rückseite beachten!   0221 ✳

druckerei MERKUR,
Frankfurt-Niedereschbach

4. Mai
1976
21 Uhr
20,—

№ 0221

4. Mai
1976
21 Uhr
20,—

GAUMONT THEATRE
SOUTHAMPTON

ADRIAN HOPKINS presents—
THIN LIZZIE
EVENING 7.30
WEDNESDAY
DECEMBER 7
STALLS
£3.50

I 18

No Tickets exchanged nor
money refunded
TO BE RETAINED   P.T.O.

Blackbushe Aerodrome, Camberley, Surrey

HARVEY GOLDSMITH by arrangement with
Hearnpond Ltd. presents

BOB DYLAN

Special guest ERIC CLAPTON and his band

SATURDAY, 15th JULY, 1978

Gates open noon

See music press for other artists appearing

Tickets £6 inc. VAT
—In advance
£7 on the day   FF № 064967

S.U.S.U.

TALKING HEADS

25/1/78

£1.00

№ 399

TO BE GIVEN UP

GAUMONT THEATRE
SOUTHAMPTON

SIOUXSIE AND
THE BANSHEES

EVENING 7.30
WEDNESDAY
NOVEMBER 24
CIRCLE
£3.50

K 10

No Tickets exchanged nor
money refunded.
TO BE RETAINED   P.T.O.

WESSEX HALL
Poole Art Centre

THE JAM
plus The Vapors

SUNDAY, 18th NOVEMBER 1979
7.30 p.m.
Admission £3.00
To be retained

№   0824

Mick Cater for Umbrella Productions

Presents

BLONDIE

plus Guests

at BOURNEMOUTH VILLAGE BOWL

on Wednesday 26th December 1979

at 7.30 p.m.

Tickets £4.00 inc. VAT

The Management Reserves the Right
to Refuse Admission

№ 4117   № 4117

Montag, 20 Juni 1983, 20.30 h.
Lundi,

Steve Winwood
& Band

LUXEMBOURG-VILLE
THEATRE MUNICIPAL

№ 1270

Concert Production MUSIKRAM S.à.r.l. Luxbg. Tél. 3 30 32

PORTENTS

COMPLIMENTARY
TICKET

EVENT BANGLES
DATE 1/2/86
ENTS OFFICER

STRICTLY NO BACKSTAGE ACCESS

122

PORTSMOUTH POLYTECHNIC STUDENTS UNION
PORTENTS PRESENTS

"THROWING MUSES"

in the Ents Hall
on Saturday 11th February 1989
Doors open 8.00 pm

Tickets £3.50 Advance   341
£4.00 On the door
This ticket does not give automatic entry to P.P.S.U.

Over 18's only

KARSTEN JAHNKE KONZERTDIREKTION

Freitag 31.Mai 1991 20 Uhr — 31.5.91

OK - Radio präsentiert
the laughter & lust tour 1991
JOE JACKSON
in concert
Tournéeleitung: Peter Rieger Konzertagentur GmbH

CCH 1

186 / 1

HOCHPARKETT MITTE

DM	Reihe	Platz
35.-	35	1

wichtige Hinweise
siehe Rückseite

PYRAMIDS CENTRE
PORTSMOUTH
FRINGE FESTIVAL '92

PORTSMOUTH VENUE CAMPAIGN
presents
THE FALL
PLUS GUESTS
MONDAY 3rd AUGUST 1992
Doors open 7:30 P.M.

£7.00
IN ADVANCE

TICKET NO
00809

RIGHT OF ADMISSION RESERVED
TO BE RETAINED

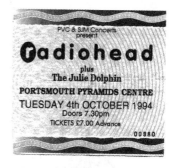

PVC & SJM Concerts
present
Radiohead
plus
The Julie Dolphin
PORTSMOUTH PYRAMIDS CENTRE
TUESDAY 4th OCTOBER 1994
Doors 7.30pm
TICKETS £7.00 Advance

00980

EMPIRE
Marshall Arts Ltd. Proudly Present
AIMEE MANN
plus special guests
Wednesday 17th April 1996
Tickets £12.50 in advance - Doors 7:00pm

DOWNSTAIRS
STANDING
00952

THE JOINERS
ST. MARYS STREET
SOUTHAMPTON
PVC & NBT Present
SILVER SUN
GRASS~SHOW
plus DON
WEDNESDAY 12th FEBRUARY 1997
8:00pm

| £ | 5.00 | Advance | TICKET No. | 00164 |

RIGHT OF ADMISSION RESERVED

THE WEDGEWOOD ROOMS
ALBERT ROAD,
SOUTHSEA
TWR/PVC Presents
CATATONIA
+ SUPPORTS
WEDNESDAY 23rd APRIL 1997
Doors 8.00pm

| £ | 6.00 | ADVANCE | TICKET No. | 00250 |

RIGHT OF ADMISSION RESERVED

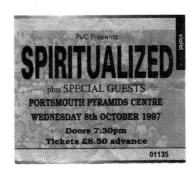

PVC Presents
SPIRITUALIZED
plus SPECIAL GUESTS
PORTSMOUTH PYRAMIDS CENTRE
WEDNESDAY 8th OCTOBER 1997
Doors 7:30pm
Tickets £8.50 advance

Violet

01135

Poole Arts Centre
OFFICIAL
BACKSTAGE PASS
SHOW... *THE CLASH*
DATE...
AUTHORISED...

MCP
GUEST
PASS
NAME O. Gray
ARTISTE U2
DATE 6/3
AUTHORIZED BY

Backstage / **PASS** Press

derek block concert promotions
16,Oxford Circus Ave., 211 Oxford St,London W1
Telephone 01-439 9881 (10 Lines)

ARTIST: *THE POLICE*
VENUE: *SOUTHAMPTON GAUMONT*
DATE: *16 DECEMBER 1979*
Authorised by:

MCP
GUEST
PASS
NAME OLIVER GRAY
ARTISTE JAM
DATE 23.6.81
AUTHORIZED BY T.G.P

MCP
GUEST
PASS
NAME
ARTISTE TALK TALK
DATE 18.11.82
AUTHORIZED BY T.G.P

Gary Revilo's Gigs

If you can't be bothered to read the book (and who could blame you), the gig list provides a summary of the horrors contained within. Just read this instead.

This selective list is far from being exhaustive. Several hundred crummy pub-rock bands have not been listed because they were not of sufficient merit. Lots of gigs have got lost in the mists of time. For example, I know for a fact that I saw the Blue Aeroplanes at least eight times but I can only identify one precise date.

* For bands like **The Time**, **The Outsiders** and **The Agency** which I saw repeatedly, only a few selected shows are mentioned.

* Gigs by the bands I "managed" (**Thieves Like Us** and **The Secret**) are listed separately.

* Festivals include only some of the bands I actually saw at them.

* Sudden gaps indicate managing bands, bringing up children or sojourns abroad.

* An asterisk indicates that I can't remember the exact date.

* I calculate that this list represents about 65 percent of the actual gigs I have attended.

* Complete accuracy is not guaranteed. Anyone spotting errors is invited to correct them ready for the reprint (ha, ha).

1964
*The Hollies, Cheltenham Town Hall
Quiffs intact. Graham Nash played an unamplified acoustic guitar.
*The Sharks, Schöningen, Germany (several times)
Unfeasible trousers but great R & B.

1965
*The Hollies, Cheltenham Town Hall
We sat on chairs positioned round the edge of the dancefloor and didn't dare ask anyone to dance.

1966
*TJ - Tours, France
TJ, a black American organist, played in the same club every night for a month. He claimed to have written "Land of a Thousand Dances".

1967
30. September: **Wynder K. Frogg,** University of East Anglia, Norwich
Hammond Heaven.
19. October: **Herbie Goins and the Night Timers,** University of East Anglia, Norwich
UK soul.
21. October: **Mike Cotton Sound with Lucas,** University of East Anglia, Norwich
Better than Geno Washington but not half as famous.
16. November: **Elmer Gantry's Velvet Opera,** University of East Anglia, Norwich
The age of psychedelia approaches.
14. December: **Jimmy James and the Vagabonds,** University of East Anglia, Norwich
Stax-type soul again, but with a white singer.

1968
13. February: **The Young Tradition,** University of East Anglia, Norwich
Early exposure to finger-in-the-ear folk. Peter Bellamy had the longest hair I'd ever seen.
25. February: **Savoy Brown,** University of East Anglia, Norwich
They got big in the States because the Americans have such good taste.
27. March: **Jeff Beck Band / Pretty Things / Pyramids,** University of East Anglia, Norwich
Rod the Mod long before he was crap.
11. May: **The Move,** University of East Anglia, Norwich
A truly great band. Even Carl Wayne acted the part.
18. May: **Chris Farlowe and the Thunderbirds,** Keswick College, Norwich
I think Albert Lee was in the band.
22. June: **Pink Floyd / Fairport Convention,** University of East Anglia, Norwich
Some double bill!
29. June: **Moody Blues,** Royal Festival Hall, London

They did make a good album, once. Pity about the moustaches.
12. October: **Tyrannosaurus Rex**, University of East Anglia, Norwich
"Elfin-like", that's what they always say about Marc.
2. November: **Spooky Tooth**, University of East Anglia, Norwich
"Sunshine Help Me".
26. November: **Cream** Farewell Concert, Royal Albert Hall, London
Didn't they go on.
*Deviants, Progressive Club, Norwich
Yes, but could they play their instruments?
7. December: **Joe Cocker and the Grease Band**, University of East Anglia, Norwich
I predicted he would go solo. He did.
18. December: **Bakerloo**, University of East Anglia, Norwich
Well-smoothed Dave Clempson's priceless trio.

1969
16. January: **The Nice / The Idle Race**, University of East Anglia, Norwich
Never mention Roy Wood to Jeff Lynne.
23 January: Free, University of East Anglia, Norwich
One of the most perfectly-formed bands of all time.
8. February: **Blossom Toes**, University of East Anglia, Norwich
Jim Cregan, later Rod Stewart's guitarist, was the leader of this sweetly-named combo.
15. February: **Bonzo Dog Doo-Da Band / Roy Harper**, University of East Anglia, Norwich
The original line-up. Sadly, less funny onstage than on record.
18. February: **Roland Kirk**, University of East Anglia, Norwich
Or rather, Rahsaan Roland. Never did get into jazz, sorry.
22. February: **The Pyramids / A Taste of Honey**, University of East Anglia, Norwich
Innocent, up-tempo reggae.
8. March: **Fairport Convention**, University of East Anglia, Norwich
We'd seen them at Colchester in the interim. Sandy Denny told me to fuck off.
22. March: **Roy Harper / Ron Geesin**, University of East Anglia, Norwich.
I can still nip down the road and see Roy at the Brook over thirty years later.
27. March: **Jon Hiseman's Colosseum / Honeybus**, University of

East Anglia, Norwich
Too much in the way of soloing, especially the old "double saxophone" bit.
But Honeybus flew like a bird in the sky.
10. May: The Barbecue, Earlham Park, Norwich with **The Hollies,**
Dave Dee, Dozy, Beaky, Mick and Tich, Gun, Soft Machine,
Marmalade and others.
"What did the students think of us?" - "Er ..."
22. May: **Fleetwood Mac**, Industrial Club, Norwich
They almost made our ears bleed and Mick Fleetwood wore a pair of wooden
testicles on a string.
7. June: **Blind Faith**, Hyde Park, London
If I hadn't rescued Stevie from the pond, this band would never have been
formed.
20. June: **Third Ear Band / Bridget St. John**, University of East
Anglia, Norwich
Everyone sat on the floor, including the band.
5. July: **The Rolling Stones**, Hyde Park, London
"Okay, see you in Hyde Park then."
4. November: **Spooky Tooth**, Mensa am Westring, Kiel, Germany
Luckily, rugby songs are a rarity in Germany.
15. November: **Ten Years After / Chicken Shack**, Ernst-Merck-Halle,
Hamburg
He's fast, isn't he? And that Christine Perfect was a bit of all right.
12. December: **Bach Weihnachtsoratorium**, St-Johanniskirche,
Lüneburg
The only classical concert I've been to in my life. I coughed all the way
through and a nice old lady gave me a sweetie.

1970
3. January: **Aspidistra Flying Blues Band**, Blue Note,
Wilhelmshaven
Who? Well, I was there and it was bloody cold.
7. January: **Hardin and York**, Mensa am Westring, Kiel, Germany
The World's Smallest Big Band.
21. January: **Soft Machine**, Mensa am Westring, Kiel, Germany
Robert Wyatt did his funny falsetto bit.
10. March: **Steamhammer**, Mensa am Westring, Kiel, Germany
Whatever did happen to Steamhammer?
10. April: **Renaissance**, Mensa am Westring, Kiel, Germany
Rather nice pastoral sounds from Keith Relf and his sister Jane.

15. April: **The Flock**, Ernst-Merck-Halle, Hamburg
"The Sound of the Seventies", said the ticket. Jerry Goodman ended up in the Mahavishnu Orchestra.
22. May: **Hardin and York**, Mensa am Westring, Kiel, Germany
The ticket price had gone up by 2 DM in four months. This can happen when you're Big In Germany.
28. May: **Deep Purple**, Ostseehalle, Kiel, Germany
The support was Alex Harvey. I thought he was brilliant but the audience hated him. A sign of things to come?
21 / 22 June: Hamburg Big Gig Festival: **Colosseum, Black Sabbath, Family, Rare Bird, Humble Pie, Uriah Heep, Gentle Giant**
We slept under the stars and woke up covered in dew.
10. July: **Free**, Spektrum Club, Kiel, Germany
Paul Rodgers pinched a bottom to celebrate the band's first hit.
25. September: **Caravan / Jackson Heights**, City Hall, Salisbury
An outing from the farm. The support was Lee Jackson from the Nice, but there was hardly anyone there.
21. December: **Strawbs / Hardin and York / Al Stewart**, Royal Albert Hall, London
A benefit for the "Conservation Society". An ill-matched bill failed to create much atmosphere.

1971
March 23: **Yes**, Norwich Lads' Club
What was the name of that irritating acoustic solo Steve Howe used to do?
April 4: **Bronco**, University of East Anglia, Norwich
It may be a loo roll to you, but to me it was my introduction to Jess Roden.
April 30: **Michael Chapman**, Norwich Folk Festival
And he's still on the road right now.
May 12th: **Traffic**, Norwich Lads' Club
It looked like members of this band would soon start to die. They did.
*****Arrival**, Rolle College, Exmouth
They had just had a big hit with "Friends": "We all have friends who have friends by the river". No we don't.
*****Mogul Thrash**, Rolle College, Exmouth
A bit like the Average White Band with guitar solos. Probably the best band John Wetton was ever in.
*****Osibisa**, Rolle College, Exmouth
"Don't talk about my girlfriend like that", I should have said.

1971 -72
*MC5: Eichhof, Kiel, Germany
"Excuse me, what means 'Kick Out Ze Jemms, Muzzerfuckers?'"
*Man: Eichhof, Kiel, Germany
You thought the Manics were the original Welsh windbags? No, Man were.
*Alexis Korner: Pupille, Kiel, Germany
I couldn't afford to go but I heard it through the floor.
*Frumpy, Förde-Hochhaus, Eckernförde, Germany
Inga Rumpf, Frumpy's singer, is now a Christian evangelist.
*Brian Auger Trinity / Status Quo, Stadthalle, Neumünster
Quo were cool. No longer a pop band and not yet a joke.

1973
15. October: **Free**, Colston Hall, Bristol
Heartbreaking performance to promote "Heartbreaker".
31. October: **Rory Gallagher**: Colston Hall, Bristol
A nice line in lumberjack shirts.

1974
*Stackridge, Victoria Rooms, Bristol
"The Stanley is for you and me." Mutter Slater wisely didn't take part in 1999's misguided reunion.
*John Entwistle's Ox, Bristol University
However did they get all that equipment up to the first floor?
18. September: **Deep Purple**, Stadthalle, Bremen, Germany
I'm afraid I always thought that Ritchie Blackmore was over-rated.
27. October: **Nektar**, Stadthalle, Bremen, Germany
Deutsch-Rock vom Feinsten.
4. November: **Gong**, Post-Aula, Bremen, Germany
Featuring Steve Hillage in woolly hat mode.
12. December: **Mungo Jerry**, Revolution, Bremen, Germany
Fantastic! Someone in the audience kept buying the band Jägermeister and they kept drinking and playing until they could no longer stand. The next night, the club burned down.
16. December: **The Sweet**, Stadthalle, Bremen, Germany
My snobby friends refused to attend on the basis that the Sweet were a "teenybop" band. Nonsense! Fabulous glam rock, with the drummer having a drum battle with a back projection of himself. They beat the Flaming Lips to this concept by 25 years.

* **Alice Cooper**, Stadthalle, Bremen, Germany
This was the classic Steve Hunter / Dick Wagner line-up featuring a guitar battle that drew blood.

1975
29. January: **Soft Machine**, University of Bremen, Germany
Robert Wyatt did his funny falsetto thing (again).
12. March: **Country Joe and the Fish**, University of Bremen, Germany
It wasn't exactly Woodstock revisited.
9. May: **Genesis**, Stadthalle, Bremen, Germany
The Lamb Lay Down on Broadway.
18. August: **Kevin Coyne**, Post-Aula, Bremen, Germany
Andy Summers was in this band.
27. September: **Camel**, Reithalle, Cloppenburg
I put up posters in Bremen to advertise this. We had to sit on bales of hay and pick our way carefully though the horse shit.
29. October: **The Who**, Stadthalle, Bremen, Germany
The main story in the local paper detailed how Moonie smashed up Bremen's poshest hotel. How could it be otherwise?

1976
8. February: **Status Quo**, Stadthalle, Oldenburg, Germany
Third time lucky (?) after the previous two shows had been cancelled.
27. February: **Uriah Heep**, Stadthalle, Oldenburg, Germany
I had a row with Birgit's sister-in-law after she falsely claimed that David Byron was a good singer.
14. March: **Udo Lindenberg**, Stadthalle, Bremen, Germany
What a shame this great character didn't catch on outside Germany. At one stage, he even recorded an album in English, but to no avail.
4. May: **The Rolling Stones**, Stadthalle, Bremen, Germany
I recall that they had a giant penis.
2. June: **Smokie**, Dorfhalle, Ritterhude, Germany
Sometimes, one gets desperate.
21. June: **Rolling Stones**, Knebworth
I think they were there somewhere.
23. July: **Heavy Metal Kids / XTC**, Brunel Rooms, Swindon
I don't remember what I was doing when I heard that JFK had died, but I do remember what I was doing when I heard that Gary Holton had died. XTC played "All Along The Watchtower", incidentally.

August: Reading Festival 1976 with **Rory Gallagher, Gong, Van Der Graaf Generator, Camel, The Enid, Black Oak Arkansas**
The year the Enid took the festival by storm! No, honestly.
17. October: **Jess Roden Band**, Southampton University
Funky British soul. His backing band came from Southampton, you know.
29. November: **Kiki Dee**, Gaumont, Southampton
She was briefly able to fill theatres like this.
1. December: **Caravan**, Southampton University
For Girls Who Grow Plump In The Night.
10. December: **Steeleye Span**, Gaumont, Southampton
They should really have kept it under their Hat.
17. December: **Manfred Mann's Earth Band**, Gaumont, Southampton
Big In Germany.

1977
28. January: **Supercharge / Ultravox**, Southampton University
This was the original Ultravox with John Foxx (better than any subsequent versions).
9. February: **Jethro Tull**, Gaumont, Southampton
Flamingos can stand on one leg as well.
13. February: **SAHB without Alex Harvey**, Top Rank, Southampton
Clever name, eh? Quite good even without the main man, because of Zal Cleminson.
5. March: **Pat Travers Band / Doctors of Madness**, Reading University
The Doctors had a bassist called Stoner who dressed up in a skelton suit.
9. March: **Graham Parker and the Rumour**, Guildhall, Portsmouth
Brinsley Schwarz is a cool name, don't you think?
15. March: **Gordon Giltrap**, Southampton University
There must be better things to do with a guitar.
21. March: **Bandit**, Village Bowl, Bournemouth
I went because dear old James Litherland was in the band. The singer was Jim Diamond, who later had a hit with "I Should Have Known Better".
13. April: **Tribo**, Mirandela, Portugal
Hitching though Portugal, I was befriended by this band which specialised in Camel covers! They gave a performance specially for me (which can happen if you are an Englishman abroad). The bassist Manuel is still a good friend today.
4. May: **Widowmaker**, Southampton University

Super-cool, motionless Luther Grosvenor had turned into crazed glam-rock axeman Ariel Bender.
7. May: **Ian Gillan Band**, Southampton University
I got to interview the man who has more brain than meets the eye.
11. May: **Johnny Thunders and the Heartbreakers**, King Alfred's College, Winchester
I'm probably prouder to have been at this gig than at any other ever. The appeal escaped most of the assembled student teachers, however.
20. May: **The Damned / The Adverts**, Southampton University
Mark Eitzel of American Music Club was at this gig. Not that I knew that.
27. May: **Queen**, Gaumont, Southampton
The tickets cost £2. What a rip-off.
4. June: **Caravan**, Farnborough Recreation Centre
Never go and see a band at a recreation centre.
16. June: **10cc**, Gaumont, Southampton
Apart from Eric Stewart, they just couldn't look the part.
21. July: **Weeke Jokes**, Henry Beaufort School, Winchester
My band, man.
30. June: **Roger Ruskin Spear**, Southampton University
He had a Kinetic Wardrobe.
3. July: **Bad Company**, Earl's Court, London
Paul Rodgers was already putting on weight and wore a stetson, for goodness' sake.
6. July: **Crawler / Boxer / Moon**, Guildhall, Portsmouth
What they call a package show. Roll on recycling.
21. July: **Roogalator**, Winchester Art School
Chunky R & B from Danny Adler.
12. August: **Freshly Layed Band**, Queen Inn, Burley
A fateful night.
August: Reading Festival 1977 with **Thin Lizzy, Graham Parker, Nazareth, Ultravox, Electric Chairs, Racing Cars, The Enid, The Motors**
The Motors had some of the most expensive promotion any band has ever received. It didn't help them much.
25. September: **The BA**, Riverside Inn, Winchester
"Bus Garage Café, well it's okay."
29. September: **Camel**, Southampton Gaumont
Well, I honestly thought the Snow Goose was good.
30. September: **Kursaal Flyers**, Southampton University

Not very exciting pub rock promoted above its station.
1. October: **The BA**, King Alfred's Boys Club, Winchester
First and last gig at this youth club. (There was a minor riot.)
2. October: **The Pirates**, Glen Eyre Hall, Southampton
Who'd have thought dear old Mick Green would end up at the Cavern with Macca? Good choice of guitarist, though.
4. October: **Ian Gillan Band**, Guildhall, Portsmouth
Their bassist appeared to be a heavyweight wrestler.
8. October: **Freshly Layed Band**, The White Buck, Burley
First of many trips into a forest hippie enclave.
11. October: **Throbbing Gristle**, Winchester Art School
I remember it well. Not many tunes, but Cosey Fanni Tutti looked a picture.
12. October: **Phil Manzanera's 801**, Southampton University
Good album but he never followed it up properly.
18. October: **Dr Feelgood**, Portsmouth Guildhall
Got to interview Lee Brilleaux, now in the Great Travel Lodge In The Sky.
19. October: **Racing Cars**, Southampton University
They had had some kind of hit.
26. October: **Caravan**, Southampton University
Still out to pasture. Do you know that Pye Hastings is now a sales rep?
27. October: **Wishbone Ash / The Motors**, Gaumont, Southampton
We got in on account of the aforementioned massive promotional push being given to the Motors. (Push the Motors, geddit?)
15. November: **Status Quo**, Gaumont, Southampton
At the end of the show, their leads were all tied up in a knot in the middle of the stage.
26. November: **The Ba**, Winchester Art College
Someone took a great photo of this.
28. November: **Wilco Johnson**, Village Bowl, Bournemouth
Do you know, he still does that "machine-gunning the audience" stuff today? Extraordinary.
6. December: **Freshly Layed Band**, Riverside Inn, Winchester
Watch those floorboards.
7. December: **Thin Lizzy**, Gaumont, Southampton
On the ticket, it said Thin Lizzie.

1978
6. January: **The Enid**, Basingstoke Technical College
At the time, they seemed revolutionary. They actually played "Land of Hope and Glory" and (blush) I actually enjoyed it. Bloody hell!

22. January: **Rich Kids**, Glen Eyre Hall, Southampton
If only Midge Ure had got frozen in this state. Mind you, they were furious at people gobbing at them, and they had a point.
25. January: **Talking Heads / Dire Straits**, Southampton University
That is not a misprint. The tickets cost £1 each.
3. February: **Tyla Gang**, King Alfred's College, Winchester
That's Sean Tyla, not Liv Tyla.
6. February: **Split Enz**, Southampton University
Before they wuz Crowded House. Better, too.
11. February: **Colosseum II**, South Stoneham Hall, Southampton
Gary Moore was in this band.
18. February: **Krazy Kat**, King Alfred's College, Winchester
In perfect harmony (but not with the Ents Officer).
19. February: **The Enid**, Victoria Palace, London
Did we really do this?
24. February: **The Soft Boys**, Winchester Art School
Wading through a ventilator.
27. February: **Rush**, Gaumont, Southampton
What about the voice of Geddy Lee, how does he sing so high?
11. March: **Freshly Layed Band**, Riverside Inn, Winchester
Slight return.
15. March: **Eddie and the Hot Rods**, Top Rank, Southampton
Barrie Masters did some good acrobatics on the lighting rig.
17. March: **David Coverdale Band**, Basingstoke Technical College
This is definitely a misprint.
22. March: **John Miles**, Village Bowl, Bournemouth
Music is my first love, and it will be my last. Soppy but undeniable.
30. March: **Freshly Layed Band**, White Buck, Burley
For the sake of the rainforests, an editorial decision has been taken at this stage not to mention the rest of the Freshly Layed gigs we attended (17 in all).
2. April: **The Soft Boys**, Nashville, London
Robyn Hitchcock didn't recognise me.
17. April: **Manfred Mann's Earth Band**, Guildhall, Portsmouth
Still Big In Germany.
25. April: **Graham Parker and the Rumour**, Mecca Ballroom, Portsmouth
Hold back the night.
26. April: **Rory Gallagher**, Gaumont, Southampton
Not a lot different from last time.

29. April: **UK**, Southampton University
That Bill Bruford, he can play a bit.
5. May: **The Tubes**, Gaumont, Southampton
A novelty band which can really play, that's rare.
12. May: **Lesser Known Tunisians**, The Saints, Southampton
First encounter with Wickham's answer to North Africa.
18. May: **Steve Hillage**, Poole Arts Centre
Surely it couldn't be the same woolly hat?
19. May: **Lesser Known Tunisians**, Tower Arts Centre, Winchester
We promoted this one.
3. June: **Black Sabbath**, Gaumont, Southampton
Another misprint.
4. June: **Sham 69 / Stratejacket**, Top Rank, Southampton
Like Madness later, Sham 69 didn't deserve their awful fans.
17. June: **The Blades**, Riverside Inn, Winchester
Previously the Amazorblades.
29. June: **Lesser Known Tunisians**, Old Mill, Holbury
The night of the Sounds review.
30. June: **Artemis**, Cricklade College, Andover
Greg Watkins was still playing Camel covers.
15. July: The Picnic, Blackbushe Airport, with **Bob Dylan, Eric Clapton, Joan Armatrading**.
First ever laminate on a string!
16. July: **Whirlwind**, Jumpers Tavern, Christchurch
Got a rather nice free T-shirt from this rockabilly band, one of whom now plays with Morrissey.
26 - 28 August: Reading Festival 1978 with **Spirit, The Motors, Status Quo, Sham 69, The Jam, Patti Smith Group**
A rather unpleasant atmosphere reigned, as the line-up might lead one to expect.
16. September: **Staa Marx**, Winchester Rugby Club
The sons of Mrs Aardvark. They were great.
20. September: **The Polar Bears**, The Cricketers, Winchester
Support came from the Erections, another Winchester band, one of whose members was called Dr. R. Slicker.
21. September: **10cc**, Gaumont, Southampton
I'm not in Love with 10cc any more. "Dreadlock Holiday", yuk.
23. September: **Camel**, Gaumont, Southampton
The "Breathless" tour, first sticky Backstage Pass!
26. September: **The Stranglers**, Gaumont, Southampton

A punk band in a seated venue didn't really work.

29. September: **The Warm Jets**, Riverside Inn, Winchester
Nothing to do with Brian Eno and nothing to do with the Nineties Warm Jets either. There you go.

6. October: **Thieves Like Us**, Riverside Inn, Winchester
Literally a life-altering experience.

11. October: **Climax Blues Band / Fabulous Poodles**, Southampton University
This was the sort of strangely mis-matched double bill which was around in those days. I am certain that the other support was Elvis Costello's Flip City, but I can't prove it.

20. October: **Press-Ups**, Riverside Inn, Winchester
One of our less wildly successful promotions.

21. October: **Identical Strangers**, Tower Arts Centre, Winchester
They begged me to review the gig and then moaned when they didn't like what it said.

27. October: **Staa Marx**, Riverside Inn, Winchester
Bognor rock.

28. October: **Boomtown Rats**, Gaumont, Southampton
It must be said, he didn't look like a future knight of the realm.

3. November: **The Enid**, Basingstoke Technical College
Oh, come on.

25. November: **The Aliens / Hazzard**, Theatre Royal, Winchester
The first show for a decade at this un-renovated theatre. When people danced, they stirred up so much dust that you couldn't see the stage. Or it could have been dry ice.

6. December: **Ian Gillan**, Southampton University
The all-in wrestler was still there.

23. December: **Tours**, Brewer's Arms, Poole
Something stirs in Poole. Tourist Information, please.

1979

10. February: **Supercharge**, South Stoneham Hall, Southampton
There was a bloke with a beard who played sax.

14. February: **Gruppo Sportivo**, Southampton University
They didn't sound Dutch, but they were.

3. March: **Fischer-Z**, Southampton University
Big In Germany, but this time deservedly so.

4. March: **Van Morrison**, Portsmouth Guildhall
Peter Bardens was playing with Van this time around.

16. March: **Screeens**, Salisbury Technical College
Yes, that's three "e"s. Thieves Like Us supported.
21. March: **The Hollies**, Portsmouth Guildhall
There is a place for nostalgia. Dunno where.
22. March: **Graham Parker and the Rumour**, Southampton Guildhall
*My friend Volker called him a little weasel. A tad unfair, I thought. Possibly
a stoat.*
23. March: **Freshly Layed Band**, Bournemouth Town Hall
This was their last ever gig. "Come and get the rest of the Ploughmans!"
24. March: **Identical Strangers**, Crown Hotel, Eastleigh
*They wanted me to re-assess them. There were only two other people in the
audience.*
4. May: **Mark Andrews and the Gents** / **The Lens**, Top Rank,
Southampton
Charity show. The Lens became IQ, a quite well-known prog-rock band.
5. May: **The Enid**, South Stoneham Hall, Southampton
*Backstage was fun for a change, because they were breaking up and yelling
at each other in a most ungentlemanly way.*
11. May: **XTC**, Glen Eyre Hall, Southampton
*I could see that Andy Partridge had stage fright. No, really. It takes one
phobic to know another.*
15. May: **Mark Andrews and the Gents**, Portsmouth Polytechnic
Although the personnel kept changing, this band was always great.
19. May: **Piranhas**, John Peel, Gosport
First of many sightings of these dangerous creatures.
30. May: **The Tubes**, Gaumont, Southampton
Still good musicians. Still high heels.
7. June: **64 Spoons**, Old Mill, Holbury
I think they had a famous guitarist.
8. June: **Writz**, Bishop Otter College, Chichester
*We went to check out the venue for a forthcoming Thieves gig. It turned
out to be a formal ball, so we stood out a bit.*
9. June: **Mungo Jerry**, King Alfred's College, Winchester
They were sober. How disappointing.
23 June: **Eric Bell Band**, Theatre Royal, Winchester
*Grand re-opening of the venue. After The Fire cancelled and this was a
poor substitute.*
5. July: **Joe Jackson**, Locarno, Portsmouth
A meteoric rise from the John Peel, Gosport
13. July: **The Stranglers**, Gaumont, Southampton

They didn't exactly have a charismatic stage show.
26. July: **Lip Moves**, Knight's, Eastleigh
Local band which might have made good. But didn't.
12. August: **Nightshift**, Jumper's Tavern, Christchurch
The new band of Roger "Fatman" Hunt from Freshly Layed.
August: Reading Festival 1979 with **The Cure, Motörhead, The Police, Cheap Trick, Peter Gabriel, The Ramones**
These were the Readings we liked.
1. September: **The Outsiders**, Pinecliff, Bournemouth
This time it was Tim Holt from Freshly Layed who had a new band.
10. September: **Patrik Fitzgerald**, Melkweg, Amsterdam
The Thieves sent me and Birgit to Amsterdam to recover from the strain. We sat behind Bob Geldof and Paula Yates in the tram.
27. September: **Leo Sayer**, Gaumont, Southampton
Merely in the line of duty.
28. September: **Siouxsie and the Banshees**, Gaumont, Southampton
This must have been shortly before the split.
29. September: **The Outsiders**, Pinecliff, Bournemouth
They wrote songs then that the Agency still play today.
5. October: **Camel**, Poole Arts Centre
Autographed backstage pass! Unfortunately there were hardly any original members left.
17. October: **Camel**, Gaumont, Southampton
And it isn't shome mishtake.
31. October: **Caravan**, Southampton University
A sales rep. Honest!
2. November: **Tours / Martian Schoolgirls**, Tower Arts Centre, Winchester
Fateful show. We promoted this one and some of the audience abused the venue. My relationship with the venue's management hasn't recovered to this day.
18. November: **The Jam / The Vapors**, Poole Arts Centre
Not that long before, the Vapors had been at the Old Mill, Holbury.
25. November: **The Enid**, Bournemouth Winter Gardens
They had turned into a parody of a parody.
6. December: **The Piranhas**, Crown Hotel, Eastleigh
I don't want my body ('cos it's so bloody shoddy).
13. December: **Last Orders**, Crown Hotel, Eastleigh
No, no, that was the name of the band.
16. December: **The Police**, Gaumont, Southampton

Of course it was me they were screaming at.
26. December: **Blondie**, Village Bowl, Bournemouth
One of the most sweatily joyful gigs ever.

1980
1. February: **Merger**, Basingstoke Technical College
Thieves supported. There were gigantic day-glo posters, but not a gigantic day-glo audience.
3. February: **Tom Robinson's Sector 27**, Poole Arts Centre
A lunchtime gig!
8. February: **Renaissance**, Southampton University
One of those bands of imposters, with no original members.
10. February: **The Clash**, Poole Arts Centre
The backstage pass was quite useful because it was a battlefield out front.
28. February: **Joe Jackson**, Gaumont, Southampton
I disapproved of the acapella "Is She Really Going Out With Him?" but now I realise it was quite good.
3. March: **Gillan**, Southampton University
Another interview. Whatever did we talk about?
13. February: **The Clash**, Top Rank, Southampton
No backstage pass, but a safe spot on the balcony. Below, it looked like the pitch at Twickenham.
14. February: **Bobby Henry and the Risk**, Knight's, Eastleigh
They could have gone far. They didn't.
27. February: **The Tourists**, Gaumont, Southampton
I couldn't understand why such a crummy band had such a high profile.
15. March: **The Limos**, The Saints, Southampton
This was an ambitious musician called Mark Easton. He later joined Mark Andrews and the Gents.
19. March: **The HGBs**, Railway Inn, Winchester
Chris Willey from Attic Theatre put together this R & B band.
10. May: **Inside Story**, Jumpers Tavern, Christchurch
Roger Hunt had already moved on from Nightshift.
22. May: **Da Biz**, Brewer's Arms, Poole
Ronnie Mayor from Tours with a new but very similar band.
3. June: **Whitesnake / Gary Moore's G-Force**, Gaumont, Southampton
I can't really explain this.
27. June: **John Otway / Wild Willy Barrett**, The Griffin, Southampton
You needed to take out personal insurance to be in this audience.

22-24 July: Reading Festival with **Samson, Iron Maiden, Slade, Whitesnake, Def Leppard**
Musicians Only! Favourite occupation: Dodge the Piss Bottles.
8. August: **The Blazers**, The Saints, Southampton
Good name. Can't remember the band.
20. August: **The Time**, Plough, Durrington
The beginning of a long and happy relationship.
22. September: **Ebony Rockers**, Top Rank, Southampton
Charity show with good local reggae band.
26. October: **Joe Jackson**, Bournemouth Winter Gardens
I'd forgiven him by then. Shouldn't have doubted him in the first place.
4. November: **Orchestral Manoeuvres In The Dark**, Gaumont, Southampton
They were boring and lightweight. Synth-pop, nein danke.
13. November: **Sad Café**, Gaumont, Southampton
They had a singer called Paul Young. How confusing.
18. October: **The Time**, Waterlooville Football Club
Big venue. Were they going to break through?
29. October: **Exploding Seagulls / Bitter Lemmings**: Solent Suite, Southampton
One of many gigs I attended (lost the details of the others) promoted by an enterprising label called Stick It In Your Ear.
13. November: **The League of Gentlemen**, Royal Exeter Hotel, Bournemouth
Robert Fripp on home ground. Very intense, naturally.
15. November: **The Enid**, Town Hall, Eastleigh
Down and very nearly out.
24. November: **The Damned**, Gaumont, Southampton
Neat Neat Neat! Yes Yes Yes!
30. November: **The Planets**, John Peel, Gosport
Super band which I assume must have been messed up by the industry.
6. December: **The Time**, Sussex Hotel, Bognor
This one was recorded live.
12. December: **The Kinks**, Gaumont, Southampton
Eye contact, that's what makes Ray Davies such a great live performer.

1981
8. January: **The Outsiders**, Railway Inn, Winchester
One of our promotions. A new venue, still going strong today.
15. January: **The Time**, Railway Inn, Winchester

This is where Richard Williams was inspired to enter the world of rock and roll.

30. January: **The Piranhas**, King Alfred's College, Winchester
They'd had a gigantic hit with "Tom Hark", which didn't represent them at all. To show their annoyance, they played a brilliant set of heavy dub reggae, which upset the audience (but not me).

14. February: **The Troggs**, Rock Garden, London
Valentine's Day with Reg.

15. February: **The Time**, Royal Hotel, Guildford
There was a terrible fight.

26. February: **The Time**, Cumberland Tavern, Portsmouth
Kevin sang one song from the gents' toilet.

28. February: **Camel**, Poole Arts Centre
The "Nude" tour this time. Rapidly losing patience!

6. March: **The Time**, John Peel, Gosport
I stayed the night and got a Chinese takeaway. Interesting stuff, isn't it?

7. March: **Dr Feelgood**, Southampton University
This line-up featured John "Gypie" Mayo.

11. March: **The Skavengers**, Railway Inn, Winchester
One of ours. Good sub-Police white reggae.

16. March: **The Who**, Poole Arts Centre
With Kenney Jones, the band just didn't feel right any more.

18. March: **Games To Avoid**, Railway Inn, Winchester
A serious-minded and really good band from Southampton.

21. March. **The Time**, Joiners Arms, Southampton.
According to the diary, I proposed to Birgit after this gig. It was obviously an inspirational performance, but romantic? I doubt it.

25. March: **The Time**, Railway Inn, Winchester
One of our promotions.

1. April: **Exploding Seagulls**, Railway Inn, Winchester
Nick Jacobs, later of the Blue Aeroplanes, was in this band.

3. April: **The Press**, New Queen's Head, Winchester
Local band which insisted I review them in this horrible pub.

5. April: **Zip Code**, The Victory, Southampton
A new venue. This was a new Winchester band.

21 April: **Xena Xerox**, Gilbey's, Southampton
They were furious because I didn't think they were as good as they thought they were.

4. May: **Cosmetics,** Royal Exeter Hotel, Bournemouth
More like it. Richard Mazda, ex of Tours, had a great band here.

11. May: **The Time / The Secret**, The Victory, Southampton.
*We caused a sensation by getting Tony Oxley (or was it Kevin Robinson?)
to announce that we were getting married the following day.*
12. May: **Duballup / The Secret**: Floater's, Southampton
Oh Lord, forgive me. I went to a gig on my wedding night.
25. May: **The Time / The Secret**: South Parade Pier, Southsea
Not many people in a very large room.
30. May: **The Time**, Railway Inn, Winchester
*This was Baz Mort's birthday party but it ended in chaos when somebody
tried to attack me.*
3. June: **Status Quo**, Gaumont, Southampton
Again and Again and Again.
23. June: **The Jam / The Time**, Guildhall, Portsmouth
*On this tour, the Jam selected local bands to support them. In Portsmouth,
The Time were the obvious choice. Bruce Foxton had checked them out in
Guildford.*
1. July: **Zip Code**, Railway Inn, Winchester
One of ours.
8. July: **Headless Horsemen / The Secret**, Railway Inn, Winchester
Initial sighting of John Parish's first post-TLU venture.
15. July: **The Skavengers**, Railway Inn, Winchester
One of ours.
22. July: **The Time**, Railway Inn, Winchester
One of ours.
31. July: **The Time**, The John Peel, Gosport
Home territory.
28-30 July: Reading Festival 1981 **with Girlschool, Gillan, Nine
Below Zero, The Kinks**
*I had been relegated to the Hants Chronicle, Musicians Only having closed
in November 1980.*
1. September: **Joe Jackson's Jumpin' Jive / The Time**, Locarno,
Portsmouth
*The critics didn't like this good-time band, but I thought they were fun.
Brilliant rhythm section: Graham Maby and Larry Tolfree.*
23. September: **Cosmetics**, Railway Inn, Winchester
*A last-minute booking. Richard Furter from Freshly Layed was in Cosmetics
by now, making them seriously funky.*
2. October: **The Bomb**, Stowaways, Southampton
*What a strange night. This was an unrehabilitated Peter Green, three-
inch fingernails and all, playing with local Southampton musicians.*

9. October: **Cosmetics**, Bournemouth Town Hall (with **Alternative TV**)
ATV were hilariously incompetent.
22. October: **The Time**, Joiners Arms, Southampton
The venue was completely laid waste by Portsmouth football thugs.
29. October: **Exploding Seagulls**, Winchester Art School
They were on the Fried Egg label, you know.
30 October: **Biz Internationale**, Jokers, Bournemouth
First encounter with a storming seven-piece band consisting of Dabiz plus a brass section.
3. November: **Madness**, Gaumont, Southampton
The ANL leaflets said "Support Madness, Not Racism". Well said.
13. November: **Bad Manners**, Gaumont, Southampton
Only because Magnet Records gave me free tickets.
22. November: **I.Q.**, Park Hotel, Southampton
I had given a bad review to a heavy metal band called Berlin. Someone pointed me out to their leather-clad supporters, so I did a bunk in the nick of time.
27. November: **Rick Wakeman**, Gaumont, Southampton
I was very, very rude about this. With good reason.
16. December: **Squeeze**, Top Rank, Southampton
Cool for cats.
19. December: **Four People I Have Known**, Railway Inn, Winchester
Ex-members of Zip code, including Paul Bringloe, were in this interesting band.
24. December: **Tom Robinson Band**, Marquee, London
Sweaty end-of-year show, backed by Cosmetics.
31. December: **Outsiders**, Pinecliff, Bournemouth
Birgit didn't like the fact that complete strangers insisted on kissing her. I didn't like that fact either.

1982
1. January: **The Time**, The Salutation, Portsmouth
Or maybe this was the one where Kevin sang from the bog.
8. January: **Sadista Sisters**, Quartier Latin, Berlin, Germany
They were scary on stage but I got to chat to them afterwards and found them charming.
24. February: **Four People I Have Known**, The Victory, Southampton
This band was beginning to catch on.
13. March: **Budgie**, Winchester Recreation Centre

Some naive promoters lost their shirts on this one. The curse of the Recreation Centre struck again.
21. March: **Haircut 100**, Poole Arts Centre
"Love Plus One" is still one of my all-time favourite singles.
28. March: **XTC**, Gaumont, Southampton
Terrible sound problems and far too loud.
6. April: **Headless Horsemen**, Cathedral Hotel, Salisbury
The début of John Parish's Spiderman pullover.
8. April: **Graham Parker**, Gaumont, Southampton
He had a new backing band and had lost a lot of his sparkle.
11. April: **Four People I Have Known**, Folly Market, Petersfield
We flogged a lot of cassettes.
16. April: **Headless Horsemen**, Crispin Hall, Street
A "Sheep Worrying" Fanzine Showcase. Apart from us, there were two paying customers. What is more, Street, being a Quaker town, has no pubs.
17. April: **Biz Internationale**, Midnight Express, Bournemouth
A cool new club with a cool new band.
24. April: **Cosmetics**, Midnight Express, Bournemouth
A cool new club with a cool not-so-new band.
28. April: **Headless Horsemen**, Joiners Arms, Southampton
Trotting around a bit.
5. May: **Four People I Have Known**, Saddle Bars, Bransgore
Nice venue in a New Forest barn.
22. May: **Camel**, Poole Arts Centre
That was it. I'd had enough.
26. May: **Biz Internationale**, The Waterfront, Southampton
The single was forthcoming. Unfortunately, it came fifth (arf!).
1. June: **Rory Gallagher**, Gaumont, Southampton
Much the same as last time. And the time before.
25. June: **Rolling Stones**, Wembley Stadium
I nearly got piles.
26. June: Burnt Offerings Showcase with **Four People I Have Known, Headless Horsemen** and **The Time**, Tower Arts Centre, Winchester
I've got a live tape of this. It was bloody good.
30. June: **Ideal**, The Venue, London
The best representatives of the Neue Deutsche Welle. I tried to start a roll in Soundmaker, but it didn't catch on.
7. July: **High Risk**, John Peel, Gosport

Heavy rock with its just about acceptable face on.
6. August: **Biz Internationale**, The Waterfront, Southampton
Now the single was out. The other day, I got it out of the shed and gave it another listen. "Stay True" - great soppy love song, ripe for covering by someone or other.
7. August: **Tiger Tiger**, Ad Lib Club, Kensington, London
Some stunning girls from Alresford. One of them went out with that blonde curly-haired drummer who's in Status Quo and we went to tea with them.
12. August: **Joe Jackson**, Gaumont, Southampton
All eyes were on his superb percussionist Sue Hadjopoulos.
11. September: **Chinatown**, Theatre Royal, Winchester
An absolutely terrible show-off heavy rock band.
25. September: **Gerry Hackett and the Fringes**, John Peel, Gosport
The latest incarnation of The Time, playing hilarious Sixties covers to pay off some debts. Quite priceless.
2. October: **The Beat**, Poole Arts Centre
Margaret didn't Stand Down, but they gave it their best shot.
4. October: **Wishbone Ash**, Guildhall, Southampton
Never! But here it is, in black and white.
5. October: **The Damned**, Guildhall, Portsmouth
Rat Scabies. Now that really is a good name.
5. November: **Look Back In Anger**, Havant Arts Centre
A Goth character called Jim Newby kept pestering me to write about his band. They briefly looked as if they might go somewhere.
13. November: **Two Finger Zen**, West End Centre, Aldershot
Performance art from Fred Bolton and other ex-Exploding Seagulls.
18. November: **Talk Talk**, Gaumont, Southampton
This mincing load of ninnies was later to throw off music biz conventions and turn into one of the greatest British bands of all time.
24. November: **Siouxsie and the Banshees**, Gaumont, Southampton
They had a brilliant light show.
3. December: **Gillan**, Poole Arts Centre
Bathing In Safe Water, said the headline. I though Gillan might one day do something interesting, but now he's back in Deep Purple.
10. December: **Whitesnake**, Gaumont, Southampton
A Bite To Sicken, said the headline. It's rare for me to walk out of a gig, but I walked out of this one.
19. December: **The Kinks**, Bournemouth Winter Gardens
We were in the front row and by the end I felt as if Ray Davies was my best friend. "Low Budget" was a bit of a classic rock song.

1981

11. January: **Factory**, Forum des Halles, Paris, France
On a course in France and in desperate need of a musical injection.

18. February: **Games To Avoid**, Joiners Arms, Southampton
Backgammon is worth giving a miss.

25. February: **Biz Internationale**, Midnight Express, Bournemouth
Still plugging away.

3. March: **Thin Lizzy**, Gaumont, Southampton
It was great the way Phil Lynott reflected the spotlight off the scratchplate of his guitar back onto the audience. Well, I thought so, anyway.

6. March: **U2**, Guildhall, Portsmouth
I thought they were pompous then and I still think they're pompous now. Bono scaled the balcony and planted a flag. Why?

9. March: **Gerry Hackett and the Fringes**, The Waterfront, Southampton
The Fareham Creek beat.

11. March: **Fun Boy Three**, Poole Arts Centre
Someone in the foyer said, "What's that old bloke doing here?" I turned round and discovered she was talking about me.

12. March: **10CC**, Gaumont, Southampton
Hardly recognised a soul in this band.

15. March: **Van Morrison**, Bournemouth Winter Gardens
What everybody should experience at least once: a terrible performance from a genius who has "off" days.

26. March: **Gerry Hackett and the Fringes**, John Peel, Gosport
Don Your Moptops.

2. April: **Spandau Ballet**, The Pavilion, Bournemouth
I thought Spandau Ballet were really good. All their effete followers came down from London and there was lots of tartan in evidence. I'd rather have Spandau than East Enders any day.

30. April: **Weapon of Peace**, Portsmouth Polytechnic
Even though I did a review, I don't remember a thing about them.

4. May: **Gerry Hackett and the Fringes**, Railway Inn, Winchester
Birgit was more than a bit pregnant, so we held a "Quick Before It's Too Late" Party.

12. May: **Roman Holliday**, Bournemouth Academy
They wore sailor suits.

21. May: **Gerry Hackett and the Fringes**, Sparsholt College, Winchester
Unfortunately, the agricultural students were all far too young to recognise any of the songs.

8. June: **Après Ski**, The Waterfront, Southampton
A variation on Biz Internationale with a new frontman. Ronnie Mayor had finally given up and emigrated to Australia.
10. June: **Chris Rea**, Guildhall, Southampton
Only because Magnet Records sent me free tickets. His allure evaded me.
20. June: **Steve Winwood**, Théâtre Municipale, Luxembourg
In my Top Ten gigs of all time. After this, he became involved in Corporate Rock and went rapidly downhill.
28. June: **Eurythmics**, Gaumont, Southampton
Not much better than the Tourists.
30 June: **Four People I Have Known**, Mash Tun, Winchester
On the way down.
8. July: **Weeke Jokes II**, Henry Beaufort School, Winchester
My band, man (again, but a different one, featuring the back of Mr Richard Williams.)
16. July: **Steve Winwood**, Gaumont, Southampton
Birgit being unavailable, I went with the girl next door. A mistake, since she spent the evening telling me unfascinating facts about the Alan Parsons Project.
3. August: **Après Ski**, Waterfront, Southampton
It just wasn't the same without Ronnie Mayor.
5. September: **Gerry Hackett and the Fringes**, The Salutation, Portsmouth
I've got it. THIS was the one where Kevin sang from the bog.
24. October: **Automatic Dlamini**, Bristol Bridge Inn, Bristol
A rare opportunity for me to do a bit of "mime mixing".
6. November: **Gerry Hackett and the Fringes**, BBC, Southampton
This was a recording of something called the Cellar Show, presented by John Sessions. He done well, didn't he?
26. November: **The Primary / Big Bear Little Bear**, New Bridge Inn, Southampton
Paul Bringloe was in Big Bear Little Bear and I liked them.

1984
3. February: **The Hollies**, Guildhall, Portsmouth
Tony's mildly flattened hamster was in good nick.
10. February: **Laughter In The Garden**, Joiners Arms, Southampton
A spin-off from Lip Moves.
27. March: **Views From A Park Bench**, Henry Beaufort School, Winchester

Students danced to my rendition of "Watch It" in this dance production. It wasn't exactly "Dance Hall at Louse Point" but the principle was similar.
13 and 14 April: **REM**, Knust Club, Hamburg, Germany
I still have the poster on my wall.
15. April: **UB40**, CCH, Hamburg, Germany
Confirmed as the most boring band of all time.
8. May: **Camel**, Guildhall, Portsmouth
Bye!
21. May 1984: **The Sound**, Marquee, London
I shed tears when Adrian Borland died. A shocking case of unrecognised talent.
2. June: **King**, La Sainte Union College, Southampton
Pop-art Doc Martens were sported by this lot. Paul King became a pop TV presenter.
11. June: **Odeon**, Greyhound, London
Tim Barron teamed up with an ex-member of Suzi Quatro's band, but it didn't work out.
22-24. June: Glastonbury Festival with **Ian Dury, Dr John, The Smiths, Elvis Costello**
I built up my biceps pushing the buggy around.
9. July: **Status Quo**, Gaumont, Southampton
... and Again and Again and Again ...
28. July: **Automatic Dlamini**, Antelope Hotel, Sherborne
Aha! Something stirs down in Dorset.
17. November: **Lords of the New Church / Wall of Voodoo**, Portsmouth Polytechnic
Richard Mazda had produced an album for Wall of Voodoo. That was the connection.

1985
4. January: **Rocking Erics**, Pinecliff, Bournemouth
A short-lived project by Tim Holt.
7. February: **Killing Joke**, Southampton Guildhall
They were supposed to be terrifying but were loud and uninteresting.
27. April: **Richard Thompson**, Dominion Theatre, London
This was the one where poor Richard was booed off by rampant Pogues fans. "Richard Thompson, who the fucking hell is he?" The Boothill Foot Tappers were also on the bill.
22-24. June: Glastonbury Festival with **Ian Dury, New Model Army, Style Council**

"The Year Of The Mud". We survived, although it took two days to clean up the buggy. At least it was character-building.
6. July: **Alvin Stardust / Mud**, South Wonston, Winchester
In the line of duty for the Hants Chronicle. Told you it was the Year of the Mud.

1986
4. January: **Sting**, BIC, Bournemouth
In his jazzy phase. Andy Summers put in a guest appearance, of course.
1. February: **The Bangles**, Portsmouth Polytechnic
Now this was a privilege. They were brilliant live.
15. March: **Wall of Voodoo**, Marquee, London
However did they get their cacti through customs? Support act was John Shuttleworth, introducing a persona which is now to be heard on Radio 4.
16. March: **The Merseybeats / Marmalade**: Theatre Royal, Winchester
Rather poor Sixties package tour.
8. May: **Talk Talk**, Hammersmith Odeon, London
Living In Another World. They were indeed, in a rather attractive one.
20-22. June: Glastonbury Festival with The Pogues, Psychedelic Furs, Robert Cray, Simply Red, Level 42
Extract from review: *It's 3 a.m. and the wind is blowing an icy gale, gusting violently at storm force speeds. High up on the hillside, a lone emaciated figure, clad only in a pair of flimsy underpants, struggles to prevent his flapping tent from disappearing over the precipice. Images of Stone Age Man are evoked as he bravely hammers at the bent tent pegs with a rough hewn flint.*
Of course, my wife and one-year old baby slept through the entire thing.
26. July: **The Agency**, Pinecliff, Bournemouth
First appearance of the Soul Searchers, made up of various Bournemouth stalwarts. The world's best party band.
12. October: **Curtis Mayfield**, Top Rank, Southampton
A fine man.
22. October: **Mighty Lemon Drops / Pop Will Eat Itself**, Southampton University
The support was a tad more interesting than the headline.
27. October: **Tom Robinson Band**, Salisbury Arts Centre
Our secret weapon to ensure that Lucy would be interested in music. Birgit was seven months pregnant. They played "War Baby" before it was released and I'm proud to say I predicted it would be a hit.

1987
1. February: **Robert Fripp**, Nuffield Theatre, Southampton
The League of Crafty Guitarists. Fripp seemed to have completely lost his sense of humour.
29. March: **Hollies**, Guildhall, Portsmouth
They didn't get any better, but they didn't get any worse either.
3. April: **The Agency**, Twyford Parish Hall
The first of a great many visits to our home village.
19-21. June: Glastonbury Festival with **Richard Thompson, Elvis Costello, New Order, The Communards**
Christ! A DOUBLE buggy! It was exhausting.
10. July: **The Agency**, St John's Rooms, Winchester
Typical bloody Winchester. This Winchester Hat Fair show was ruined by an invasion of beermonsters.
18. September: **Kelly McGuinness Rhythm Method**, Boar's Head, Wickham
A new blues venue which had opened in a country and western club called the Ponderosa. It felt like being in an American roadhouse.
28. October: **Flik Spatula / Who's In The Kitchen**, Southampton University
Two really good Southampton bands.
2. November: **Bad News**, Guildhall, Portsmouth
The Comic Strip being comic. The TV joke did not transfer well.
11. November: **10,000 Maniacs**, Basins, Portsmouth
A horrible venue at the top of a multi-storey car park voted Europe's ugliest building. A loss-leading gig for Natalie Merchant's band, the first UK date of the "In My Tribe" tour.
11. December: **The Agency**, Henry Beaufort School, Winchester
They got lost and arrived late but played a stormer for the staff "do".
13. December: **Cranes / Bushbabies**, Portsmouth Polytechnic
Early exposure to the work of Portsmouth's Bite Back label.
14. December: **Automatic Dlamini / Betty Pages**, Railway Inn, Winchester
Aha! One of ours. The greatness of this band was becoming apparent.

1988
26. January: **Stitch,** Joiners Arms, Southampton
This was the first-ever Next Big Thing gig. Stitch had previously been Games To Avoid and had shortened their name from Stitched Back Foot Airman.

3. February: **Roachford**, Basins, Portsmouth
A promo for "Due South". Sensibly, the band refused to play until they got paid. If we'd done that with our articles, there wouldn't have been a magazine at all.
9. February: **Blurt**, Joiners Arms, Southampton
First of three Joiners appearances from Bristol avant-garde screechers.
24. March: **Automatic Dlamini**: Railway Inn, Winchester
Back again and more and more exciting.
20. March: **FSK**, Joiners Arms, Southampton
"I Wish I Could Sprechen Sie Deutsch" sang these John Peel favourites on a rare visit to Blighty.
22. June: **M Walking On The Water**, Joiners Arms, Southampton
Another groovy German band. I have NINE albums by M Walking On The Water, even though one of them tried to chat up my wife.
23. August: **Rainbirds**, Riverside Studios, Hammersmith, London
This is where that horrible Chris Evans records TFI Friday. Yet another German band, and one that made two really good albums.
17. September: **Duck Soup**, Twyford Parish Hall
Portsmouth r & b band played at a 40th birthday party for me and Will Thallon.
5. October: **Steve Winwood**, Royal Albert Hall, London
I got vertigo in the upper balcony. And Winwood had lost it.
14. October: **The Hollies**, Poole Arts Centre
Jochen Schmidt and his girlfriend Vicky turned up out of the blue. **Oliver:** *"Vicky, what did you think of the Hollies' version of 'Purple Rain'?"* **Vicky:** *"It was Scheisse".*
27. October: **Roachford**, Quartier Latin, Berlin, Germany
"Cuddly Toy" sounded good.
19. November: **The Agency**, White Buck, Burley
New Forest Frolics.
25. November: **Billy Bragg / Michelle Shocked / Beatnigs**, Guildhall, Portsmouth
The ultimate package tour. The Beatnigs attacked sheets of metal with electric saws, just like Einstürzende Neubauten.

1989
12. January: **Wolfhounds**, Joiners Arms, Southampton
They were supported by the Mild Mannered Janitors from Portsmouth.
11. February: **Throwing Muses**, Portsmouth Polytechnic
A great US band which opened the doors for a whole lot more great US bands.

11. March: **The Agency**, Mean Fiddler, Harlesden, London
I took Craig Whipsnade, but he wasn't keen on them.
19. April: **REM**, Portsmouth Guildhall
Wonderful double bill with the Blue Aeroplanes. Michael Stipe appeared to be wearing a straitjacket. This was an early UK date of the "Green" tour.
23. May: **Big Dipper,** Joiners Arms, Southampton
Good American band. Supported by Strange Fruit, later to become Trip.
16-18 June: Glastonbury Festival with **Suzanne Vega, Van Morrison, Elvis Costello**
Extract from the review: *I observe a curry stall for half an hour and do some sums. Veg curry and pitta costs £4. There are six people serving, on average, one customer a minute each. This means they're making £1440 an hour. Nice work! One festival a year and the rest of the year on the Costa Brava.*
26. July: **Senseless Things**, River Park, Winchester
Winchester's pathetic attempt at a "festival".
6. August: **The Templemeads**, Mash Tun, Winchester
What a great name. A truly likeable "raggle-taggle" band, which made an album with the marvellous title "Ate My Kitchen".
26. August: **The Agency**, White Buck, Burley
More stirrings down in the Forest.
9. September: **Flik Spatula / Eat**, Joiners Arms, Southampton
Later, Flik's guitarist actually joined Eat.
14. October: **Van Morrison**, Gaumont, Southampton
*Back to top form. My ribald friend Malcolm Payne pretended he thought it was **Jim** Morrison.*
14. December: **Automatic Dlamini**, Railway Inn, Winchester
The first ever sighting round these parts of Polly Jean Harvey.

1990
11. January: **Automatic Dlamini**, Joiners Arms, Southampton
I videoed this classic gig. Support came from ex-Chesterfields the Betty Pages.
15. February: **Giant Sand**, Joiners Arms, Southampton
Howe Gelb found an old upright piano and spent most of the show improvising blues on it. He couldn't have hated me then because we'd never met.
18. March: **Kevin Coyne**, Tower Arts Centre, Winchester
His hair had gone white but he still had the magic.

27 March: **The Brilliant Corners**, Joiners Arms. Southampton
First of four Joiners appearances from these under-recognised Bristolians.
7. April: **The Hollies**, Mayflower, Southampton
Sorry Suzanne.
14. June: **Whisky Priests**, Railway Inn, Winchester
Bloody typical Winchester again. There was a punch-up, wasn't there.
23-25. June: Glastonbury Festival with **The Cure**
On the way home we crashed into exactly the same bridge outside Salisbury that the Rolling Stones had crashed into decades earlier. I promise we didn't do it on purpose.
9. July: **Spirit of the West**, Railway Inn, Winchester
An American band at the Railway. Blimey!
28. August: **An Emotional Fish,** Joiners Arms, Southampton
Hilarious. They brought an articulated lorry full of gear and got it stuck in St Mary Street. Serve them right.
5. September: **John Otway**, Railway Inn, Winchester
He couldn't get far up the step ladder because the ceiling was so low.
10. October: **Die Toten Hosen**, Subterrania, London
Mad German punks. "Dead Trousers" - that's a good name.
10. November: **Van Morrison**, Mayflower, Southampton
When he's good, he's very very good.
15. November: **The Becketts**, Joiners Arms, Southampton
John Parish produced this Bristol band which specialised in controversial posters.
24. November: **Happy End**, Hope Centre, Bristol
Improvised jazz in the mould of Loose Tubes.This was interesting. It was the first evidence that John Parish was a star in Bristol. Every two minutes, people came up to shake his hand.

1991
11. January: **The Agency**, Bournemouth Pavilion
It was a trifle chilly on the seafront.
2. February: **Return to the Forbidden Planet**, Cambridge Theatre, London
The return of Tim Barron, starring in this blockbuster musical.
14. February: **Trip**, West Indian Club, Southampton
They'd just been signed and everything was set fair.
23. March: **Maria McKee**, Academy, Manchester
Maria can knock spots off all the Alanis Morissettes of this world.

25. May: **BAP / Bob Geldof's Vegetarians of Love**, Hamburg, Germany
A sort of festival. Dave Stewart's band played as well. All the music was lamentable and I froze half to death.
31. May: **Joe Jackson**, CCH, Hamburg
The Laughter and Lust tour. Not much of either, unfortunately.
5. August: **John Otway / Attilla the Stockbroker**, Guildhall, Winchester
Hat Fair Cabaret, compèred by Arthur Smith.
22. August: **Trip**, West Indian Club, Southampton
Never was a band more "up for it". I was propositioned by a hooker. Never was anyone less "up for it".
29. August: **Thin White Rope**, Joiners Arms, Southampton
This was the 200th Next Big Thing gig.
8. September: **The Blues Band**, City Hall, Salisbury
Chilling. In the audience was the Languages Adviser who for years ensured that I didn't get promotion. If she was a Blues Band fan, I couldn't be.
26. October: **Runrig**, Modernes, Bremen
Christmas in Germany makes you desperate. One good thing: The roof of the venue swung open to reveal the stars.
21. December: **PJ Harvey**, Joiners Arms, Southampton
Hadn't we seen this girl somewhere before?
29. December: **Cropdusters / Trip**, East Point Centre, Southampton
A horrible old school hall.

1992
17. January: **Robyn Hitchcock / PJ Harvey**: ULU, London
Poor Robyn was upstaged and the press was out in force. I had a nasty experience in the bar. A bloke called Jon Driscoll from Waltham Chase, who years before had successfully hassled me to plug his fanzine "Teenage Kicks", had become a music media darling by the name of Jon Beast. I spotted him and went over to congratulate him on his success. He blanked me.
15. February: **Gallon Drunk**, Joiners Arms, Southampton
The support band was Asphalt Ribbons, later to become Tindersticks.
12. March: **John Campbell**, Boar's Head, Wickham
In my Top Three gigs of all time.
13. March: **Birdland / Trip**, Southampton University
I cycled there and left after my boys had finished.
28. March: **The Hamsters / The Producers**, Boar's Head, Wickham

The Hamsters did annoyingly pointless Hendrix covers.
24. April: **The Fall**, Grosse Freiheit 36, Hamburg
I nearly died. See the book.
5. May: **Dr Feelgood**, Boar's Head, Wickham
Farewell, Sir Lee. We shall not hear his like again.
27. May: **PJ Harvey**, Pyramids, Portsmouth
This was shattering. Got to go again tomorrow.
28. May: **PJ Harvey / Automatic Dlamini**, Bierkeller, Bristol
So we did. John Parish nearly fell off the stage when he saw me leering out of the audience.
3. June: **Automatic Dlamini**, The Gardens, Yeovil
A night club complete with palm trees. I scattered flyers to the winds.
26-28 June: Glastonbury Festival with **Van Morrison, Lou Reed, PJ Harvey, Shakespear's Sister**
Watching PJH, my children had their first view of crowd surfing.
14. July: **Rolling Stones**, Wembley Stadium
Actually it was Wilco Johnson. Some idiot lost the Stones tickets.
24. July: **K-Passa**, Gosport Festival
"Bollocks", we shouted. It's a compliment.
3. August: **The Fall**, Pyramids, Portsmouth
Less eventful than Hamburg.
25. August: **Eugenius / Urge Overkill**, Joiners Arms, Southampton
There was little sign that the American support band would end up in the charts.
7. September: **Throwing Muses**, Pyramids, Portsmouth
Good birthday present.
9. October: **Joe Ely / Coal Porters**, Boar's Head, Wickham
Right, I must go to Austin, Texas. Immediately.
28. October: **Guitar Orchestra / Passing Clouds**, BID, Berlin, Germany
I attended this in an effort to promote the Dlamini album, and bumped into ex-pupil Adam Green as well.
26. November: **That Petrol Emotion**, Pyramids, Portsmouth
Another band which deserved to do far better than it did.
8. December: **The Sundays,** Pyramids, Portsmouth
It was hard to see what made this band at all special.
15. December: **Automatic Dlamini**, The Cricketers, Oval, London
This was their last ever gig. I was the only paying customer.

1993

12. January: **Otis Grand**, Boar's Head, Wickham
He did a guitar walkabout and nearly trampled me to death.
13. January: **The Wishplants**, Powerhaus, Islington, London
After the band had gone off, a curtain was pulled across the stage and a disco started up.
2. February: **Stereo MCs**, Pyramids, Portsmouth
They still haven't made a second album.
23. February: **Belly**, Pyramids, Portsmouth
Belly had a gorgeous heavy metal bassist.
24. February: **Suede**, Pyramids, Portsmouth
Concave stomachs a go-go.
3. March: **The Auteurs**, Joiners Arms, Southampton
They thought they were pretty wonderful. Last time they had played at the Joiners, they had been supporting Suede.
9. March: **Birdland**, Joiners Arms, Southampton
Funniest Joiners gig ever. They asked Mint to turn out the lights so they could make a spectacular entrance. Unfortunately, they forgot to ask him to turn them on again and thus played their first two numbers in complete darkness.
22. April: **The Heartthrobs**, Joiners Arms, Southampton
A great band built around the Carlotti sisters. Should have been a lot better known.
22. May: **PJ Harvey**, Guildhall, Southampton
Support band Gallon Drunk were destroyed by the soundman. PJH were inspiring.
12. June: **The Agency,** Twyford Parish Hall
The support band, Moosehead, featured Mark Meredith from TLU and his brother Guy.
24. June: **Arthur Brown**, Joiners Arms, Southampton
No flaming headdress. A cautionary warning of the possible consequences of a rock & roll lifestyle.
25-27 June: Glastonbury Festival with **Donovan, Barenaked Ladies, Page and Plant, Midnight Oil** and **The Kinks**
I have a video of this weekend.
20. July: **Underground Lovers / ILA**, Joiners Arms, Southampton
ILA was a Henry Beaufort school band I was looking after.
24. July: **Richard Thompson**, Gosport Festival
He annoyingly didn't bring a band with him.
26. July: **The Blues Band**, Gosport Festival

Phew! No sign of the Languages Adviser.
24. August: **U2**, Pairc Ui Chaoimh, Cork, Ireland
This involved a lengthy journey through the night. Was it worth it? Was it heck.
18. September: **Richard Sinclair's Caravan**, The Gantry, Southampton
They were all in an awful state. Andy Ward, Camel's original drummer, was unrecognisable.
24. September: **Smokin' Joe Kubek / The Hoax**, Boar's Head, Wickham
Sometimes, a band is just a revelation. The Hoax was such a band.
4. October: **Clive Gregson**, Railway Inn , Winchester
Some folk is good.
7. October: **The Breeders**, Pyramids, Portsmouth
The Deal sisters looked like they'd done a few too many Deals.
28. October: **The Wedding Present**, Joiners Arms, Southampton
Indie cult favourites. Not with me.
21. November: **Robyn Hitchcock**, Wedgewood Rooms, Portsmouth
Not many people present. He will never be more than a cult, admit it.
2. November: **World Party**, Portsmouth Poly
Actually I do Wanna Sail In This Ship of Fools.

1994
15. January: **The Soft Boys**, Astoria, London
How sweet: a reunion. It sold out, too.
27. January: **Cornershop**, Wedgewood Rooms, Portsmouth
I loved their wilful non-commerciality. What a thrill when they finally got a hit, much later. On this occasion, there can't have been more than 30 people there.
7. February: **The Blue Aeroplanes**, Wedgewood Rooms, Portsmouth
It looked as if they were finally going to achieve a breakthrough. The place was packed. Almost exactly six years later, you couldn't give tickets away.
9. March: **Trans-Global Underground**, Southampton University
Everybody in the audience appeared to have been taking Ecstasy or something.
11. March: **Paul Weller**, Guildhall, Portsmouth
He had that bloke from Ocean Colour Scene with him.
18. March: **Silver Rattles**, Twyford Parish Hall
A Beatles tribute? Why would I book such a thing? Because Phil Campbell, from The Time, was on bass. I very nearly electrocuted myself by fiddling

about with things I knew nothing of.

21. April: **Walter Trout Band**, Pyramids, Portsmouth
A horrible over-the-top guitar show-off.

2. May: **Oasis**, Wedgewood Rooms, Portsmouth
"Marginally less interesting than a slumbering lugworm". I don't feel ashamed of this verdict. It just took everyone else a few years to catch up with the truth.

8. June: **Peter Perrett and the One**, Joiners Arms, Southampton
Having never seen the Only Ones, this was the next best thing. But he was a bad advert for heroin.

24-26. June: Glastonbury Festival with **Nick Cave, The Levellers, Paul Weller, James**
Not one of the most memorable festivals.

19. July: **The Agency**, Twyford Parish Hall
Back again.

16. September: **The Steamkings**, Joiners Arms, Southampton
Good local band which kept plugging away for years.

27. September: **Pretenders**, Guildhall, Portsmouth
Nobody can wear leather trousers like Chrissie can.

4. October: **Radiohead**, Pyramids, Portsmouth
I don't remember whether they were any good. But they were sniffy about playing "Creep". Shouldn't have bloody written it then.

13. October: **Sugar**, Pyramids, Portsmouth
The trouble with Bob Mould is that after a while it all begins to sound the same.

22. November: **Electrafixion**, Wedgewood Rooms, Portsmouth
Effectively it was Echo and the Bunnymen. And it wasn't very good.

25. November: **Tom Robinson**, Tower Arts Centre, Winchester
Now completely solo. Support was TV Smith from the Adverts.

21. December: **The Agency**, Twyford Parish Hall
Public demand.

1995

6. January: **The Surfing Brides**, Boar's Head, Wickham
They came highly recommended, but they weren't that good.

20. January: **Joe Jackson**, Guildhall, Portsmouth
The "Night Moves" tour. It began brilliantly with "Home Town", starting to coincide with the chiming of the Guildhall clock. Then it went downhill.

9. February: **Supergrass / Bluetones**, Joiners Arms, Southampton
A typically inspired Mint double bill. I preferred the Bluetones.

14. February: **Richard Thompson**, Pyramids, Portsmouth
Why doesn't he ever bring a band? How can you promote an electric album with an acoustic set?
6. March: **Sleeper**, Joiners Arms, Southampton
They did several Joiners shows, including a free one in 1993.
11. March: **PJ Harvey**, Shepherds Bush Empire
Tricky was the support act. He didn't get on with Island Records either.
17. March: **John Otway**, Tower Arts Centre, Winchester
Not exactly the most responsive audience in the world.
19. March: **David Thomas and Two Pale Boys**, Joiners Arms, Southampton
Almost like having Pere Ubu in your living room.
4. April: **Elastica**, Pyramids, Portsmouth
Hard to believe that we'd have to wait five years before a chance to see them again.
11. May: **PJ Harvey**, The Forum, London
We went there via Swindon. Unintentionally.
22. May: **Kirsty McColl**, Pyramids, Portsmouth
A little Twyford charabanc outing, culminating with fish and chips.
15. June: **Bettie Serveert**, Wedgewood Rooms, Portsmouth
Really good band from Holland, who turned out to have a surprisingly large UK following.
24-26. June: Glastonbury Festival with **Oasis, PJ Harvey, Portishead, Pulp**
This was the year of the pink catsuit.
6. July: **Elastica / Gene**, The Forum, London
An NME Brat show. They purposely positioned the lights to highlight Justine Frischmann's breasts. Or maybe I would have noticed them anyway.
18. July: **Black Grape**, Wedgewood Rooms, Portsmouth
This was one of their first ever shows. A good moment to catch them, as they were still bursting with enthusiasm and something approaching good health.
19 July: **Duffy**, Joiners Arms, Southampton
Yes, Steven "Tin Tin" Duffy. An artist who deserved more recognition. The audience kept calling out for Duran Duran numbers! Drummer James Powell (Georgie Fame's son) had played with Automatic Dlamini.
24. July: **Tom Robinson**, Gosport Festival
He brought a band with him but they weren't much good.
5. August: The Feile Festival, Cork, Ireland, with **M People, Sleeper, The Boo Radleys** and **Blur**

What a shame! There was hardly anyone there, so the girls got to be on Irish TV just by dancing around in front of the stage. In a Guinness-fuelled frenzy, I finally got my ear pierced.

10. August: **Kinky Machine**, Joiners Arms, Southampton
Later to become Rialto, they played at the Joiners four times.

11. October: **Sleeper**, Pyramids, Portsmouth
I took my friend Trevor but he wasn't impressed: "She can't sing!"

19. October: **Echobelly**, Joiners Arms, Southampton
Drummer Andy Henderson had been in Automatic Dlamini. Me, I tried to square the apparent picture of innocence that was Sonja Aurora Madan with a lascivious interview with her which I had read in that week's NME.

1996

17. January: **Perfume**, Joiners Arms, Southampton
They had five different styles of promotional postcard. Five!

22. January: **Björk**, BIC, Bournemouth
We first had to sit through the Brodsky Quartet caterwauling for an hour.

24. January: **Placebo**, Joiners Arms, Southampton
My idea of a truly terrible band.

25. January: **Catatonia**, Joiners Arms, Southampton
First sight of Cerys in action and one thing was obvious: This is a star.

5. February: **Northern Uproar**, Joiners Arms, Southampton
A lot of fuss about nothing.

11. February: **Number One Cup**, Joiners Arms, Southampton
Is this a bra size?

22. February: **Alan Price and the Electric Blues Company**, Bridport Arts Centre
Awful to behold. Sub-standard pub rock from musicians who had once been star attractions.

23. February: **The Producers**, Tower Arts Centre, Winchester
This was something rare: A Brit blues band with taste and flair.

26. February: **Echobelly**, Pyramids, Portsmouth
They had a fantastic soppy slow song at the end.

3. March: **Audioweb / Mansun**, Joiners Arms, Southampton
One of those "whoo" moments. Mansun are absolutely my kind of band. "We are destined to be stars and nothing will stop us".

4. March: **Screeper / Velcro**, Wedgewood Rooms, Portsmouth
Screeper's manager Tony Rollinson reminded me so much of me in Thieves days that I suspected I'd died and been reincarnated.

12. March: **The Bluetones**, Pyramids, Portsmouth

They found the transition to a big stage problematic.
2. April: **Tiny Monroe**, Joiners Arms, Southampton
Four-piece in the style of Echobelly / Sleeper. Great stage presence.
14. April: **Catatonia / Space**, The Brook, Southampton
Some Welsh double bill. Unfortunately, this super venue is now used almost exclusively by bloody tribute bands.
17. April: **Aimee Mann**, Shephards Bush Empire, London
In the audience was Tony Banks, a future government minister. A good reason to vote Labour, then.
27. April: **Pete Harris Blues Band / XL5**, Twyford Parish Hall
An unpromising name for actually a quite swinging dance band. Dear old Mark Andrews fronted XL5.
17. May: **Bottomless Pit Orchestra**, The Eagle, Winchester
This was Chris Willey back again, playing in a fleapit.
26. May: Essential Festival, Brighton with **Audioweb, Bis, Drugstore, Echobelly, Baby Bird, Whipping Boy**
I went with Lucy and it pissed all day. Whipping Boy were brilliant, whatever became of them?
6. June: **Sleeper**, Southampton Guildhall
They failed, like every other band here, to overcome the acoustics.
16. June: **Freakpower**, Portsmouth Polytechnic
This time I went with Annabel and the bouncers were awkward. We had a backstage pass, however, courtesy of the bassist Jesse, who had been in a musical with Tim Barron. Norman Cook is a better rhythm guitarist than a DJ.
17. June: **Mansun**, Joiners Arms, Southampton
Headlining now.
5. July: **The Agency**, Twyford Parish Hall
More soul searching.
17. July: **Tiger / Linoleum**, Joiners Arms, Southampton
I put my name on Linoleum's mailing list and for the next few years, I kept receiving bits of lino through the post. I nearly accumulated enough to finish the kitchen floor.
20 - 21 July: **Womad Festival**, Reading
Lots of good people whose names I can't spell.
26. July: **Bottomless Pit Orchestra**, The Eagle, Winchester
More fleas.
4. September: **Sneaker Pimps / Screeper**, Joiners Arms, Southampton
Chris Corner of the Sneaker Pimps took a call on his mobile phone on stage. Cool or what?

7. September: **Howe Gelb**, The Pit, Farnham
My birthday treat. As Howe was a friend of John Parish's, we offered to help him get to the nearest railway station, but he refused. He doesn't like me.
9. September: **Robyn Hitchcock / Homer**, Joiners Arms, Southampton
Someone wrote an incomprehensible letter to the Chronicle about Homer.
18. September: **Linoleum**, Joiners Arms, Southampton
I spotted a brilliant guitarist in this band, and lo and behold, he later joined Elastica.
24. September: **Longpigs**, Pyramids, Portsmouth
A Crispin and a Crispian within a fortnight. What's rock & roll coming to?
27. September: **XL5**, The Bridge, Shawford
Not even Mark Andrews could awaken the audience in this "Ignore the band" pub.
1. October: **Kula Shaker**: Pyramids, Portsmouth
When I went to the bar, I looked to the left and saw Richard Branson (record company boss). Then I looked to the right and saw Sir John Mills (Crispian's grandfather).
2. October: **Nils Lofgren**, The Brook, Southampton
Quite nice to drive ten minutes down the road and see a legend in a pub.
5. October: **John Parish and PJ Harvey**, The Cavity, Bridport
The best night of my life.
6. October: **The Hoax**, The Brook, Southampton
Would they break through? They'd already been on Later With Jools Holland.
8. October: **John Parish and PJ Harvey**, Fleece and Firkin, Bristol
We stayed at a guest house in Whitchurch called Revilo. It wasn't very good.
12. October: **The Producers**, The Brook, Southampton
They kept playing until they more or less had to be carried offstage.
13. October: **Nut**, Joiners Arms, Southampton
A girl singer briefly touted by some record company. The name wasn't too promising.
16. October: **Audioweb**, Wedgewood Rooms, Portsmouth
The press hated this band but I thought the combination of soulful vocals and chunky guitars was quite clever.
4. November: **Drugstore**, Wedgewood Rooms, Portsmouth
The crowd was small but the amount of red wine consumed on stage was

quite large.
5. November: **Catatonia**, Wedgewood Rooms, Portsmouth
The buzz was growing fast now.
16. November: **Edward II**, RKL Club, Gosport
The most danceable band on the planet, it said. Unfortunately, the audience was clinically dead.
18. November: **Scheer**, Joiners Arms, Southampton
Good band from Northern Ireland. "Head" from Yeovil was doing the sound.
30. November: **La Cucina**, RKL Club, Gosport / **K-Passa**, The Brook, Southampton
A trawl for a danceable band to play in Twyford.
12. December: **Peter Green Splinter Group**, Wedgewood Rooms, Portsmouth
Cozy Powell was on drums!
20. December: **The Hoax**, Salisbury Arts Centre
In my top ten gigs ever.
21. December: **The Producers / XL5**, Twyford Parish Hall
Unprofessionally. I got drunk and couldn't remember if I'd locked up the hall or not. Had to go back in the middle of the night to check.

1997
11. January: **The Producers**, The Brook, Southampton
More of the same.
21. January: **Super Furry Animals, Kenickie**, Astoria, London
This was an NME Brat show. Kenickie were just beginning to attract attention.
2. February: **Screeper**, North Pole, Winchester
Their manager, Tony Rollinson, wrote a book about music in Portsmouth, not by any means as short a volume as you might think.
5. February: **Candyskins**, Joiners Arms, Southampton
Oxford band on the way down.
6. February: **John Parish and PJ Harvey**, Queen Elizabeth Hall, London
Sumptuous surroundings for the Louse Point dance show.
12. February: **Silver Sun**, Joiners Arms, Southampton
Spunky harmony pop.
26. February: **Gene**, Guildhall, Southampton
The Supernaturals supported and were better than Gene.
28. February: **The Agency, The Producers**, Winter Gardens, Bournemouth

A fund-raiser for Bournemouth Football club!
6. March: **Rosa Mota**, Joiners Arms, Southampton
Certainly the loudest band ever to play the Joiners.
12. March: **Pavement**, Pyramids, Portsmouth
My favourite US band at the time. Check out the mad drummer.
20. March: **Symposium**, Joiners Arms, Southampton
Spoilt brats.
25. March: **Gorkys Zygotic Mynci**, The Brook, Southampton
Gorkys on top form before record company tomfoolery.
28. March: **T-Rextasy**, Wedgewood Rooms, Portsmouth
Ugh! A tribute band. Paul made me go.
3. April: **K-Passa**, The Brook, Southampton
Mass pogoing.
15. April: **Gold Blade**, Joiners Arms, Southampton
My pet goths Gretschen Hofner supported and were more interesting than the self-aggrandising Gold Blade.
20. April: **Billy Bragg,** Salisbury Arts Centre
Very special Bragg show: It was just before the General Election!
21. April: **Gorkys Zygotic Mynci**, Wedgewood Rooms, Portsmouth
On an upward trajectory.
23. April: **Catatonia**, Wedgewood Rooms, Portsmouth
And another.
25. April: **La Cucina**, Twyford Parish Hall
The conga went right the way round the outside of the hall. One of those bands where it's impossible to believe that such thrilling music can't make a living for itself.
1. May: **Mansun**, Pyramids, Portsmouth
The perfect rock & roll attitude.
13. May: **Ian Hunter**, The Brook, Southampton
Not nearly as good as his past had led one to believe.
14. May: **Fejl Garvie**, Joiners Arms, Southampton
Adam Green's latest effort. Even less likely to succeed than the previous ones.
17. May: **Jackie Leven**, Tower Arts Centre, Winchester
I really wanted to be positive about Jackie. He was good but still took himself too seriously.
20. May: **Kenickie**, Wedgewood Rooms, Portsmouth
At their best. It wouldn't last long.
21. June: **Pete Harris Blues Band,** Twyford Parish Hall
This was Birgit's 40th birthday party. Support was the first (and last)

performance by Revilo and Ricardo. I demonstrated my love by forcing myself to go on stage with Richard Williams and sing "Stay", "The One I Love" and "Don't Ask Me". We got an encore.

23. June: **Ash**, Wedgewood Rooms, Portsmouth
Glastonbury warm-up bedlam.

24. June: **Primal Scream**, Wedgewood Rooms, Portsmouth
Every Sister is a Star. What a brilliant, brilliant band. And this was them allegedly not on top form.

27-29 June: Glastonbury Festival with **Sting, Radiohead, The Prodigy, Primal Scream**
I fail to see the charm of Radiohead. It seems I am not in the majority.

4. July: **World Party**, Guildhall, Portsmouth
Hello Jumbo. Now the brains behind Robbie Williams.

10. July: **Vex**, North Pole, Winchester
They got "Indie Album Of The Month" in MOJO.

12. July: **La Cucina**, The Brook, Southampton
All their families were there.

19. July: **The Agency**, Twyford Parish Hall
They brought the hall down as usual.

26 - 27 July: **Womad Festival**, Reading
We had a go at a drum workshop.

6. September: **Paul Jones and Dave Kelly**, The Pit, Farnham
My birthday present again. A sweet little venue which holds about thirty people, but the food was awful.

13. September: **The Cage**, Tower Arts Centre, Winchester
The grand debut of Richard's band. I was in a furious mood because of having been refused admission to see Eric Bibb at the same venue the previous night on account of arriving five minutes late.

24. September: **Tanya Donnelly**, Wedgewood Rooms, Portsmouth
Considerably more mellow music than last time round.

2. October: **Stereolab**, Wedgewood Rooms, Portsmouth
I love a band that sets up its own gear.

8. October: **Spiritualized**, Pyramids, Portsmouth
I hated it. Dunno why. Within a couple of months I'd decided they were brilliant.

9. October: **Strangelove**, Wedgewood Rooms, Portsmouth
Fantastic. Patrick Duff was a complete natural. Fail to understand why he's so unpopular with the press. Maybe because he's got a brain?

28. October: **Seventeen Reasons Why**, Hotel Utah, San Francisco
A visit to the home of American Music Club. We ate salsa and corn chips.

13. November: **Flaming Stars**, Joiners Arms, Southampton
The natural successors to Gallon Drunk. Nice, seedy, skinny blokes in dark, baggy Oxfam suits.
14. November: **The Hoax,** Salisbury Arts Centre
Birgit's brother Harald flew in from Germany specially to see them. It was worth it.
2. December: **Echobelly**, Pyramids, Portsmouth
They had really sweet twinkly lights on their backdrop but all their albums sounded the same.
3. December: **Robyn Hitchcock**, Joiners Arms, Southampton
Our feet nearly froze to the floor.
13. December: **The Producers**, Twyford Parish Hall
Xmas special.
18. December: **Chris T-T**: Railway Inn, Winchester
My brave ex-pupil (previously in ILA), striking out on his own.
29. December: **The Hoax**, Wedgewood Rooms, Portsmouth
Videoed for posterity. I can see all my friends in it (well, not all of them).

1998
17. January: **The Agency**, BIC, Bournemouth
Gulp! A Harley Davidson convention!
20. January: **Spiritualized**, Salisbury Arts Centre
So this is what it's like to take drugs!
22. January: **Richard Thompson**, Salisbury City Hall
He still didn't bring a band, only his son.
29. January: **Catatonia**, Wedgwood Rooms, Portsmouth
You could hardly get in there.
5. February: **User / Screeper**, Wedgewood Rooms, Portsmouth
"Showcase" recording for a TV show called SFX.
18. February: **Colin John**, The Cavity, Bridport
I met a couple I'd last seen on the Rochdale Canal. We unforgivably chatted in loud voices all the way through the performance.
23. February: **Sleeper / Rialto**, Pyramids, Portsmouth
"But she can't sing!"
21. March: **The Hollies**, Mayflower, Southampton
Please don't tell me I look as old as this audience.
27. March: **Asian Dub Foundation**, Wedgewood Rooms, Portsmouth
What sprung dance floors were invented for.
28. March: **La Cucina**, Twyford Parish Hall

They broke up soon afterwards. No connection.
30. March: **Bobby Mack and Night Train,** The Brook, Southampton
He said the competition in Austin, Texas is so fierce that he can't get a gig there. We gotta go to Austin!
31. March: **Drugstore,** Wedgewood Rooms, Portsmouth
They have an album out and even the prospect of a hit single with Thom Yorke. Success for Drugstore? That would ruin everything.
18. April: **Preacher Boy,** The Brook, Southampton
From Tenderloin, San Francisco.
25. April: **Catatonia,** Southampton University
We took Annabel. She was amazed by the crowd surfers. This band was about to go ballistic.
28. April: **Jesus and Mary Chain,** Wedgewood Rooms, Portsmouth
They seemed a bit bad tempered.
2. May: Creamfields Festival, Winchester with **Beth Orton, Finley Quaye, Primal Scream**
Surrounded by wild-eyed maniacs shouting, "Ello Mr Gray! What're you on then?"
6. May: **Heather Nova,** Wedgewood Rooms, Portsmouth
She was marvellous and had a really good band as well.
31. May: **Kenickie,** Wedgewood Rooms, Portsmouth
They were terrible and obviously about to break up.
2. June: **Embrace,** Wedgewood Rooms, Portsmouth
I wouldn't want to cuddle them.
5. June: **Billy Bragg,** Wedgewood Rooms, Portsmouth
The crowd was unconvinced by the Woody Guthrie stuff. Don't worry, you'll get used to it eventually.
14. June: **Eric Bibb,** The Brook, Southampton
Got to see him at last but he was a bit too Mr Perfect for me.
16. June: **The Cage,** Tower Arts Centre, Winchester
The plan was to sell lots of CDs. The plan failed.
26 - 28. June: Glastonbury Festival with **Blur, Catatonia, Pulp, Robbie Williams**
Independent on Sunday! Fame at long, long last!
1. July: **Spleen.** The Thekla, Bristol
A fantastic noise from Rob Ellis and co. On a ship, as well.
4. July: **Preacher Boy,** Red Eye Club, London
I don't recommend wandering round Kings Cross late at night, unless you're getting paid for it.
5. July: Party In The Park, Hyde Park, London, with **Tom Jones, All Saints, Boyzone**

I got to stand in a queue with Sir David Frost. Lucy got David Duchovny's autograph and then spoke to Prince Charles. The music was shite.

11. July: **The Hoax**, Twyford Parish Hall
The summit of my promoting career. People said they were too loud and I just didn't care.

18. July: **Noel Redding Band**, Tower Arts Centre, Winchester
Probably the most depressing gig of my life. How could a rock legend demean himself so?

25 - 26 July: **Womad Festival**, Reading
I remember dancing to "White Lines" in the Rough Guide tent at 2 am.

3. August: **PJ Harvey**, Bridport Arts Centre
An intimate warm-up for the "Is This Desire?" tour. Great support band too: White Hotel.

10. August: **Ian Dury**, Dingwalls, London
On great form despite ill health.

11. August: **Lodger**, Dingwalls, London
Island records showcase for a new signing. Just for once, I could look around at all the journalists and think, "I'm one of you!"

15. August: **The Producers**, The Brook, Southampton
You'd think one would get bored. One wouldn't.

5. September: **Thieves Like Us, The Agency, Trip, The Cage, Z.inc**, Twyford Parish Hall
Or maybe this was the best day of my life. My 50th birthday party.

19. September: **Bop Brothers**, Ashcroft Arts Centre, Fareham
Checking out a Brit Blues outfit for a possible booking. The venue was a school hall. Shudder!

27. September: **Jackie Leven**, The Brook, Southampton
He told a lot of rude stories.

28. September: **Daheebiejeebies**, Lucy's Retired Surfer's, Austin, Texas, USA
Jet lagged and in heaven.

29. September: **Maceo Parker**, Antone's, Austin, Texas
Funk Overload, the Real Thing! And we met someone who had been at Glastonbury.

30. September: **Monte Montgomery**, Saxon Bar, Austin, Texas
Tequila overdose! The next day, I bought his album.

3. October: **R.L. Burnside**, House of Blues, New Orleans
Genuine toothless blues.

4. October: **John Carey**, Tipicino's, New Orleans
Kill that digital sound system.

8. October: **Hurricane No. 1**, Joiners Arms, Southampton
One of these ended up in Oasis.
12. October: **Rialto / Lodger**, Wedgewood Rooms, Portsmouth
Overblown and over-hyped. Rialto, not Lodger.
14. October: **Ash**, Guildhall, Portsmouth
Ash have one of the wildest audiences ever, but the songs were great and Charlotte Hatherley had transformed the band.
19. October: **Grandaddy**, Wedgewood Rooms, Portsmouth
The lowest-fi imaginable. A quiet electric band - how refreshing.
20. October: **Mansun**, Guildhall, Southampton
Annabel fell asleep.Well, she was tired.
26. October: **Bob Mould / Mercury Rev**, Reading University
Just a minute, who's that support band? The candelabra gave them away. I made the fatal mistake of going to the front during Bob Mould's set and couldn't hear for a week.
27. October: **Silver Sun**, Wedgewood Rooms, Portsmouth
*I'm sorry, but I **like** harmony vocals.*
11. November: **Morcheeba**, Pyramids, Portsmouth
Quite pleasant to listen to but not much of a live spectacle.
16. November: **Roddy Frame**, Wedgewood Rooms, Portsmouth
Very impressive. Just as lively and inspired as in Aztec Camera days.
26. November: **Edward II**, The Brook, Southampton
Could we afford to book them? No.
28. November: **John Cooper-Clarke**, Tower Arts Centre, Winchester
Bernard Manning lives.
2. December: **Drugstore**, Wedgewood Rooms, Portsmouth
Yes, well, by now it had all gone horribly wrong, of course.
11. December: **PJ Harvey**, Colston Hall, Bristol
We all went down in a gang. We walked out of the car park and someone threw a bottle at us. Thanks a bunch.
12. December: **The Producers**, Twyford Parish Hall
They stayed over and played a lunchtime gig at the Bugle the next day, despite having consumed the best part of a bottle of whisky before going to bed. Hard livin' bluesmen.
18. December: **PJ Harvey / Howe Gelb**, Olympia, Dublin, Ireland
I stayed in Swords, where Boyzone come from. Howe Gelb still doesn't like me.

1999
8. January: **Orko**, Railway Inn, Winchester

Briefly managed by Mint. Probably a mistake.
9. January: **Reconsider**, Talking Heads, Southampton
A young blues band. So bad that I decided not to review it for fear of being too offensive. Getting old at last.
19. January: **Mercury Rev**, Wedgewood Rooms, Portsmouth
Putting in a bid to be my favourite band of all time.
25. January: **John Parish**, Wedgewood Rooms, Portsmouth
A live version of his "Rosie" film soundtrack. It really worked.
8. February: **Heather Nova**, Salisbury Arts Centre
Twyford village outing. Heather is a suitable role model for any teenage girl.
13. February: **Miller Anderson**, Vintage Inn, Shedfield
And this was the man who wrote most of the songs on the Keef Harley albums.
20. February: **Colosseum**, The Brook, Southampton
Oh God! Dave Clempson was half bald and wore glasses. They hadn't progressed at all in 25 years. There was really no need to insult the audience like this.
24. February: **Los Pacaminos**, The Brook, Southampton
Paul Young's hobby Tex-Mex band.
26. February: **The Creatures**, Salisbury Arts Centre
The audience seemed to have taken a wrong turning from the Rocky Horror Show.
5. March: **Wilco Johnson**, Tower Arts Centre, Winchester
He wasn't getting any better either.
9. March: **Rumdum**, Joiners Arms, Southampton
The grand re-opening of the Joiners after re-furbishment. They put the stage against the only wall which hadn't been tried before.
16. March: **Glenn Tilbrook**, The Brook, Southampton
You can't half singalong to those old Squeeze songs.
20. March: **Bop Brothers**, Twyford Parish Hall
Undemanding blues evening.
1. April: **PJ Harvey and John Parish**, Improv. Theatre, London
They were sensational. It was supposed to be John Peel's birthday party but turned out to be the first of many. Echo and the Bunnymen were so bad that Birgit was yelling "Boo, get off", like the guys in the Muppet Show.
9. April: **K-Passa**, Talking Heads, Southampton
Should I book them?
12. April: **Rosita**, Joiners Arms, Southampton

Kenickie spin-off, hardly worth the bother.
13. April: **Bobby Mack and Night Train**, The Brook, Southampton
Southampton, Texas, what's the difference?
16. April: **The Hoax**, The Brook, Southampton
Recording their farewell live album.
19. April: **Ultrasound**, Wedgewood Rooms, Portsmouth
Fat people being not very good. My unerring antennae for a band about to break up proved reliable again.
27. April: **Howe Gelb**, The Cumberland, Bristol
He STILL doesn't like me.
9. May: **Handsome Family**, Tower Arts Centre, Winchester
Murder in the woods. Sylvia Sims is a big fan (You'll have to read the book).
10. May: **John Cale**, Wedgewood Rooms, Portsmouth
The fact that it was billed as a "Spoken Word" event didn't put people off calling out for Velvet Underground songs.
12. May: **dEUS**, Wedgewood Rooms, Portsmouth
Belgium's finest. They'd gone a bit "alt-country" but none the worse for that.
15. May: **Colin Blunstone**, The Brook, Southampton
The Zombies' "Odessy and Oracle" is one of my favourite albums. Colin was encouragingly elegant and unravaged.
29. May: Homelands Festival, Winchester, with **Dot Allison, Asian Dub Foundation, Black Star Liner**
More pop-eyed maniacs.
30 - 31 May: Bishopstock Festival, Exeter, with **Taj Mahal, Buddy Guy, Magic Slim**
It rained and there weren't many people, but it didn't matter because this weird event was bankrolled by rich people for our entertainment. There are certainly worse things to spend your money on.
3. June: **The Producers**, Tower Arts Centre
They'd just been voted British Blues Band of the Year.
6. June: **A**, Joiners Arms, Southampton
It was very rumbustious but not much else.
17. June: **Scott 4**, Joiners Arms, Southampton
An unsuccessful attempt to appear cool in stetsons.
20. June: **Tom Robinson**, Tower Arts Centre, Winchester
He downloaded some of his own lyrics on the internet in the interval.
22. June: **Wilco**, Wedgewood Rooms, Portsmouth
Jeff Tweedy wins my vote for seediest rocker of the century. He also hurled

himself backwards through the drumkit during the encore.
25 -27. June: Glastonbury Festival, with **Hole, Blondie, REM, Manic Street Preachers**
But more importantly, Marianne Faithfull.
10. July: **The Agency**, Twyford Parish Hall
Probably their best ever performance. They wanted to make up for being pissed on my birthday.
23 - 25 July: **WOMAD Festival**
We handed out 2000 Robyn Hitchcock flyers.
14. August: **Chris T-T**, Railway Inn, Winchester
Still brave. If I didn't know better, I'd have offered to manage him.
26. August: **Ten Benson**, Joiners Arms, Southampton
Loony local support, Rumdum, were better.
27. August: **Robbie McIntosh**, The Brook Southampton
Desperately disappointing solo effort from Macca's sideman.
1. September: **Death In Vegas**, Wedgewood Rooms, Portsmouth
One of those wild nights, full of excitement. Spiritualized revisited.
4. September: **Willard Grant Conspiracy**, Melkweg, Amsterdam
Robert Fisher assured me: "When we come to England, we'll be visiting some small towns like Manchester, Birmingham and Winchester." They did.
5. September: **Luscious Jackson**, Melkweg, Amsterdam
Luscious by name, luscious by nature.
6. September: **Sparklehorse**, The Garage, London
John Parish wangled me in. People annoyingly talked in the quiet bits.
9. September: **Edward II**, The Brook, Southampton
We definitely couldn't afford to book them. And then they split up.
10. September: **Llama Farmers**, Joiners Arms, Southampton
Trevor's "stag night"! Forever to be known as a Llama Night.
11. September: **Trevor's wedding**, Oxford
A live performance by me of a re-written version of "Clever Trevor". All because I was too scared to make a speech.
13. September: **Arab Strap**, Wedgewood Roms, Portsmouth
I didn't care at all about that ugly Scottish bloke's troubled love life.
18. September: **The Hoax**, South Parade Pier, Portsmouth
Nearly the end.
24. September: **Robyn Hitchcock**, Tower Arts Centre, Winchester
All the elements were there: Guest appearance by Kimberley Rew, nearly a fight in the audience and Robyn Hitchcock still didn't recognise me.
30. September: **Chris T-T,** Railway Inn, Winchester

No, no, I won't be tempted.
6. October: **Campag Velocet**, Wedgewood Rooms, Portsmouth
Objectively, not a promising format. Subjectively, hugely enjoyable because the attitude was so good.
13. October: **The Hoax**, Astoria, London
The absolute end. The autograph session continued afterwards in Tottenham Court Road.
16. October: **Sonny Black and the Dukes**, Tower Arts Centre, Winchester
Anaemic Brit blues in a cabaret style.
18. October: **Dan Penn and Spooner Oldham**, Tower Arts Centre, Winchester
Quelle scoop! The old boys and their Do Right Women done good.
3. November: **Reg Presley**, Tower Arts Centre, Winchester
He said he knew where to mine for gold. But since "Four Weddings and a Funeral", he doesn't need to bother.
8. November: **David Gray**, Wedgewood Rooms, Portsmouth
Good name, good bloke.
12. November: **Eugene Hideaway Bridges**, Tower Arts Centre, Winchester
Hideaway? Good idea.
16. November: **The Flaming Lips**, Wedgewood Rooms, Portsmouth
Brilliant performance art. In my Top Three ever.
25. November: **Paddy Casey**, Joiners Arms, Southampton
A bit like Marc Bolan. Are we coming full circle?
11. December: **John Otway / K-Passa**, Twyford Parish Hall
This is where we came in.
26. December: **The Agency**, Liquids, Bournemouth
Finishing the Millennium in traditional style.

The Flaming Lips: Second best gig of all time?

Gary Revilo's Top Three Gigs Ever:

1. **John Parish and Polly Jean Harvey**, The Cavity, Bridport
2. **The Flaming Lips**, Wedgewood Rooms, Portsmouth
3. **John Campbell**, Boar's Head, Wickham

Thieves Like Us

Complete gig list during the time I "managed" the band:

1979

9. January: **Portsmouth Polytechnic**

12. January: **Elm Tree, Ringwood**

13. January: **Bedales School, Petersfield**

17. January: **Old Mill, Holbury**

19. February: **Dorset Institute, Bournemouth**

22. January: **White Horse, Rogate**

26. January: **Old Mill, Holbury**

31. January: **Pinecliff, Bournemouth**

1. February: **Crown Hotel, Eastleigh**

2. February: **Bridge House, Canning Town**

3. February: **Alex Wood Hall, Cambridge**

8. February: **Swan, Hammersmith**

9. February: **Royal Oak, Passfield**

10. February: **Charterhouse School**

13. February: **The Tramshed, Woolwich**

16. February: **Wokingham Rock Club**

17. February: **Magnums, Basingstoke**

21. February: **Old Mill, Holbury**

22. February: **Lottsbridge Arms, Eastbourne**

23. February: **The Onslow, Southampton**

24. February: **Bishop Otter College, Chichester**

2. March: **Banbury College**

3. March: **Ancaster School, Bexhill**

4. March: **Poole Arts Centre**

7. March: **Swan, Hammersmith**

9. March: **King Alfred's College, Winchester**

10. March: **Bridge House, Bracknell**

11. March: **Elm Tree, Ringwood**

13. March: **Western Counties, Paddington**

15. March: **Bournemouth Town Hall (with Wild Horses)**

16. March: **Salisbury Technical College**

17. March: **Cranbrook School**

19 - 21 March: **Crockers, Bristol**

22. March: **Culham College, Oxford**

26 March: **Corn Dolly, Oxford**

28. March: **Old Mill, Holbury**

29. March: **Brockenhurst College**

30. March: **Brewers Arms, Poole**

31. March: **Swan, Hammersmith**

1. April: **Windsor Castle, Harrow Road, London**

2. April: **White Horse, Rogate**

4. March: **Pinecliff, Bournemouth**

5. March: **Crown Hotel, Eastleigh**

7. March: **Magnum's, Basingstoke**

27. March: **Capone's, Bournemouth**

28. March: **Triad Leisure Centre, Bishops Stortford**

29. March: **Laker's Hotel, Redhill**

30. March: **White Horse, Rogate**

4. May: **Top Rank, Southampton**

8. May: **Target Club, Reading**

10. May: **Pinecliff, Bournemouth**

13. May: **Windsor Castle, Harrow Road, London**

14. May: **South Bank Polytechnic, London**

17. May: **Old Mill, Holbury**

18. May: Langrish House Hotel, Petersfield

23. May: Eton College

24. May: Crown Hotel, Eastleigh

25. May: Brewers Arms, Poole

28. May: Corn Dolly, Oxford

31. May / 1. June: Crockers, Bristol

2. June: Nowhere Club, Bicester

(Single recorded at Surrey Sound)

17. June: Buccaneer, Brighton

20. June: Pinecliff, Bournemouth

21. June: Swan, Hammersmith

22. June: Magnums, Basingstoke

23. June: Theatre Royal, Winchester

24. June: Jumpers Tavern, Christchurch

25. June: White Horse, Rogate

28. June: Swan, Hammersmith

30. June: Bridge House, Bracknell

5. July: Old Mill, Holbury

7. July: Cellar Vino, Weymouth

10. July: Windsor Castle, Harrow Road, London

13. July: Pinecliff, Bournemouth

14. July: Plume, Hungerford

15. July: Three Lions, Farncombe

18. July: Henry Beaufort School, Winchester

19. July: Joiners Arms, Southampton

25 July: Fagin's Kitchen, Taunton

31 July: Windsor Castle, Harrow Road, London

4. August: Swan, Hammersmith

5. August: Jumpers Tavern , Christchurch

11. August: Gloucester Bars, Weymouth

12. August: **Poole Arts Centre**

13. August: **Corn Dolly, Oxford**

17 - 17. August: **Crockers, Bristol**

18. August: **Salisbury City Hall**

19. August: **Laker's Hotel, Redhill**

22. August: **Swan, Hammersmith**

23. August: **Old Mill, Holbury**

24. August: **Magnums, Basingstoke**

25. August: **Cellar Vino, Weymouth**

(This was the gig at which John Parish first saw the band)

26. August: **Pinecliff, Bournemouth**

28. August: **Joiners Arms, Southampton**

29. August: **Windsor Castle, Harrow Road, London**

30. August: **Gloucester Bars, Weymouth**

31. August: **Camelot Suite, Yeovil**

3. November: **Tower Arts Centre, Winchester**

7. November: **Moonlight Club, West Hampstead**

8. November: **Dorchester Tavern**

9. November: **Magnums, Basingstoke**

11. November: **Pinecliff, Bournemouth**

14. November: **Portsmouth Polytechnic**

15. November: **Windsor Castle, Harrow Road, London**

16. November: **101 Club, Clapham**

17. November: **Moira House School, Eastbourne**

22. November: **Windsor Castle, Harrow Road, London**

23. November: **Salisbury City Hall**

24. November: **Swan, Hammersmith**

(Tony Oxley's final gig.)

1980

(Barry Mizen joins the band.)

18. January: **Yeovil Technical College**

20. January: **Pinecliff, Bournemouth**

21. January: **101 Club, Clapham**

31. January: **Southampton University**

1. February: **Basingstoke Technical College** (with Merger)

2. February: **Swan, Hammersmith**

3. February: **Poole Arts Centre** (with Tom Robinson)

7. February: **Windsor Castle, Harrow Road, London**

13. February: **Dorset Institute, Bournemouth**

15. February: **Cellar Vino, Weymouth**

20. February: **Greyhound, Fulham**

23. February: **Griffin, Southampton**

29. February: **Kings College Hospital**

(Barry leaves the band. Five or six other January / February gigs - not listed - had had to be cancelled owing to his non-appearance).

(Seven March / April gigs blown out for auditions and rehearsing in Dorset.)

24. April: **Swan, Hammersmith** *(Craig's first date)*

26. April: **Tower Arts Centre** *(Launch of "Mind Made".)*

4. May: **Laker's Hotel, Redhill**

17. May: **Pinecliff, Bournemouth**

19. May: **Moonlight Club, W. Hampstead** *(with Doll By Doll)*

21. May: **Greyhound, Fulham Palace Road**

23 May: **Southampton Rugby Club, Southampton**

7. June: **Windsor Castle, Harrow Road, London**

7. June: **Swan, Hammersmith**

8. June: **Griffin, Southampton**

9 - 10. June: **Bremen, Germany** for TV

15. June: **Pinecliff, Bournemouth**

21. June: **Cellar Vino, Weymouth**

28. June: **John Peel, Gosport**

30. June: **Thomas a'Beckett, Old Kent Road**

4. July: **Windsor Castle, Harrow Road, London**

5. July: **Swan, Hammersmith**

18. July: **Windsor Castle, Harrow Road, London**

19. July: **Riverside Inn, Winchester**

18. July: **Royal Holloway College, Egham**

(John was teaching some Italian students and this was a morning gig for them!)

August: Recording, overdubbing and mixing at Park Gate Studios, Marcus Music and the Marquee.

4. October: **Jumpers Tavern, Christchurch**

9. October: **Greyhound, Fulham** *(This the one where we had no PA.)*

20. October: **Golden Lion, Fulham**

17. October: **Queen Mary's College, Basingstoke**

19. October: **Royal Exeter Hotel, Bournemouth**

24. October: **Yeovil College** *(Hunt Sabateurs' Society Benefit.)*

25. October: **Cellar Vino, Weymouth**

26. October: **Crown Hotel, Hailsham**

1. November: **Three Tuns, Kingston**

14. November: **Music Machine, London**

27. November: **London College of Printing**

28. November: **Grange Centre, Midhurst** *(Tony Oxley did the P.A.!)*

29. November: **King Alfred's College, Winchester**

6. December: **Bognor College**

15. December: **Greyhound, Fulham** *(with Punishment of Luxury.)*

18. December: **101 Club, Clapham**

This was Craig's - and indeed the band's - last gig.

The Secret

1981

11. May: **Victory, Southampton**

12. May: **Floaters, Southampton**

14. May: **Majestic Hotel, Bournemouth**

15. May: **Tower Arts Centre, Winchester**

16. May: **The Plough, Durrington**

19. May: **Majestic, Bournemouth**

(Pause for Stuart to do his O-levels)

18. June: **Maybush, Southampton**

21. June: **Victory, Southampton**

23. June: **Gilbies, Southampton**

24. June: **Railway Inn, Winchester**

25. June: **The Plough, Durrington**

26. June: **The Egmont, Midhurst**

8. July: **Railway Inn, Winchester**

15. July: **Badger Bar, Bournemouth**

19. July: **Park Hotel, Southampton**

21. July: **Bisterne Festival, Ringwood**

30. July: **Plough, Durrington**

9. September: **Railway Inn,Winchester**

10. September: **Chequers, Lytchett Matravers**

2. October: **Elm Tree, Ringwood**

8. October: **Pinecliff, Bournemouth**